D1588545

THE GREAT MOTOR HIGHWAYS OF THE ALPS

Other books by the same Author

Novels
    Pillar of the Sky
    Andreas at Sundown
    Savoy Episode
    The Breaking Strain
    Out of the Night

Photography and Travel
    Rambles in the Alps

Translations (Mountaineering and Exploration)
    To the Third Pole   Prof. G. O. Dyhrenfurth
    Worlds beyond the Horizon   Joachim Leithaüser
    Nanga Parbat Pilgrimage   Hermann Buhl
    The Everest-Lhotse Adventure   Albert Eggler

Editorial
    " Athletics " by the Achilles Club, 1951
    " Athletics " by the Achilles Club, 1955
    " Modern Athletics " by the Achilles Club, 1958

The Val Tremola windings on the southern side of the St. Gotthard

THE GREAT
MOTOR HIGHWAYS
OF THE ALPS

by

HUGH MERRICK

London
Robert Hale Limited
63 Old Brompton Road, S.W.7

Printed in Great Britain by Richard Clay and Company, Ltd.,
Bungay, Suffolk

ACKNOWLEDGMENTS

THE AUTHOR wishes to record his indebtedness to all those who have assisted him in the compilation of this book. While it is impossible to mention everybody by name, special thanks are due to the following bodies and individuals.

The Swiss National Tourist Office in London, particularly its Director Mr. O. Ernst and Mr. E. Kunz, Chief Publicity Officer, for their assistance throughout, for their enlisting the additional services of Herr Oscar Honegger of the Postal Administration in Berne and for thus making available a large amount of detailed information about the Swiss roads and a number of fine photographs which will be found among the illustrations.

To Count L. de Hoyos, Vivian Rowe, Esq., and Dr. R. Guerrieri, the Directors of the Travel and Tourist Departments of Austria, France, and Italy in London, for similar assistance in the provision of information, books of reference, and several splendid photographs; and for their valuable help and advice in the final stages.

To Prof. Ingenieur Wallack of Vienna, personally, for sending me a copy of his excellent history of the birth of the Glocknerstrasse, which I found invaluable.

To the Automobile Association for the provision of detailed information and the great general help afforded by their highly informative Foreign Touring Guide, which contains a mine of useful matter for those motoring on the Continent.

To the Editor of the 'Autocar' for tracking down an item of obscure statistical information.

To the Assistant Secretary of the Alpine Club, T. S. Blakeney Esq., for the loan of several books of reference, ancient and modern, the use of which has lightened my task considerably; and to C. Douglas Milner Esq., for his encouragement from the inception of the project.

Finally, to Alan A. Meyer Esq., for many hours devoted to assisting me with the selection, processing, and arrangement of the photographic material.

CONTENTS

LIST OF ILLUSTRATIONS

Photographic Acknowledgments

The author wishes to record his thanks to the following, for the kind permission given to reproduce their photographs:

Jacket, Nos. 1, 5, 6, 7, 8, 14, 15, 17, 20, 22, 23, 24, 25, 26, 27, 28, 30 and 31: Swiss National Tourist Office, London. No. 18, the same source in connection with Swissair, Zürich. Nos. 9, 21, 32: Austrian State Tourist Department, London. No. 36: French Government Tourist Office, London. No. 2: Italian State Tourist Office, London. Nos. 4, 16, 29, 37, 43: Alan A. Meyer Esq. No. 33: Cdr. D. H. T. Ll. Jenkins R.N. Retd. Nos. 3, 10, 11, 12, 13, 19, 34, 35, 38, 39, 40, 41, 42 and 44 were taken by the Author.

PREFACE

THIS BOOK is definitely not for moles.

I have always had a soft spot for the furry little creatures, partly because I am sorry for them; so much determination, so much effort, so close to the surface, so near the light, yet 'missing so much and so much', saddens me infinitely.

There are already half a dozen major railway-tunnels beneath the Alps, advertising for motorists a safe, swift, and sightless passage from one side to the other as passengers in a railway compartment, their car unsuitably enthroned on a flat truck.

Now we are to go one—or possibly two—better.

For two gigantic road-tunnel schemes are, as I write, well on the way to realization; though, by the time this book appears a fierce commercial struggle between rival parochial interests may well have been resolved. It seems improbable that there is room for both the present propositions in such close proximity to one another—the long-standing project for a tunnel under Mont Blanc from Chamonix to Courmayeur, drawing all its northern traffic through the gateway of Geneva; and the more recent proposal for a route under the Great St. Bernard from above Martigny to Aosta, which would, of course, draw its main traffic through Lausanne, cold-shouldering poor Geneva altogether.

True, the motorist would then at least be spared the indignity of immobilizing the good engine under the bonnet of his car and converting himself into a railway-passenger. He could still retain his self-respect by proceeding—whether by one hole in the ground or another—from one side of the Alps to the other under his own juice, and—however much a straight, tiled tube might reduce the operation to a formality—seated at his own steering-wheel and controls.

To both types of Alpine burrower—rail or road—I ask leave to extend the same kindly sympathy as to our little friend in the black coat, and for the same reasons; for it seems to me a pitiful thing to come by considerable effort to within an ace of so much loveliness and then to forego it all for an intrusive covering of earth. So, I repeat, this book is not for moles.

Nor is this book for greyhounds.

Though no one could appreciate the grace and beauty of those lean-ribbed flashes of canine lightning more than I do in their proper place, that place seems to me more appropriately on a green strip under the flood-lights of the White City or Harringay than on the white windings of an Alpine road in the dapple of mountain sunshine and cloud-shadow.

This book is therefore not for those hardy and technically motor-conscious folk who, equipped with every kind of gadget, slide-rule and ready-reckoner, ganging up as driver, relief driver, and navigator, regard the mountain roads as nothing more than an exciting sector of a rally route. They are a race of supermen, bent on maintaining (but not exceeding) by night and by day, a stipulated average speed of a very high order, dodging the snares of the hidden control and cheerfully risking a spin off the road—preferably iced, or the thing becomes a mere 'piece of cake'—into a friendly wall, a kindly rock-face, or a rather amusing ravine. Hats off to their courage and skill; but this book is not for them.

It is a hundred years since Ruskin lambasted the climbers who were then defiling his beloved 'cathedrals of the earth' by treating them as 'soaped poles in a bear-garden'. Quite wrongly, for a splendid literature of Alpine endeavour stands there today to prove his error; but I wonder whether he would have been so wrong in suggesting that those who use the Alpine roads as a testing-ground for their latest, modified, over-tuned 'Popular' in this fashion are not for all their watchfulness, blind eyes indeed —unable to see the route for the road?

Less still is this book for those who see in the banked-up hairpin corners of the Stelvio or Klausen nothing more than an ideal race-track-cum-hill-climb combined and who have successively reduced the record for the forty-eight bends from Trafoi to the summit to so many minutes and seconds, or an average speed of—maybe?—over fifty miles an hour. A performance I find incredible, from every point of view.

To whom, then, is my book addressed?

In the first instance, to all those who share my life-long joy in and passion for the mountain scene in all its lovely aspects—an enthusiasm and a recreation dating from the days before the motor car and, later still, the motor coach became a regular visitor to the white threads of the Alpine roads etched zig-zag into the great flanks of the hills. Those were the days of the yellow *diligence*, drawn by three white horses, straining their way from corner to corner up the immense rises, rattling down from the summit with the braking-shoe hard on; the days of the postal guard blowing his long coaching horn, and of the drawn-out day from the valley of departure to the valley of hopeful arrival. It is all done a great deal more quickly nowadays; perhaps—unless one is careful and, above all, knows what to look for and at along the road—a little too easily and too quickly. But the purpose of those wonderful roads has not changed with the heightened tempo nor their essence altered one whit.

They are there, of course, to link valley to valley, district to district, by the shortest possible route and to provide direct highways from one side of the great mountain barriers to the other. But they are also there, as I see it, for another and fully complementary purpose—to take the traveller into and through high, remote, and otherwise less accessible tracts of the great mountain masses of the Alps, unfolding for him a continually changing panorama of peak and glacier, forest and lake, township and hamlet, enabling him to stop where he likes and take his fill of sublime mountain scenery, of vistas into wide valleys and narrow gorges or out over the distant carpet of the multi-coloured plains.

In other words, they are an extension of mountaineering itself, throwing open the wonders of the high places to countless thousands who, for lack of ability or inclination, for reasons of age or disability, or for mere want of time in which to cover so vast an area of ground, would never otherwise have come to the high flower-starred alps, the dark mountain tarns, to the very rim of the glittering glacier-ice itself or to the lofty saddles between the ultimate crests of rock or snow still towering above them.

There is no doubt that for the motorist who is also a lover of mountain scenery 'pass-bagging' can become something of a mild obsession, much as a certain type of Fell-walker in our own Lake District will proudly boast that he has collected 177 map points of over 2,000 ft. during his rambles, or a certain peculiar brand of mountaineer will not rest till he has set foot on all the 'Four Thousanders'—the peaks of over 3,000 metres or, to all intents and purposes, 13,000 ft.

Something has perhaps been lost since the motor car has reached a standard of reliability and performance which has robbed the crossing of a high Alpine pass of the sense of courageous and challenging adventure. In the early days there was all the added excitement of the very material doubts—would she get up it at all? Would she groan triumphantly up at a snail's pace, boiling at intervals and demanding great draughts of radiator refreshment from a collapsible canvas bucket? Would the brakes run hot or even fail altogether on the long descent down the other side?

As a small boy, when first introduced to those intriguing banks of hair-pin corners bulging tier upon tier from the mountain-side, I sat beside the driver with a heavy balk of wood on my knees; when the car occasion-ally stalled on a steep turn, it was my duty to leap out, rush round the back and plant the 'sprag' as accurately as possible behind one of the rear wheels. With the relative inefficiency of engine and brakes at the time, this could be quite an exciting experience. A great deal of this sort of thing was dictated by a combination of poor steering-locks and the extreme sharpness of the hairpin Vs, which had, of course, been designed for the less-exacting needs of horse-drawn traffic. On most of the passes we crossed in those days, reversing was constantly necessary in order to get round the hairpins, if lucky, at the second bite. I thus early acquired a useful acquaintance with the steep edges of things above winging slopes and sufficiently deep gulfs and also learned the desirability of a fair degree of accuracy; in the event, we never actually rolled backwards over any-thing, though occasionally there was not a great deal to spare. Other cars we met at the time were fitted with a mechanical version of our some-what Heath Robinsonian arrangement; this was a steel rod fixed under the chassis which, when lowered in an emergency, descended at an angle of forty-five degrees and dug its slightly sharpened end into the roadway. Modesty forbids any discussion of the relative efficiency of the methods employed.

As to boiling, it was all part of the accepted fun. The thing boiled away every few minutes and you just stopped to let it cool down. This was actually a great advantage, because it gave you time to familiarize yourself with the details of the road and to take in the loveliness of the scenery along it. Mountains are bounteous things, and there was usually an adequate supply from streamlet or minature waterfall not very far away. When the engine was cool enough you took the bucket to the torrent's edge and did a shuttle service till the radiator was topped up again. Occasionally one came across a novice who hadn't waited long enough before feeding ice-cold glacier water to his overheated mount and had consequently acquired a nice line in cracked cylinder blocks. It was, of course, very sad, but one learned about these things; and, no doubt, whatever might happen to him on his next visit to the passes, it wouldn't be just that . . .

Nowadays, with water-service stations and telephone rescue boxes every few yards along even the mildest routes and with the problems mainly eliminated by the competence of the modern car, some of the excitement of those pioneering days and a little of the sense of high adventure has inevitably been drained away. But the main thrill is still there, and each crossing is still an undertaking and an adventure.

I cannot help feeling that only a dull heart would fail to respond to the crescendo of pleasure involved in the ascent of one of these remote high saddles in a formidable range of peaks barring the way to the plains beyond. The swift recession of the valley as the car noses its way in low gear up the first steps into a lateral rift; the sense almost of winged flight as you swing steadily up the rocky face of an immense mountain wall by wide, well-graded, finely surfaced hairpin bends, banked bewilderingly one above the other, as the engineering wonder of a road twists and turns, doubling back above itself, towards the cloud-capped peaks; the long climb along a ledge in a precipitous face, high above the brawling torrent in the gorge below, on a safely walled or iron-fenced road, with the summit-gap now visible ahead. Then the last short sweep to the crest of the saddle and the sudden dazzling vista of snow fields, creaming glaciers, and rock spires close at hand; the blue folds of the valleys remotely below, with perhaps a lake shining up from their mysterious depths; a distant view, maybe, of great shining peaks lifting above the jumble of bare intervening ranges, fifty, eighty miles away . . .

And, an hour later, when all that is to be seen has been seen during a mild scramble by neighbouring paths to one or other of the rocky knobs dominating the saddle, comes the enchantment of the long, floating descent down the looped ribbon of the road—down, down, down into the soft, welcoming green of wooded valleys and rushing streams of brown-beamed châlets and villages clustering around white church towers in the warm afternoon sun. As the car glides endlessly down some thousands of feet of the opposing mountain wall, the snows and rocks, which a little while ago almost touched the road, retire to the remote sunlit recesses of the sky, fantastically far and high above; and the familiar world of fields and cows and yellowing corn lifts up to meet and greet your return to the gentler, less awesome world you left behind in the cool of the morning. Presently you are running on the level again along the rim of a blue lake, back in the heart of a world which has flat, rail-fenced meadows and straight, tree-lined roads in the repertoire.   Can you really have been up there, in the cold, thin air, where now a golden streak of snow lies against the clear evening sky, only a couple of hours ago?   It is, of course, more fun for the driver, who has the whole thing under his watchful control, than for his passengers, but I cannot imagine any except the most craven of back-seat drivers who would not respond to the experience.

Nor is this mechanized variant of the sport of mountaineering exclusive, and a joy only to those who are fain to climb but fear to fall.   It is a different but complementary form of high-mountain travel.   I have walked and climbed among the Alps since I was a boy, and nobody could have enjoyed the delights of reaching a high summit or glacier pass on his own feet and by his own exertions more than I have; but I cannot remember the time when the passage of one of the great Alpine roads by Postal Motor or car did not give me a different, but hardly less satisfying, kind of mountain thrill; and the roadside picnic in such a setting can be almost as rewarding as a summit snack.   It is very good to have leisure at times to look at the familiar peaks, on which one has perhaps laboured and toiled, from those half-way heights from which they look their shapely best—unutterably high, withdrawn and unattainable, and, above all, magnificently related to the shadowed valley depths below.

The man who wants to go up to the top can, moreover, combine the pleasures of the Alpine road with his more strenuous ambition.   He can stop at high villages, summit hospices, or mountain hostels along the way, and from their high springboard climb his chosen peak, returning exalted from the heights to continue his arm-chair voyage to the valley beyond. And if it pleases him, he can use his car to link a climb in the Valais with another in the Ortler or the Dolomites, enjoying the rest and enchantment of the mountain-roads uncoiling their ribbons between the far-flung groups.   While the mere lover of a long uphill walk can always find somewhere to improve upon the roadside view by idling up the mountain slopes for an hour or two before coming down again to his parked car and continuing his pursuit of new prospects, ever-unfolding around the next corner.

I am, incidentally, a firm believer in 'surprise' views, yielding the gem one has come to seek only at the end of the least repaying part of the journey.   All through the sweat and toil of the 'dull' side—and most Alpine passes have a more and a less exciting side—there is the thrill of mounting anticipation, the stimulating promise of the big moment towards which one is climbing and swinging at each banked hairpin in the screen of the intervening wall.   Then, at last, there it is, at the saddle between the defeated ridges—disclosed in a blinding moment of revelation and overwhelming impact—the great view of towering snow peaks, the expanse of fretted glacier, of glittering turquoise lakes, of infinitely deep valley-levels, blue-shadowed and minute toys of villages and threads of roads at the foot of a 5,000-ft. wall—whichever happens to be the crowning glory of your chosen pass.   That way you come upon it as a reward for patient uphill toil, and the splendour of the newly revealed wonders, which had lain hidden till a moment ago behind rocky curtains, is tenfold enhanced.

Taken the other way, the view is already with you as you swing up the turns, and there is the disadvantage of its being for the most part behind you as you go. When you reach the saddle, instead of a revelation, you enjoy the fitting together of parts with which the eye is already familiar, as if you were assembling a jig-saw puzzle to complete a set picture already before you.

It is an entirely different approach, but for me there is no comparison, and however many times I have driven one pass or another, the blind-side approach remains infinitely more rewarding, when one definitely exists.

It is for this reason that I have attempted to describe each of the roads pictured in this book—where there seems to be a clear choice—from the direction in which I feel it yields the greatest rewards of anticipation and fulfilment. As this is probably a matter of temperament and personal prejudice, I will not be surprised if any given reader thinks the *Aussichts-joch*, the *Col de Sijarrive*, or the *Passo della Speranza* much better when driven in the opposite direction. In any case, over the years, most drivers will have the desire and, it is hoped, the opportunity of driving their favourite passes a second or a third time and then they can make up their minds how good or bad was my advice.

.   .   .   .   .

For those, then—be they already mountaineers in the true sense, or never likely to attempt a serious mountain climb—whom the thrill and beauty of this less exacting sport of motor-mountaineering has already enthralled, and for many, many more, I hope, who have yet before them the almost limitless and varied joy of what the mountain-roads can hold for him who drives their lofty, winding ways, this book has been compiled.

In it I have tried not only to describe the individual roads, their infinite variety of character, interest, and scenery, and to pin point the high lights of mountain beauty along their course; but also to give as full a picture as possible, within the scope of a book of this size, of the Alpine and holiday amenities of all kinds to which they lead or which may be found along their routes.

The motorist who drives these highways may be a non-stop traveller, using them only as a means to an end, a sector of a long international tour, and he will be primarily interested in how they can further his progress from stage to stage. For him I have tried to indicate the lie of the major trans-Alpine and other links, providing as much description as possible of what there is for him to see in passing along his selected through-route.

Conversely, the motorist who is using his car mainly as an adjunct to an Alpine holiday may not only wish to drive this or that pass as an end in itself—a day's 'outing' or motor-mountaineering expedition within the framework of his sojourn at one or more resorts or centres in the mountains. In the intervals between driving he may be in search—within the mountain framework—of a luxury hotel, an Alpine Club Hut, a golf-course, a swimming-pool, gentle walking to woodland view-points, high climbs to snowy or rocky summits, a picturesque village to sketch or photograph, a cable-railway lifting him above the snow line, or a lakeside siesta among the sheltering pines.

For him I have tried to include as much useful information as possible about the district adjacent to each road, its holiday resorts, its valleys, and its ranges, in the hope that he will find along its route or at its either end precisely those pursuits and pleasures he is seeking from his mountain holiday.

It has, of course, been possible to attempt this only in the broadest possible outline. The guide-books are there to fill in the detail—*Baedeker*, the *Guides Bleus*, and many others.

If I have succeeded in helping or entertaining the experienced Alpine motorist, even in a nostalgic sense, and—far better still—in opening up the vast and lovely field of Alpine motoring to the uninitiated, bringing them a pleasure and an enthusiasm which can be a life-long source of joy, the object of this book will have been attained.

H. M.

Note on Alpine driving

A gentle word of warning is perhaps necessary for the motorist new to Alpine roads and accustomed only to the broad speedways of the Plains.

Exaggerated care is the first rule on mountain roads; fast driving is not only bad manners but usually an offence as well. For instance, Swiss law requires that a vehicle anywhere on any mountain road can be brought to a standstill inside 20 feet; it will be obvious that this is an impossibility, especially when descending a steep gradient, unless a very modest speed is observed. The continuous use of gears for additional braking-power when travelling downhill is compulsory; coasting is forbidden. The foot-brake should be used to reduce speed before changing down and the hand-brake to ensure control until the change has been safely effected; otherwise you should brake as sparingly as possible (see also p. 249).

On narrow roads the *descending* car must be prepared to pull in to the very right-hand edge of the road and, if necessary, stop, to allow ascending traffic to pass (see also p. 250).

Unfortunately, none of this ensures that you will not meet the occasional road-hog driving like a lunatic on steep and narrow mountain roads. So drive with meticulous care yourself.

PART I

INTRODUCTORY

Note on the Maps

In Maps no. 2 (p. 56), 3 (p. 76), 4 (p. 167), 5 (p. 197), 6 (p. 222) and Sketch Maps no. 1 (p. 28) and 2 (p. 30), the broad stippled area indicates the main Alpine watershed or ' Backbone '.

I

MOUNTAINS, PASSES, AND RIVERS

Every year some two hundred thousand motorists, using one or other of seven sea-routes and three air-ferry services, cross the narrow waters which through the centuries have denied this Island to the successive menaces of Philip of Spain, Napoleon Bonaparte, Adolf Schickelgruber, and, so far—though the project has recently revived its hoary head—to a fifty-year-old Channel-tunnel project.

Crossing guardian seas at varying degrees of discomfort and expense, by sea and air, through half a dozen ferry ports on the coasts of France and Belgium, they stream eastwards across the straight, tree-lined avenues of the main Continental highways in search of change, sunshine, and recreation, in every variety of holiday resort, throughout the limited number of countries still left free to access short of the great political barrier which now divides Western from Eastern Europe.

The lay-out of this book is designed primarily for the very large proportion of motorists whose destination lies south of a line drawn due east from Nantes to Vienna—roughly the dividing line between the great subtemperate plains of Northern Europe and the sunnier, more genial lands fringing the northern coasts of the Mediterranean Basin. This arbitrary line corresponds closely with a far more solid physical barrier which has since time immemorial sundered the dourer, tougher peoples of the more physically exacting North from the more mercurial and voluble races of the softer, kindlier South. For along it stretches 600 miles of the great backbone of Europe, the almost unbroken complex of mountain ranges, varying in altitude from 5,000 to nearly 16,000 ft., which forms the chain of the Alps.

This huge concatenation of linked mountain-groups is rarely more than 30 miles deep from north to south, but it tends throughout its length to build up to maximum height towards its southern fringe, and then to plunge steeply to the plains in an immense wall with a relatively short belt of foothills at its base. This tendency is less noticeable the farther eastward one goes. Exceptions to the rule are provided, from the eastern shores of Lake Como onwards, by several subsidiary 'island' groups, separated from the main watershed, now lying a little withdrawn to the north, by the deep and sometimes broad furrows of considerable river systems.

In this long spine of Europe, stretching from the first westerly ramparts of the Alps on France's eastern frontiers, where rise the Vosges, the Jura, and the far loftier ranges of Savoy and Dauphiné, to the Carpathians in the distant East, there are only a dozen or so major breaches, allowing the passage of a first-class highway.

The Passes

To be strictly accurate, if all the main motor-roads which cross the true Alpine watershed are faithfully enumerated, they number twenty-five. Starting from the Mediterranean coast and working up the long sector which runs northwards through the Maritime Alps to the Cottians, where the great mountain belt at last bends eastwards into the highest part of the wall, and then continuing to its eastern end, just short of Vienna, the following passes make up the list:

1. Colle di Tenda (4,331 ft.)
2. Col de Larche (6,545 ft.)
3. Col du Mont Genèvre (6,100 ft.)
4. Col du Mont Cenis (6,834 ft.)
5. Col du Petit St. Bernard (7,178 ft.)
6. Col du Grand St. Bernard (8,110 ft.)
7. Simplon Pass (6,594 ft.)
8. St. Gotthard Pass (6,926 ft.)
9. Lukmanier Pass (6,289 ft.)
10. San Bernardino Pass (6,768 ft.)
11. Splügen Pass (6,930 ft.)
12. Maloja Pass (5,960 ft.)
13. Bernina Pass (7,644 ft.)
14. Ofen Pass (7,070 ft.)
15. Resia (Reschen-Scheideck) Pass (4,947 ft.)
16. Brenner Pass (4,495 ft.)
17. Glocknerstrasse (8,212 ft.)
18. Tauern Pass—(Katschberg) (5,700 ft.)
19-25. To the East of the Tauern there are eight minor passages through the diminishing range, none of them over 4,500 ft. high.

These twenty-five can be further subdivided into three categories:

1. The International Passes, whose names are for the most part known throughout the world, which cross the frontier between two states as well as the main watershed off the Alps.

These are the Tenda, Larche, Mont Genèvre, Mont Cenis, Petit St. Bernard, Grand St. Bernard, Simplon, Splügen, Bernina, Resia, and Brenner.

2. Those which, although forming part of a through route from one country to another, are in fact entirely internal to one country.

These are the St. Gotthard, Lukmanier, San Bernardino, Maloja, and Ofen, all of which lie in Swiss territory; while the Glockner-strasse, the Tauern Pass, and the minor passages to the east of them, all lie entirely in Austrian territory.

Of the passes mentioned, the most significant are, from west to east:

1. *Linking France and Italy*

The *Mont Cenis*, leading from the valleys of Haute Savoie, between the major blocks of the Dauphiné Alps and the Cottian-Graian complex, into the upper basin of the Po, descending on Turin.

The *Petit St. Bernard*, just to the south of the Mont Blanc massif, the highest group in the Alps, connecting Savoy with the Aosta valley in Northern Italy, also descending eventually on Turin and the Po valley.

2. *Linking Switzerland and Italy*

The *Grand St. Bernard*, cutting due south from the western end of the great Rhone valley trench in southern Switzerland to scale the main wall of the Pennine Alps at a great height, between the two lofty groups of Mont Blanc and the Grand Combin to its east, descending direct on Aosta, and so again on Turin.

The *Simplon*, 30 miles away to the east, at the other end of the Rhone valley's lower rift, forcing a way between the Fletschhorn and Monte Leone massifs to come down through the southern gorges on Domodossola and thence, by way of Lake Maggiore's western bank, to Milan.

The *St. Gotthard*, some 20 miles farther eastwards, finding a long and gradual route from the Central Swiss uplands at Lucerne to the high, bare crater-like Urseren valley, 'the navel of Switzerland'; thence over the adjacent Alpine backbone to plunge into the mild Italianate canton of Ticino, descending by way of Bellinzona to the Lake of Lugano and its renowned holiday resort. From the frontier at the lake's southern end it is only another 40 miles to Milan.

The *Splügen Pass*, though (like its neighbours the San Bernardino and Lukmanier) minor in character, is the traditional and most direct link between the upper basin of the Rhine and the head of Lake Como by way of Chiavenna and on by the western shore of the lake to Como and Milan. It must consequently qualify for the description of an important gap in the main structure of the Alpine chain.

This route from north to south is thus triplicated, for the two other passes named both afford more circuitous routes between the upper Rhine valley and Chiavenna.

A fourth road, falling on Chiavenna and linking the Como–Milan area directly with the Alpine areas eastwards towards the Inn Basin and Austria is the *Maloja Pass*. To do so it utilizes the long, narrow groove, some 30 miles in length, of the Upper and Lower Engadine.

As will be seen presently, the Maloja is not a true pass in the usual sense. It is indeed unique among the Alpine 'Passes' in being unilateral; for only the southern side exhibits one of the main characteristics of a mountain pass—a noticeable ascent to the watershed. It does, however, afford one of the lowest and most accessible breaches in the whole length of the Alpine rampart, and must, by virtue of its ease of combination with a number of other important mountain roads, assuredly classify as a major passage from North to South of the Alpine backbone.

A subsidiary and circuitous variant of the Maloja route, the *Bernina Pass*, can also be used as a link between the valleys of Western Austria and the head of Lake Como.   It leaves the direct Engadine route 12 miles short of Maloja and crosses a convenient gap close to the magnificent peaks and glaciers of the lofty Bernina Group, whose name it bears.   In this case Chiavenna is by-passed by a mile or two, but the final route into the Italian plain is essentially the same; for at Tirano the Bernina road strikes the main highway descending the broad sub-Alpine valley of the Adda from the foot of the Stelvio (see below), and this road again debouches into the Chiavenna–Como–Milan road at Colico, near the head of the lake.

These complementary routes, the *Maloja* and the *Bernina*, thus afford the least exacting routes between the Vorarlberg country and the southern frontier regions of Germany (Garmisch, etc.) to the north, and the plain of Lombardy to the south of the main Alpine chain.

The Resia (*Reschen–Scheideck Pass*).   This easy road, the third lowest of all the true trans-Alpine crossings, affords a direct link from Eastern Switzerland, Southern Germany, Liechtenstein, and the Vorarlberg Region of Western Austria to the central part of the Northern Italian plain, by way of the Adige valley and Lake Garda; also to the south-eastern provinces of Austria itself, lying south of the main Alpine chain, by way of Merano and Bolzano and thence by the valley road along the beautiful Pustertal to Lienz.

In order to reach the Resia Pass from the western plains, however, it is necessary first to cross the Arlberg (not in itself a trans-Alpine crossing) to Landeck, where the Resia turns south to force its passage of the 'Backbone'; so that it does not strictly fall into the category of major *single* passes across the Alps from plain to plain.   Yet, apart from its value as a passage from north to south of the main chain, it also affords an easy approach to the northern foot of the Stelvio, which, for all its magnificence and altitude, traverses an isolated mountain-massif, sundered from the main chain to its north by the upper Adige valley, and not the 'Backbone' itself.

The *Adige Valley*, which separates the 'island' of the Ortler Group* from the Alps and, in its lower reaches, also from the Dolomite region, 20 miles farther east, bites more deeply into the mountain mass of the central and eastern Alps from the south than any other valley route, for it connects with the considerable valleys of its tributaries the Isarco (Eisack), the Rienz, and the Drave (Drau) north-eastwards, without anywhere reaching an altitude of much more than 3,000 ft.

The Alps, however, are more stubborn than the Himalaya, since nowhere between the Franco-Swiss frontier and Vienna does a single river succeed in carving a passage through the main watershed from north to south, as do the Arun, the Sun Kosi, the Kali, and the Dhauli in the case of the world's highest mountain range.   In order to reach the northern side of this uncompromising backbone from the southern valleys at this point it is therefore necessary even for users of the Adige valley to cross

* The historic name Ortler has been retained for a historic mountain throughout this book.   The Italianized form is Ortlès.

one or other of the few available saddles between continuing mountain masses all more than 10,000 ft. high and bristling with snow peaks and extensive glacier systems.

Due south of Innsbruck, the relatively low and easy *Brenner* depression has, since time immemorial, offered a comfortable passage, broad enough to accommodate, in modern times, a double line of international main railway line as well as one of the less exacting of the great Alpine motor-roads. Through this artery, during the Second World War, poured much of the vital traffic, by road and rail, which sustained the German effort in Italy when the Allies were at last able to strike upwards from Churchill's 'soft underbelly of Europe'.

The other main road-artery connecting Austria with the districts of northern Italy lying to the south of the Oetztal, Zillertal, and Hohe Tauern groups of the Alps is the magnificent and fairly recent *Glockner-strasse*, converted in modern days into one of the finest of Alpine motor-roads, skirting the very rim of the glaciers and peaks of the Grossglockner (Austria's highest and easiest summit) to debouch over an 8,000-ft. saddle on to Heiligenblut on the southern side. Thence it continues to Lienz, beyond which valley high-roads in opposite directions connect it with Klagenfurt and Bolzano.

The grooming of the Glockner road for stardom has displaced in importance as a main link from north to south the high, steep, and difficult Hohe Tauern Pass–Katschberg route, parallel to it and some 30 miles farther east. For that route, frequented *faute de mieux* in earlier days, cannot now compete with its celebrated neighbour either in quality as a highway or in the magnificence of the scenery it traverses; though the driver who revels in pass-driving for its own sake will still be glad to visit it and add another considerable mountain pass to his collection of scalps.

Of the twelve passes enumerated above as main arteries yielding essential passage across the Alpine backbone, only four are relatively easy—the Mont Cenis, the Maloja Gap, the Resia, and the Brenner; all the others have to struggle up to more or less rugged and narrow depressions in the huge sundering wall, at heights varying from 6,000 to 9,000 ft., in order to save long, circuitous valley journeys entailing many extra hours of travel between points often only 20 or 30 miles apart.

Almost all of them are marvels of engineering skill and enduring monuments to the courage and tenacity, not only of the men who originally planned and built them but also of those who tend, maintain, and annually restore them after the ravages of the summer traffic and the winter storms and snows.

This engineering skill and devotion is, however, by no means confined to the great international highways already mentioned. Besides the major and minor passes which cross the main 'Backbone' of the Alps, there are numerous other great roads providing internal connections between the main arteries and forming invaluable inter-regional links. Indeed, a dozen of the finest passes are to be found among the subsidiary class.

From it I have selected for description, in greater or less detail, those I consider the most interesting in themselves and of the greatest use to motorists in planning their Alpine journeys and in bringing them to close quarters with the most important groups of mountains and to the most attractive resorts among them.

In this category I have included:

1. *In the French Alps*

The Lautaret and the Galibier; the Izoard, Vars, Allos, and Cayolle; and the Iseran.

2. *In Switzerland*

The Susten, Furka, Grimsel, and Klausen; the Oberalp, Julier, Albula, Flüela, and Umbrail.

2. *In Italy*

The Sella, Pordoi, Falzarego, Tre Croci, Rolle, Mendola, Costalunga, and Campiglio passes, all in the Dolomites.

It may be argued that this selection and grouping is arbitrary and that a number of highly attractive Alpine roads have been omitted. In defence I can only say that consideration had to be given to the size of the book and that in making the selection consequently enforced I have chosen from the lesser roads those which have given me—and will, I believe, give others—the greatest service and pleasure. Wherever possible, I have, however, tried to mention the alternative or complementary passes which, owing to considerations of space, it has been impossible to describe in detail.

THE RIVERS

In order to understand fully the main trends of the network of major passes across the Alps and the subsidiary mountain roads linking them, it is useful to study the relationship of the great rivers of Europe, all of which find their sources or tributary head-waters in the Central Alps, to the general mountain structure of the range.

A study of the map of Switzerland will show that at some time or other the great mountain masses underwent their severest pressure and up-heaval at a point almost precisely in the centre of the country, over an area only a few miles long and broad, whose only town of any importance is the small traffic-centre and hotel-cluster of Andermatt.

At this point in the Alpine chain the granite substructure was heavily compressed and flung up to great heights, to be covered in primeval days by an immense layer of ice thousands of feet thick, whose base would appear to have been not lower than the 8,000-ft. level. The peaks and glaciers of this upheaval have long since been worn away, and the chief mountain group of the area now contains no summits of more than 11,000 ft. The basic structure, however, from which the dividing range rise, remains the loftiest and largest solid core in Switzerland; and from its flanks, within a radius of only a few miles, five important European rivers set out on their courses, to flow in different directions and eventually to empty their waters in seas as distant and diverse as the North Sea, the Adriatic, the Western Mediterranean and the Black Sea. For it is here in this mountain nexus, without parallel in the whole length of the Alps, that in a space 10 miles long and 5 miles broad we find the sources of the Rhine, the Rhone, the Aar, the Reuss, and the Ticino.

Of these, the two first-named great rivers spring from watersheds just 6 miles apart, to turn their backs frigidly on one another and start out on courses running due east and due west respectively, rather as the Severn and the Wye rise in close proximity high among Plynlimmon's ridges, to flow at first in diametrically opposite directions. The two great Continental rivers, however, later on take a right-angled change of direction, the Rhine to flow almost due north on its 960-mile journey by way of Bâle to Holland and the North Sea; the 850-mile Rhone turning due south a little above Lyons, to traverse the breadth of southern France to its Mediterranean mouth.

Only 5 miles to the north-west across the Grimsel watershed from where the Rhone Glacier gives birth to its grey foaming torrent, in the glaciers of the Finsteraarhorn, lies the source of the Aar. This considerable but brief river flows due north till, at Meiringen, it strikes the deep trench which cradles the Lakes of Brienz and Thun and leads to the fertile Bernese plain. Traversing the lakes, between which lies Interlaken, and the 30-mile-long plain, the river swings back north-eastwards at Berne, to find its way through a gap in the foothills beyond Aarau and join first the Reuss, then the Rhone, at a point in its course where it is flowing due west between Chur and Bâle, before its final swing to the North.

The Reuss, though the smallest and least important of the five, is, in its early course, perhaps the most remarkable. Springing from a small glacier to the east of the Furka–Rhone watershed, only about 2 miles from the Rhone's source, it first flows east along the extraordinary Urserental. This elevated plainlet, occupying the floor of a trench 5 miles long by a mile wide at an elevation of 5,000 ft., frowned down upon from all sides by high, rocky combs is truly the 'navel of Switzerland' and indeed of the Continent. A deep depression in the most fiercely compressed upthrust in the Central Alps, it forms a kind of bath-shaped basin between the Furka and Oberalp watersheds, with no normal outlet for the waters draining into it from the surrounding peaks. But for one circumstance it might indeed have provided one of the most remarkable lake-basins in the Alps. Nature, however, arranged otherwise; for at its north-eastern corner she left a weakness in the containing walls of rock, through which the Reuss gratefully bored a most sensational passage, fully described in the chapter dealing with the St. Gotthard Pass. The waters are thus able to escape through what almost amounts to a tunnel and find their way steeply down to the great valley rift which falls from Goeschenen, at the foot of the mountain barrier to the head of Lake Lucerne. Passing through the lake, the Reuss then continues northward and eastwards to fall into the Rhine.

The other important arm of this star-shaped quintet of river basins is that of the Ticino, which again rises only a mile or two away, but on the southern side of the main Alpine watershed, among the glaciers of the Gotthard Group. Draining the whole southern flank of that mountain massif, this river brawls its way steeply down into the smiling, sub-Alpine trench of the Ticino valley, which gives its name to Switzerland's Italianate canton. Through this broad valley it then flows less tempestuously to reach the head of Lago Maggiore, through which its waters are carried on into the Po, and are thus emptied into the Adriatic Sea.

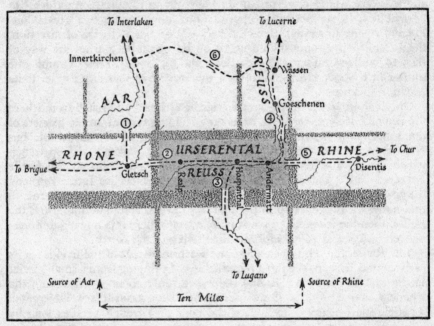

SKETCH MAP No. 1. THE CRADLE OF FIVE RIVERS

Passes
1. Grimsel   2. Furka   3. St. Gotthard   4. Schoellenen Gorge   5. Oberalp   6. Susten

Note: The fifth river is, of course, the Ticino, flowing south from the St. Gotthard.

Each of these five river valleys carries, as might be expected, its important high-road.

The Rhone valley road brings traffic up from the lowland levels of Geneva via Brigue to Gletsch; the first sector almost level, the second rising steadily.

The Rhine valley highway affords an unbroken and easy approach from the Lakes of Constance and Zürich by way of Liechtenstein and Chur to Disentis, just short of one of the main sources of the great river.

The Aar rift houses the road from Interlaken, the plain of Thun and Berne to the Grimsel watershed.

None of these approach routes breaches the main Alpine barrier without the necessity of crossing an intervening pass in a lateral range first—the

Rhone route is barred above Gletsch by the Furka; the Rhine above Disentis by the Oberalp; the Aar by the Grimsel. Yet each of them thus affords a connection with the Urseren basin and the St. Gotthard.

The St. Gotthard Pass alone cuts a miraculous way through this vertebra in the spine of the Alps, from the pine-fringed lowlands of Northern Switzerland beyond Lucerne to the palms and passion-flowers of Lugano— still in Switzerland—and the lakes and foothills at the corresponding low level to the South. It is for this reason that the St. Gotthard has a very special place among the great trans-Alpine arteries. The significance of this remarkable highway to Swiss political and economic history is fully dealt with in the relevant chapter (VIII).

It has thus been shown that three of Europe's great river-systems—the Rhine, Rhone, and Po—are nourished by streams rising in this extraordinary 10-mile area. The fourth—the Danube—debouching 1,500 miles away into the Black Sea, is fed by Switzerland's other great river, the Inn.

This river, destined to traverse Austria from West to East and later part of Eastern Germany, before falling into the Danube at Passau, rises in the mountains of the Bergell (Bregaglia) close to Maloja and affords another curiosity in the way of 'near-misses'. For at Maloja it flows within a quarter of a mile of the strangest watershed in the whole Alpine chain. This tiny neck, a few hundred yards long and certainly not more than 50 ft. high, is all that here separates the infant stream from a 2,000-ft. drop into the Val Bregaglia on the southern side of the Alps; by only this much is the great river to be diverted from a southward course by way of Lake Como into the great river basin of the Italian plain—a course actually taken by the Mera, whose waters originate a few yards on the other side of this lowest and slenderest of Alpine divides.

Instead, the Inn is pushed quietly away to the north-east and immediately sets off on its long straight course down the gently graded Engadine, whose floor is at first almost level, as the rivulet flows through the adjoining lakes of Sils, Silvaplana, Campfer, and St. Moritz. For 30 miles the river descends comparatively gently through the successive terraces of the Upper and Lower Engadine till at Nauders it cuts its way through a narrow neck to cross the Austrian frontier and at last bends eastwards on its long journey to Innsbruck and to the Danube far beyond.

The Inn valley and Engadine thus afford the traveller from anywhere east of the Arlberg on the northern side of the Alps the easiest approach and lowest Alpine crossing to Milan and the central Italian plain. For, rising steadily from the Austrian frontier over more than 30 miles of road, almost entirely free from the banks of hairpin turns which are a feature of every other major pass, it never exceeds a height of 6,000 ft. This is reached at Maloja without the traveller being in the least conscious of having ascended a pass or climbed the northern side of the Alpine watershed—indeed, the last 10 miles have led him along the flat floor of a smiling valley, studded with charming, pine-fringed lakes. The descent on the southern side is only a degree less remarkable for unspectacular ease and the absence of all sense that a major road-crossing of the Alps has been achieved, being accomplished in a dozen easy hairpin-bends down the 2,000-ft. escarpment south of Maloja, through dense and lovely pine-woods. Thence, to its end at Chiavenna, at the level of the Italian lakes, it descends gently and as a normal valley highway from terrace to terrace in the deep rift of the Val Bregaglia—a fall of 5,000 ft. spaced gradually over 20 miles.

These great valley-routes, affording easy approach from the plains and

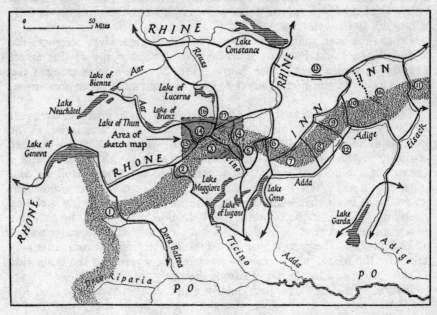

SKETCH MAP No. 2.   THE VALLEY ROUTES TO THE MAIN
CROSSINGS

Crossings

1. Grand St. Bernard	6. Splügen	10a. Timml Joch	13. Arlberg
2. Simplon	7. Maloja	11. Brenner	14. Furka
3. St. Gotthard	8. Bernina		15. Grimsel
4. Lukmanier	9. Ofen–Umbrail	*Other connecting Passes*	16. Susten
5. San Bernardino	10. Resia (Reschen Scheideck)	12. Stelvio	17. Oberalp

Note: The shaded rectangle refers to Sketch Map no 1, page 28.

lowlands of Germany, Switzerland, and Austria to the high gateways in the Alpine roof-ridge are thus cruciform in pattern; or perhaps more like a starfish sprawling limply on a beach at high-tide. By the Rhone from the West, the Rhine from the North, the Inn from the East, and the Ticino from the South, the great motor trunkways impinge upon Switzerland's half-dozen crossing places, set like gateways in a 30-mile sector. Considering that these final approach routes thread their penetrative way between mountain-groups rising to 13,000 ft. and more, at a distance of only a few miles on either side, and that the walls of the valleys containing them often rise to 7,000 or 8,000 ft., these roads thrusting at comparative low-level to reach the feet of the passes are good, well-graded highways, more characteristic of a lowland main-road than of a mountain route.

The Rhone route runs almost flat to Brigue, where it reaches a modest 2,200 ft. in elevation; the Rhine route rises unsensationally to Chur and then a little more hastily to Disentis; the Ticino road runs almost level from Bellinzona to Faido and never exceeds 4,000 ft. till its abrupt collision with the sheer south wall of the Alps at Airolo. These and the equally straightforward routes along the valleys of the Inn and Adige, farther East, are the true keys which readily unlock the gateways of the main Alpine crossings.

II

THE APPROACH ROUTES

1. ACROSS GERMANY
2. ACROSS FRANCE

In these days of haste and hustle many motorists prefer to approach the Alpine areas of Switzerland, Austria, and Italy by air or sea routes converging on the German Autobahn system through Belgium or Luxembourg. Once on those tremendous multi-lane, one-way race-tracks, it is possible to cover enormous distances in a day at average speeds which which would a few years ago have sounded fantastic for the ordinary motor tourist. In this way, it is by no means impossible to 'get through' to the northern borders of Switzerland or Austria in little more than one long, heavy—and boring—day's motoring, with one's foot on the accelerator and the needle on seventy or more for most of the time.

I personally do not care for that kind of motoring, in which everything worth seeing is by-passed, the sustained speed is utterly detrimental to enjoyment of the countryside, the road itself is a concrete race-track, and anyone who does not keep up the crazy speed which such conditions invite is subjected to the scowls and vituperations of an unbroken stream of lorry and coach drivers travelling at over a mile a minute and extremely critical of anyone who happens to want to do less.

Moreover, there is always the pleasant thought at the back of one's mind that if, for some unforeseen reason, someone has to check suddenly, half a dozen cars and buses will inevitably be involved in a more or less cataclysmic multiple shambles. This is, I fear, not my idea of a good holiday.

I have therefore confined myself to a bare list of the approach routes through Germany, but have given a fairly detailed description of the main routes across France, which still remain good, fast, honest country highways pursuing their course through villages and towns. Along them one can drive as fast or as slowly as one pleases; there is frequently the pleasant shade of long avenues of trees; halts can be made on little grassy roadside arbours instead of formal lay-bys, often by streams or on riverbanks; and one has the time and the right to admire the lovely countryside, its red-roofed villages and their fine churches, the workers in the corn-fields and among the vines, the ox-drawn hay-cart lurching to meet one in the evening.

It may take a day longer to arrive, but in this respect I am a firm Stevensonian and find great delight in travelling hopefully.

Besides which, the *Routes Nationales* across France still offer the most direct approach to all the vast mountain area piled up on her own eastern

32

borders south of a line drawn through, say, Dijon and Bâle, and to Southern Switzerland and Italy beyond her frontiers.

1. Across Germany

Those who wish to make use of the speed-track provided by Germany's great Autobahn, running down the Upper Rhine valley from Cologne to Karlsruhe and thence south-eastwards to Munich, can approach it by a variety of routes from the coastal ports.

If, as is probable, speed and time-saving are the prime requirements, the

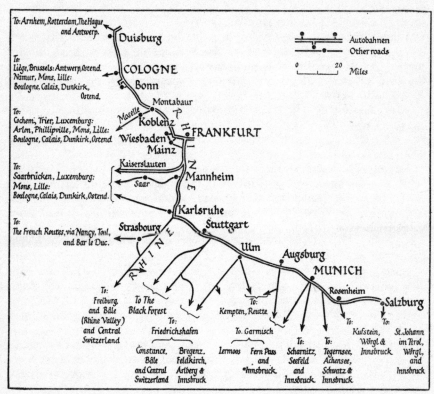

Sketch Map No. 3. THE GERMAN AUTOBAHN ROUTE
and the connecting links with the passes in the Alpine areas

motorist will converge from Boulogne, Calais, Dunkirk, or Ostend on Brussels, by way of Lille in the first case and by the coast road and the direct *Autoroute* speedway in the others. (The motorist who has shipped his car to Rotterdam or the Hook of Holland will come down on the German Autobahn system through Arnhem, Emmerich, and Wesel, striking it just north of Duisburg, at a point some 40 miles north of Cologne.)

From Brussels the most direct route is through Liège and Aachen, to

c

strike the Autobahn at Cologne.   A more leisurely variant is provided by turning south-eastwards at Liège and driving through the pretty wooded hills of Eupen and Malmedy, delaying one's arrival on the speedway till the Montabaur junction beyond Koblenz.

For those less pressed for time and able to enjoy a longer but much more interesting approach to the Autobahn, there is a very attractive route.

Keep on at Lille through Tournai to Mons and there head south-east to Luxemburg, which is well worth seeing in itself.   Thence, down the valley of the Moselle, through Trier and Berncastel, to Koblenz is as lovely a riverside journey as anyone could wish for.   Lateral roads at various points afford links between the valley road and the Autobahn farther south, through Wiesbaden and Mainz, by-passing Koblenz.

A direct road from Luxemburg through the industrialized Saar territory leads to the Autobahn, by way of Saarbrucken at a point much farther south, near Karlsruhe; it is uninteresting and, moreover, loses most of the advantages in view for the user of the special speedway, by striking it so late in its course.

From Karlsruhe, where the Autobahn turns eastwards, the old Rhine valley highway runs south to Freiburg and Bâle, thus affording a direct link with northern and western Switzerland and the main routes through the central Alps.

The Autobahn now sweeps on through Pforzheim, by-passing Stuttgart, Ulm, and Augsburg to Munich, about 130 miles of swift motoring which need not occupy much more than, say, a couple of hours, so that the boredom is at least short.   Beyond Munich it continues for another 90 to Salzburg.

At Pforzheim and near Stuttgart southerly roads give access to the lovely hills and woods of the Black Forest and through it to the northern borders of Switzerland at Constance, where the Arlberg and Rhine valley routes to Austria and Italy are easily picked up.   The roads running south from Ulm will serve the same connections by way of Friedrichshafen on the north (German) shore of Lake Constance and through the principality of Liechtenstein.

From Augsburg a road due south through Landsberg leads to Garmisch-Partenkirchen at the foot of the Zugspitze, and thence by the Fern Pass through the Limestone Alps to the valley of the Inn, Landeck and Innsbruck being equally accessible.

From Munich and Salzburg, and all along the sector between them, half a dozen roads strike out to the south and penetrate the rocky Limestone Alps into the Inn valley and upper Austria by way of minor mountain passes.

The direct road from Munich to Innsbruck runs through Walchensee, Scharnitz, and Seefeld; a parallel road crosses the Achen Pass between the Tegern See and the Achen See, famous for Pertisau and 'White Horse Inn', to come down on the Inn east of Innsbruck at Schwaz.   A third, between Rosenheim and Wörgl, penetrates the Kufstein gap.

From Salzburg, the Loferer Stein Pass and the Strub Pass cross a

German 'isthmus' to St. Johann-im-Tirol, Kitzbühel, and Wörgl; the Lueg Pass gives direct access to the Glocknerstrasse, by way of St. Johann-im-Pongau and Bruck, and with the Tauern Pass by way of Radstadt.

2. ACROSS FRANCE

I would like to make it quite clear at the outset that this section is written in the context of the main theme of this book and is intended for

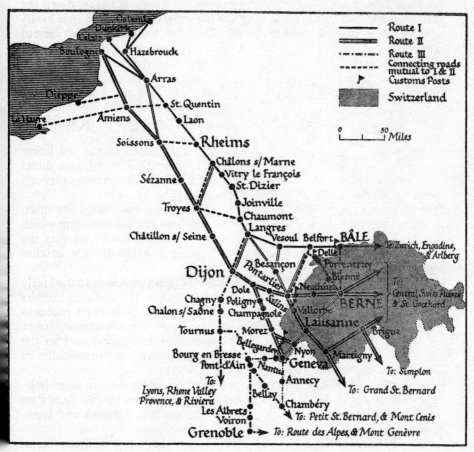

MAP No. 1. THE MAIN ROUTES ACROSS FRANCE

the motorist with limited holiday time at his disposal, who wishes to reach his destination, among or beyond the Alps, as soon as he can and to spend as long as possible there. It is therefore a study of the quick routes through France designed to get him to his Swiss, Italian, or Austrian destination or at least to the foot of his selected Alpine crossing, in the shortest possible time. Without this declaration I might lay myself wide open to justifiably savage attack on the ground that my eyes are ridiculously shut to the wealth of beauty, natural and architectural, which lies along the great tree-lined avenues of France.   I should therefore like to repeat that the French routes described here are, for this special purpose, regarded purely as the quickest and most direct approach-routes to the Alpine passes which form the main subject of this book.   Were I to treat them in any other way, stopping to look aside at lovely stretches of countryside, historic cities, and incomparable ancient monuments within measurable distance of the trunk routes, we might never get far enough even to see the foothill fringes of Central Europe's great mountain barriers lifting blue and distant above the vineyard-covered slopes and ripening corn-fields of Eastern France.

ROUTE I:

(i) *Coastal Ports—Soissons or St. Quentin—Rhiems—Châlons sur Marne—Chaumont—Langres—Vesoul—Belfort—Bâle—(Zürich) (Lucerne)—(Arlberg and Gotthard)*

(ii) *Langres—Gray—Besançon—Pontarlier—(Berne) or—(Lausanne—Simplon)*

(iii) *Belfort—Delle—Porrentruy—(Berne)*

The main through-route from the northern ferry-ports to the Swiss frontier is the combination of *Routes Nationales* 37, 39, 43, 44, and 19 to Bâle. It is the most direct and the fastest—though nowhere really fast in its early stages through northern France—and is normally maintained in the best condition.

For this route, whether you come off the boat at Dunkirk, Calais, or Boulogne, and whichever of alternative connecting roads you select, Rheims is the focal point for the long highway to the northern entries into Switzerland.

Rheims is, moreover, an excellent staging post if you have crossed the Channel in the middle of the day and only cleared the customs by mid-afternoon.   Roughly 170 miles from the coast, it can be reached in the late evening without undue speeding—some people need a little time to get used to driving on the right of the road.   Here, in these days of heavy traffic, as at all first-and-last night points along the main routes, it is as well to have rooms booked in advance, especially if you intend to arrive later than dinner-time.   It can be very uncomfortable to arrive in the dark, hungry and tired, to be faced with a frantic search for a bed from hotel to hotel, already crammed to overflowing with earlier arrivals.

Other good first-night points to aim at, according to the road you are taking from the coast, are Soissons and Laon, about an hour's shorter run than Rheims; St. Quentin and Amiens, an hour shorter still; or Arras, less than three hours from Dunkirk or Boulogne, if a short stage is preferred.   If Boulogne is the port of entry and a minimum of motoring is desired after a midday crossing, Le Touquet is only an hour away along the coast and very little off the Amiens road.

The direct road from Dunkirk to Rheims runs through Hazebrouck and Bethune to Arras, narrow, twisty at times, and with a number of abominable sections of *pavé*. It then improves and is reasonably fast through Bapaume and Peronne to St. Quentin. From there on through Laon to Rheims is typical good, fast *Route Nationale*.

From Boulogne you can either take the Montreuil–Hesdin–St. Pol road, narrow and slow, to Arras (see above). Or you can continue on the faster but slightly longer route through Abbeville and Amiens, thence striking north to join the other route at St. Quentin. Both involve typical sections of *pavé*, an abomination which is, fortunately, being gradually replaced everywhere.

If Soissons is the objective, the deviation point on the Dunkirk road is at a point a few miles north of Ham, where the right-hand turning to that place is taken, instead of taking the left-hand turning to St. Quentin. From Ham to Soissons, through Chauny, is another 34 miles. From Amiens through Roye and Noyon to Soissons is a straight run of 60 miles. (Soissons cathedral is at least as well worth a visit as the more renowned one at Rheims.)

The continuation of the through-route beyond Soissons to points on the more southerly sector of the Swiss frontier and in the French Alps is dealt with under Route II on p. 39.

From Rheims—even an early morning start should allow of a visit to the Cathedral—the N.44 runs fast and straight through Sillery, where a sector of the immortal battlefields of the First World War has been preserved as a permanent memorial, for 27 miles to Châlons-sur-Marne. Châlons, at the heart of the champagne country, boasts a hostelry with a remarkable name and a world-famous cellar, but in my opinion, overrated in other respects.

From Châlons to Vitry le Francois and St. Dizier is the straightest and fastest sector of the whole route, and a high average can be safely maintained for 40 miles. Beyond St. Dizier the road enters the delightful upper valley of the Marne, through whose peaceful, wooded landscape it takes a curving, tree-lined way past Joinville for 50 miles to Chaumont, with consequent slight reduction of speed.

Here the road climbs momentarily high above the lovely valley, with wide views over the hills bounding it on the other side and then swings on through more open country to Langres, a remarkable old fortress town, magnificently set on a steep hill. Its battlemented walls, under which the road passes through massive archways, and the towers of its fine Abbey church dominate the country for miles around. Here a connecting link branches off to the right, reaching Dijon on Route II (Soissons–Troyes–Dijon) in a fast, undulating, almost straight 40 miles' run (see p. 40).

Here, too, is the point for leaving the main Bâle highway if you are aiming at the more southerly entries into Switzerland by Pontarlier and Les Verrières or Les Joux, depending on whether you are bound for Neuchâtel or Lausanne. This route starts along the Dijon road, but almost immediately leaves it and strikes off to the left through Gray (35 miles), then by a slow and hilly 28 miles to Besançon, continuing by typical Jura main road through twisting gorges, allowing of no great speed, to Pontarlier, another 38 miles on.

While this variant of Route I is certainly one of the direct ways to Pontarlier and the Swiss entries beyond it, the last sector is slow and tortuous for a much greater distance than the final sector of Route II beyond Dijon. I have therefore treated that route (pp. 41–2) as the fastest and most direct route for the motorist bound for Neuchâtel and Berne or for Cossonnay and Lausanne.

Reverting to the main Bâle highway, beyond Langres, it is a long, rather uninteresting run of 46 miles through scrubby, wooded, more undulating country to the railway junction of Vesoul, where there is another turning south to Besançon and Pontarlier, by a subsidiary road. From Vesoul through Lure to Belfort is another 40 miles without any particular distinguishing marks till, a few miles short of that busy city, you become aware with surprising suddenness that you are on the threshold of the great hills. A long, straight piece of collar-work lifts the road to an altitude of 1,000 ft. at the Ban de Champagney, whose summit view, in clear weather, marks it out for one of the obligatory halts on this long and, for the last 80 miles, tedious rush across Eastern France. This hill-top provides a lovely unobstructed sweep over the great green backs of the Vosges, rising only a few miles to the north, with a vista beyond into the unseen gap of the Rhine valley and away to the soft outlines of the Black Forest, 30 miles ahead.

The road now drops sharply into Belfort, another important rail and road junction point; for here, again, the roads divide according to where you have decided to cross the Swiss frontier. If you are bound for Bâle, Zürich, or Constance, you keep straight on along N.19; the frontier is still 42 miles ahead of you. But if you are going in through Delle and the Swiss Jura you must now turn off to the right and take the Pontarlier road (N.437) for a mile or two before striking off to the left again to Delle, only 12 miles away, crossing the Rhone–Rhine canal on the way. This entry into Switzerland leads on through the fine ancient Swiss town of Porrentruy only a few miles over the border, across the hump of the Jura by the Col at Les Rangiers, with its huge memorial to the Swiss frontier guard, at a height of 3,000 ft., to Délémont, Moutier, and through a series of fine Jura gorges to Bienne, on its pleasant lake, a picturesque run of 45 miles of mountain road. From there it is only 22 miles to Berne, across the plain.

This, then, is the shortest and most direct route to Berne, the Central Swiss plain, and the Bernese Oberland resorts beyond it, Thun, Spiez, Interlaken, Kandersteg, and Meiringen, at the foot of the Susten–Grimsel–Furka triangle of passes. It also affords an alternative link with Lucerne and the Gotthard, taking the valley road from Berne onwards, through Langnau.

From Belfort, however, N.19 is the main highway to Bâle, continuing through a delightful countryside of old timbered farm-houses and shady pine-woods to picturesque Altkirch (20 miles), on a low ridge above its bridge over the Ill. Then, gaining height a little, it runs along the crest of a beautifully wooded ridge almost all the remaining 20 miles to the frontier just short of Bâle, with glorious views all round you as you drop gently into Switzerland. On the left, the lofty Vosges sweep round to the broad gap of the Rhine basin, beyond which rise the pine-clad slopes and gentle contours of the Black Forest; to the right, the long, smooth line of the Jura swings away to the south-east with all the promise of the great lakes and peaks screened by their modest intrusion. At last, after his long, hot day's motoring across the plains and dales, the mountain-lover will feel, with a lift of his heart, that he is on the threshold of the promised land. This entry into Switzerland is particularly lovely in the cool of the evening, when the whole wide prelude to the hills is bathed in the low light of the westering sun. If you have driven from Soissons or Rheims since breakfast—or, if driving one of the really fast cars, you have taken the whole dusty 400-miles plus since the night ferry decanted you at Dunkirk in the dawn—it is an indescribably lovely welcome at journey's end for hot and tired eyes.

From Bâle two main arteries fan out, according to your ultimate destination. There is the direct Zürich–Sargans–Bludenz route over the Arlberg Pass to Austria and Innsbruck (this can be varied by the slightly longer and less interesting approach to Bludenz through Constance and Rorschach). Or, south-eastwards, lies the direct approach by Olten and Lucerne's lovely lake to the Gotthard Pass, Lugano, and Milan.

For these two objectives Bâle is the proper point of entry into Switzerland, and Route I, as described, the most direct and quickest road across France. From the coast at Dunkirk or Boulogne it is roughly 450 miles; from Rheims about 270 and from Soissons about 300. And this is a road on which a small modern car can comfortably average thirty-five overall, even if heavily laden with passengers, luggage, and holiday gear.

I have purposely omitted a description of the alternative route (N.394) which branches off from the main highway shortly after Rheims to Bar le Duc and appears so straight and attractive on the map. By continuing south-eastward along it and N.66 beyond Bar le Duc through Neufchâteau—and, incidentally Joan of Arc's birthplace, Domrémy—Contrexeville and Luxeuil les Bains, it can be used to bring one back into N.19 at Lure, just short of Belfort. But the proper function of this road, in my view, is to carry the eastward traffic on from Bar to Toul and Nancy (along N.4) and to serve the northern Vosges and Strasbourg. As an alternative route to Switzerland it is slightly longer, definitely slower, on the whole less attractive scenically, and mostly in a less good state of repair; if there is any advantage, it is that, in the high season, the traffic may be rather less dense.

ROUTE II:

    (i) *Coastal Ports—Soissons—Montmirail—Sézanne—Troyes—Châtillon-sur-Seine—Dijon—Dole—Salins-les-Bains—Pontarlier—Les Joux—Cossonnay—(Lausanne–Simplon) or Pontarlier—Les Verrières—(Neuchâtel–Berne)*

    (ii) *Dole—Poligny—Champagnole—Lons le Saunier—Morez—La Cure —Col de St. Cergue—Nyon—(Lausanne) or Morez—Col de la Faucille—(Geneva)*

If you are intending to enter Switzerland by one of the three main Jura frontier-posts south of Delle ; Les Verrières on the Pontarlier–Neuchâtel–Berne road; Les Joux on the road from Pontarlier to Cossonnay and Lausanne; or La Cure on that from Dole, through Morez and then by St. Cergue, to Lausanne (this also serves Geneva over the Col de la Faucille, the roads dividing after Morez, and in this case the frontier post is on the outskirts of Geneva itself)—the most direct approach across France lies through Soissons (N.37) by N.373, N.71 and N.5 to Dijon and Dole. There the route divides, the northerly arm leading to Pontarlier, the southern to Geneva or Nyon, also at the western end of the lake. Beyond Pontarlier, the road offers two frontier crossings, that at Les Joux providing the direct main road to Lausanne, the Simplon, the Italian Lakes (Maggiore), and Milan; while the secondary left-hand turn to Les Verrières–Suisse leads to Neuchâtel and Berne.

From the coastal ports the first stages are identical with those of Route I, already described.

The most direct way to Dijon runs through Soissons, which will again offer a convenient staging post (about 135 miles) and Troyes; but the road onwards from Soissons over the heights of the Marne and from the valley of the Marne to that of the Seine, though shorter by many miles, is hillier and generally slower than Route I. So there are probably not more than a couple of hours in it if you prefer to go by Rheims and remain on the Bâle route either till Châlons, whence a very fast, almost dead-straight road runs south-east to Troyes, or even as far as Langres, cutting across to Dijon from there by the link already mentioned (p. 37).

From Soissons the direct road (Route II) runs over the uplands between the Marne and the Seine, through Montmirail and Sézanne, beyond which it crosses the Aube, just before its confluence with the Seine. It then follows the Seine valley, with some delightful stretches of woodland scenery, to the busy manufacturing and railway centre of Troyes (90 miles from Soissons).

Beyond Troyes the road enters the upper valley of the Seine, and from here to the charming little summer resort of Châtillon-sur-Seine (40 miles), near the river's head-waters, it winds its rather slower way, rising and falling on either side of the pretty valley, which boasts some fine country houses and châteaux dominating the wooded slopes.

Châtillon is separated from Dijon (52 miles) by the high, scrub-covered plateau of the Côte d'Or, intersected by the deep limestone ravines of several minor rivers. In and out of these the road is presently forced to wriggle, with resultant steep hills and sharp—occasionally even miniature hairpin-bends, which considerably reduce the rate of progress. Between these fine, wooded gorges, with their steep limestone cliffs, lie wonderful straight sections over high ground, yielding enormous vistas to immensely distant horizons under a wide, vaulting sky.

In one of the gentler folds, not far short of Dijon, lies St. Seine L'Abbaye, finely seen from the road, lying below with its russet roofs clustering round its ancient Abbey, before you sweep down through its narrow main street and up again over the brow beyond. A few miles farther on, the road dips into the very pretty Val Suzon, then climbs steeply again to the plateau, which continues to within a mile or two of Dijon, where it ends abruptly in the vine-covered Côte d'Or escarpment, overlooking the vast, luxuriant plain of eastern France, which sweeps away beyond the basins of the Ain, the Saône, and the Rhone to the Jura and the Alps.

This is a truly magnificent view, and no place along the route offers a better choice for a roadside halt. At your feet lies Dijon, its outlines little changed since Corot rendered this very scene so marvellously nearly a hundred years ago. The old peasant I spoke to at his ploughing on the brow of the hill assured me that on clear mornings he looks out across the intervening hundred miles to Mont Blanc's glittering crown, though I have never been lucky enough to see more than a vague blue promise of the Alps from here.

A few wide curves take the road steeply down to Dijon's hot and busy streets. This city of 100,000 inhabitants is a fascinating mixture of modern industry, a railway junction on the scale of Crewe, and a spacious ancient cathedral-and-fortress town, with handsome parks, squares, and boulevards, the ruins of a well-preserved Roman gateway and a lofty medieval citadel, from whose ramparts, once again, Mont Blanc is reported to be visible, though the right weather conditions have so far eluded me.

At Dijon my Routes II and III separate, the former being the continuation of the direct route to Switzerland, the latter serving the French Alps of Savoy and Dauphiné away to the south-east, the Mont Cenis route to Turin and Italy—the most direct and lowest pass route to Piedmont—and, of course, the splendid highway to Lyons and the Mediterranean by the lower course of the Rhone; though the last-named hardly falls within the scope of this book (see below p. 44).

From Dijon Route II runs fairly straight on across the fertile Burgundy plain to Dole, of vineyard fame, by way of Auxonne, with its picturesque bridge over the Saône. After crossing the Doubs at Dole the road begins to lift into the hills, and a long ascent, the last part through a fine gorge crowned by typical limestone ramparts, leads, by way of Poligny and the high, open, and well-wooded valleys of the Jura, to Champagnole, where there is a famous hotel, renowned for the crayfish which lead a short but gay life in the courtyard tank.

Beyond Champagnole the Jura road winds on through the woods for 21 miles to Morez, where it divides. The left-hand branch rises almost immediately to the Swiss frontier post at La Cure, from which it drops down, with glorious views ahead, through the beech woods of the Col de St. Cergue to Nyon on the lakeside road from Geneva to Lausanne.

The right-hand arm falls away for a while, then climbs over the Col de la Faucille, with its classic view over the whole lake-basin and the great snow-ranges swinging away behind it in a wide arc from Mont Blanc due south and only 30 miles distant, to the far Valaisian giants and the still farther Bernese Oberland peaks on the horizon. From the Col the road sweeps down the steep flank of the Jura by broad windings to Gex and the Swiss frontier just outside Geneva. From Morez to Geneva is 35 miles;

and beyond Geneva a choice of roads leads onwards through the Savoy Alps to Chamonix, Annecy, Aix-les-Bains, and Chambéry.

Striking a little more to the north from Dijon, and following the above route as far as Dole, is the most direct of all the roads through the Jura, by way of Salins-les-Bains, a delightful stopping-place, and the curving woodland road to Pontarlier, the last railway and road junction on the French side of the frontier. Here it joins the offshoot from Route I, by Gray and Besançon and the gorges of the Loue referred to as an alternative approach to Pontarlier on p. 37.

A mile or two beyond Pontarlier, directly after passing through a narrow defile crowned by the impressive ancient and ruined fortress of La Cluse, the road to Neuchâtel and Central Switzerland goes off at right-angles eastwards. This is a slow, narrow, up-and-down journey of some 35 miles, with nothing much to look at till the final long descent on Neuchâtel and its lake, which is lovely and, like all the views from the Jura ridge behind the fine old town, takes in a magnificent sweep of the central plain and the distant wall of the Alps, 80 miles away. A *détour* to the local Chaumont, 2,000 ft. up and half an hour's drive away, to see the full extent of this wonderful spectacle, will set a seal of unforgettable beauty on this otherwise rather tame entry into Switzerland. From Neuchâtel to Berne, through Kerzers and Mühleberg, it is a delightful drive of 25 miles, with the snowy chain of the Bernese Alps lifting their heads above the undulating, cultivated folds of the plain ahead of you all the way, as you draw nearer to them.

From the Pontarlier road-junction, the direct route to Lausanne and the Simplon continues delightfully between the Jura pines, through the small summer resort of Jougne, to enter Switzerland at Les Joux, in the open valley of the Orbe, and then accompanies the main Paris–Vallorbe–Simplon railway line down the gentle slope to the Cossonnay plateau. This it crosses, with glorious views across the lake-basin to the Savoy Alps, backed by the snows from Mont Blanc to the Oberland, as well as towards Yverdon and the Lake of Neuchâtel to the north-east; the Lake of Geneva does not really come into sight till very late in the proceedings, as the road drops over the edge of the plateau and down the last steep little escarpment to Lausanne.

Pontarlier to Lausanne is 40 miles, and from the customs at Les Joux 26 miles of very attractive motoring; and at Lausanne you are poised for the continuation along the wonderful Rhone highway to Milan over the Simplon; Turin over the Great St. Bernard; to the Central Swiss passes, affording a direct link from Visp with the Rhine valley and the Grisons (Engadine); or to half a dozen lovely lateral valleys stabbing off the main road into the mountains on either side.

ROUTE III :

   (i) *Dijon—Beaune—Chalon-sur-Saône—Tournus—Bourg-en-Bresse—Pont d'Ain—Belley—Chambéry—Aiguebelle—St. Jean de Maurienne—Modane—Lanslebourg—Mont Cenis Pass—(Suze–Turin)*

(ii) *Pont d'Ain—Les Abrets—Voiron—Grenoble—Lautaret and Galibier Passes—Briançon—Mont Genèvre Pass—(Susa–Turin)—Route des Alpes—Mediterranean*

(iii) *Bourg-en-Bresse—Nantua—Geneva—Simplon Pass—(Milan)*

(iv) *Tournus—Macon—Lyons—Mediterranean*

(v) *Grenoble—Gap—Digne—Mediterranean*

Both the routes already described to the Central Alps and their high passes approach them through Switzerland.

At Dijon the third direct high road to and across the Alps turns due south, and for 60 miles, as far as Tournus, shares the broad, swift highway across the Burgundy plain with the main routes to the Mediterranean, either by Lyons and Provence or by Grenoble and a choice of more or less mountainous roads beyond.

This third route lies entirely on French soil and gives direct access to one of the major trans-Alpine crossings, the Mont Cenis, which besides being the shortest way to Turin, is also the lowest and least exacting of the great roads across the backbone of the Alps dividing France from Italy. From Aiguebelle, beyond Chambéry, where the Mont Cenis approach turns south-east into the valley of the Arc, a road forks north-east to Albertville and runs by the Isère valley to the foot of the Petit St. Bernard Pass—another relatively easy Alpine crossing, leading to Aosta and Turin—at Bourg St. Maurice. This approach thus serves two of the major passages from France to Italy over the Alps; though the Petit St. Bernard may be more directly approached by taking one or other of the roads through the Alps of Savoy beyond Geneva (see Route II, p. 42).

Motorists bound farther south to the Dauphiné and its internal passes, over the Route des Alpes to the Mediterranean, and to those subsidiary crossings of the Alpine chain into Italy stemming from the long mountain road to the coast—the Mont Genèvre, the Col de Larche, and the Colle di Tenda—follow the Mont Cenis approach to a point a little beyond Pont d'Ain. Here the road through Voiron to Grenoble—the gateway to the great Dauphiné Passes, the Col du Lautaret, and the Galibier, as well as to the many minor mountain roads running south more directly to the Côte d'Azur—diverges southwards to the right (see below p. 45).

Leaving Dijon, all these routes share the great Burgundy highway, broad and fast, through Beaune and Chalon-sur-Saône, both good stopping-places at the end of a long day; along its lovely course every side turning bears the name of a famous Burgundy vineyard—Nuits St. Georges, Montrachet, and all.

From Chalon the road follows the broad Saône valley for 16 miles to Tournus, with its magnificent Abbey. Here the road to the Alps branches off leftwards at right-angles, to cross the river, and forges first east and then south-east, under trees often arching across the roadway to provide much-needed shade, to Bourg-en-Bresse, 34 miles away along N.79, another good staging post, whose chief glory are the fine churches of Notre Dame and, in the outskirts, St. Brou, whose interior is well worth a visit. This is a cross-country stretch of slightly slower *Route Nationale*, but by no means a secondary road.

(The main road on which we turn our back at Tournus goes straight on down the Saône valley to Macon and Lyons (80 miles) and thence onwards along the plain of the Rhone by the lowland route to Vienne and Valence.)

At Bourg a picturesque Jura road, slow and tortuous for much of the way, strikes off due east through Nantua, a pleasant hill-resort on a small but pretty lake, to Bellegarde and through the *Zone Franche* (double customs posts) to Geneva (90 miles). The high ridges crossed during the early part of this drive yield fine wide vistas over the Jura landscape, and the final section lies through the very impressive gorges carved out by the Rhone after issuing from the Lake of Geneva on its southward course to Lyons and the Mediterranean. This road through Nantua can also be reached more directly by striking eastwards earlier, from Chalon-sur-Saône, through Lons le Saunier.

Continuing from Bourg along the joint Mont Cenis–Dauphiné approach route the road draws steadily nearer to the southern Jura on the left till, just beyond the Ain crossing at Pont d'Ain, the two roads diverge at an important fork.

The Chambéry–Mont Cenis–Italy route continues through pretty but hilly country to Belley, beyond which it climbs to the miniature pass of the Col du Chat,* which not only has a good hotel, but commands delightful views of the wide basin of the Lac du Bourget, with Aix-les-Bains on its far shore, and away to the Savoy Alps behind it and to the fringes of the Tarentaise Alps beyond Chambéry. The road then falls away for 18 miles past the foot of the lake, to that ancient town and road junction, beyond which it enters the broad valley of the Isère.

It then proceeds north-eastwards up the valley towards Albertville (see p. 43 above) till at Aiguebelle, where the Arc flows into the Isère, it swings abruptly south-east into the long, deep valley of that tributary river, hurrying down from the Cottian Alps ahead, and for 40 miles follows the main Mont Cenis railway line and the river at close quarters, through St. Michel and St. Jean de Maurienne, to Modane, where the so-called Mont Cenis tunnel begins (see Chap. IV, p. 57).

The only side turning of any note along this lengthy valley road is at St. Michel, where a rather narrow and extremely sinuous approach, winding up and up the enormous, well-wooded southern flank of the valley for more than 2,000 ft., leads to the small summer resort of Valloire and thence by a splendidly graded, wide, modern road—often, however, seriously damaged just short of the summit tunnel by the ravages of winter—to the Col du Galibier, 8,399 ft. (see Chapter XXX, p. 201) and so down to join the Grenoble–Col du Lautaret–Briançon artery of the Dauphiné.

From Modane it is an hour's lovely drive at the foot of the great Tarentaise mountains to Lanslebourg, where the gentle windings of the Mont Cenis Pass suddenly strike southwards over a low saddle in the main chain

---

* Several hundred feet of climbing are avoided by taking the tunnel, at 2,050 ft., underneath the summit, but this misses the best of the view.

of the Cottian Alps to Susa and so down to Turin in the Piedmont Plain still 60 miles on the other side of the huge mountain wall (Chapter IV).

As has been said above, the road to Grenoble and the Dauphiné leaves the through-route to Italy soon after Pont d'Ain, taking a more southerly course. A mile or two later, at Sault Brenaz, it suddenly strikes the wide glacier-grey Rhone, flowing swiftly between steep limestone bluffs which rise above the wooded hill-sides. If it happens to be lunch-time and you carry your own commissariat, the little water-front here, in the shade of clumpy trees, makes a delightful picnic place, by the way. The broad, swirling river is crossed by a fine, many-arched concrete bridge, and the road then continues across the uplands on the other side for 35 miles to Les Abrets, Voiron 17 miles farther on, and Grenoble.

For a long while it climbs gently and deceptively over rolling, cultivated slopes, with wide forward views to the distant Chartreuse and Dauphiné ranges, as well as down on to the adjacent lake of Paladru on the other side, to a height of nearly 2,000 ft. So long and gentle is the gradient that I have known people to keep their foot down on the accelerator as if they were on the flat and end up with a boiling radiator. It then descends to Les Abrets and, passing through a charmingly wooded valley, reaches the pleasant holiday resort of Voiron, backed by the steep limestone massif of the Chartreuse, now close at hand.

From Voiron to Grenoble (13 miles) is a fast, modern stretch of road across the plain of the Isère and, as it approaches the great gap in the hills which suddenly tower immensely overhead, it frequently skirts the river's northern bank. The gateway narrows rapidly and, passing through it close under great rocky faces to the left, the road enters the magnificent University city of Grenoble, spread out across its lush green plain at the western foot of the Belledonne and Dauphiné massifs.

From Grenoble a number of important roads radiate; through Savoy by Annecy to Geneva; to Albertville and the Little St. Bernard Pass (Chapter V); to Chambéry and the Mont Cenis (Chapter IV); and south-wards to Gap, Sisteron, Digne, and the Mediterranean by several less mountainous routes which skirt or circumvent the major snowy ranges. But its own particular glory among high mountain roads is that striking due east through the heart of the great massif of the Dauphiné Alps by the Col du Lautaret to Briançon, whence the Col du Mont Genèvre carries it forward over the Cottians into Italy; and from Briançon sharply south over a series of minor linked passes, all on the French side of the border range, which penetrate the rocky spurs of the *Alpes Maritimes* to Puget-Théniers and Nice—200 miles of magnificent mountain scenery and thrilling roads—the *Route des Alpes* (Chapter XXIX).

Car-sleeper Expresses.

For those who wish to cut out the road-approach across France or Germany, car-sleeper expresses are now available, daily (except Wednesdays) during the summer, from Boulogne to Lyons and, on Saturdays and Tuesdays, from Ostend to Munich. Readers of this book will presumably be less interested in the latest addition, on Saturdays, from Ostend to Milan, as it cuts out the Alpine road-crossings as well.

III

THE MAIN MOUNTAIN HOLIDAY REGIONS
AND RESORTS

FROM WEST to east, it is convenient to divide the holiday regions of the high Alps, along the routes described in this book, into four main areas.

1. The French Alps. Savoy—Dauphiné and the Maritime Alps.
2. Switzerland. The Bernese Oberland—The Valais—The Grisons (Engadine).
3. Northern Italy. The Lakes—The Graian and Cottian Alps—the south side of the Pennines—the Ortler Group—the Dolomites.
4. Austria. The German/Austrian Limestone Alps—the Zillertal, Oetztal, and Stubai Alps—the Hohe Tauern (Grossglockner).

THE FRENCH ALPS

Savoy

Savoy (Savoie and Haute Savoie) embraces the mountainous tract from the south shore of the Lake of Geneva southwards to the Mont Blanc group, the highest massif in the Alps, and the lower but very attractive Tarentaise and Frontier Ranges (Cottians) farther south and south-east.

In this area is to be found every kind of holiday resort, higher or lower, larger or smaller, luxurious or simple, according to the traveller's taste.

At the lower levels, Chambéry, Aix-les-Bains, and Annecy are the main centres, all of them towns of some size and providing standards one would expect to find there, ranging to a high level of luxury and sophistication, particularly at Aix.

Aix and Annecy are lake-side resorts—the former on the sunny, open Lac du Bourget, the latter on its own charming and smaller lake, enclosed by steep limestone escarpments. The other large lake-resort is Evian-Thonon on the south shore of Geneva's vast expanse, looking across to Lausanne and the Jura behind it. The swimmer, the water-skier, the lover of speed boats will find everything he wants here and, for variety, the mountains are within easy reach.

At moderate heights, and bristling with hotels and holiday facilities, are the popular resorts of Megève and St. Gervais, on sunny slopes within close call of the Mont Blanc range and its scenic wonders.

In the Tarentaise (Vanoise Alps) Brides-les-Bains, still almost at the level of the Isère valley, offers a less-pretentious thermal station, while high up along the winding roads behind it lie the mountain walking and climbing resorts of Pralognan, at the heart of the Vanoise peaks and glaciers, and the rapidly developing post-war resort of Courchevel.

Continuing up the Isère valley through Bourg St. Maurice, a typical valley resort, at the foot of the Petit St. Bernard Pass into Italy, the upper Isère road climbs to the mountain-walking and climbing centre of Val d'Isère, in a high but sunny and open situation between the eastern fringe of the Vanoise massif and the high frontier peaks of the Cottian Alps.

Across the Col d'Iséran from Val d'Isère are the smaller and less pretentious valley resorts of Bonneval sur Arc and Lanslebourg in the upper valley of the Arc, at the foot of the Mont Cenis. Both offer magnificent mountain scenery and scope for fine walks and splendid climbs.

The most famous Savoy resort of all is, of course, Chamonix at the northern foot of Mont Blanc. Everything is to be found here, cinemas, a lido, luxury hotels, a casino, *telefériques* to high above the snow line; and yet it remains one of the great mountaineering centres, visited by thousands whose luggage is a rucksack and their hotel a mountain hostel or hut. Situated at a modest height of 3,500 ft., it is an ideal centre for peak gazing, motor-excursions, magnificent walks, and, of course, some of the world's most sensational climbing.

Dauphiné

The Dauphiné lies southwards of Savoy, sundered from it by the lower Isère valley and the deep trench of the Maurienne, from which it sweeps away to the borders of the Maritime Alps far to the south and south-east.

Grenoble, its capital, is a magnificent University city, spreading finely across the Isère plain at the western fringe of the Dauphiné Alps. It is a splendidly equipped centre for motoring excursions, and a stay of several days would not exhaust its attractions.

The massif of the Dauphiné Alps, to the east and south-east of Grenoble, while less well provided with up-to-date and well-appointed resorts than any other great Alpine region, contains some of the most rugged, awe-inspiring, and magnificent high-mountain scenery in the Alps.

The main valley resorts at the heart of the great peaks are Briançon, a fine old fortified town with numerous hotels, the smaller valley-centre of Bourg d'Oisans and, beyond the southern fringe of the main massif, such well-known centres as Gap, Embrun, Guillestre, and Barcelonnette.

Of the high-level resorts, Alpe d'Huez, a post-war development, stands at 6,000 ft. at the top of a magnificent new road from Bourg d'Oisans. Here are hotels of every standard from modest pension to luxury-cum-chromium. and the views over the peaks are magnificent if distant.

Of the climbing centres, the most famous—accessible only by a narrow and highly exciting road along the Vénéon Gorges—is La Bérarde, a hamlet with only primitive accommodation, set at the foot of truly stupendous rock walls. The motorist with strong nerves will find a day's drive up and down this cul-de-sac a wonderful experience if he is also a lover of mountain scenery at its most savage and magnificent.

La Grave, half-way along the Lautaret road, nestles in a scene of fantastic beauty at the foot of the Meije. This is a glorious centre for walking as well as for mountaineering; but accommodation is limited to 80 rooms, in two good though not luxurious hotels, besides other plainer lodgings.

Vallouise, at the eastern fringe of the massif, is again a purely climbing and high walking centre; but a drive up the side road to it from the main Durance valley road is recommended for lovers of grand mountain scenery.

Valloire, on the descent from the Col du Galibier to St. Michel de Maurienne, is a small but charming medium-level summer resort, in sunny meadows backed by shady woods, and affords a convenient place for breaking a journey northwards from Dauphiné to Savoy.

The Alpes Maritimes

The Riviera resorts are too well known to require mention. Inland, on the roads leading to the mountains of Dauphiné, lie Grasse, Puget-Théniers, Castellane, Digne, and numerous smaller resorts and staging posts.

SWITZERLAND

Switzerland is so well documented in guide-book, pamphlet, and folder that only the briefest outline seems necessary.

The Northern Plain

The northern plain and the foothills provide innumerable holiday opportunities, particularly on the shores of a dozen lakes—Constance, Zürich, the Walensee, Bienne, Neuchâtel, the north shore of Geneva, the lovely Lake of Lucerne, its neighbour Zug, and the twin lakes of Thun and Brienz. The choice for the lover of a lowland, bathing, and boating holiday is endless, and there are good hotels everywhere in Switzerland.

The Bernese Oberland

Along the roads through this most northerly of the great Swiss mountain groups lie countless resorts of all sizes and at all levels, most of them offering scenic attractions, recreations such as tennis and swimming and, of course, the more strenuous mountain pursuits.

Interlaken, bestriding the plain at the gateway to the Bernese mountains, is a world-famous tourist-centre requiring no description.

At the head of their respective valley roads, but still definitely valley resorts, stand Grindelwald, Lauterbrunnen, Kandersteg, and Adelboden. Meiringen, at the foot of the Brünig, is a large and pleasant valley centre; Innertkirchen, only a few miles away at the approach to the Grimsel, smaller but no less charming.

Wengen (4,400 ft.) and Mürren (5,500 ft.), opposing one another across the rift of the Lauterbrunnen valley, stand higher than the others. Neither is accessible by road, but there is ample garage accommodation at Lauter-

Susa, at the Italian foot of the Mont Cenis, with the Roccia Melone above

Mont Blanc from above Pré St. Didier (Val d'Aosta)

brunnen, from which both are reached by short journeys on mountain railways.

The Valais

Till lately the valleys of the Valais, cutting deep into the group of far larger and even more magnificent mountains to the south of the Rhone, have been relatively neglected by motorists.   Recent road improvements should result in their being visited by steadily increasing numbers, for they lead to some of the finest scenery in Switzerland.

Verbier, above the Val des Bagnes, south of Martigny, is now approached by a fine modern road and is a rapidly developing resort with all holiday facilities; its position on a sunny shelf at 6,000 ft., facing the vast snowy bulk of the Grand Combin and also commanding the more distant Mont Blanc range, is superb.

In the Val d'Hérens, Evolène is a charming resort at a moderate height and gives access to the famous climbing centre of Arolla, beyond and above.   The road leaves the Rhone valley highway at Sion.

The Val d'Anniviers is one of the loveliest valleys in the Alps.   The recently modernized road climbs into it from Sierre, and brings the motorist without difficulty to the charming high-mountain resort of St. Luc.   Some rather more tricky motoring up the narrow valley road beyond Vissoie and Ayer leads the more adventurous to the climbing-centre of Zinal, at the foot of a dozen mighty peaks.   The whole length of this valley affords glorious walking possibilities.

Zermatt is, at the time of writing, still only approachable by rail, but a fine, if narrow, new road from Stalden now brings the motorist to the famous climbing and walking centre of Saas Fee, in incomparable surroundings at the very foot of the huge Mischabel peaks and glaciers.

The Grisons (Engadine)

Chur, an historic old town, in the Rhine valley, is the largest centre and the urban gateway to the mountains of the Grisons.   Farther up the main valley lies Disentis, while on a high shelf overlooking the Rhine Gorges between Chur and Ilanz is the finely equipped holiday centre of Flims-Waldhaus, with its famous bathing-lake, the Cauma See, a golf-course, and every imaginable holiday amenity.

Higher up in the valleys which climb southwards towards the main ranges of the Grisons are a number of celebrated resorts—Klosters, Davos, Lenzerheide, all ideal centres for sub-Alpine holiday delights—and a great many very pleasant smaller places, Thusis, Tiefencastel, and Savognin among them.

It is, however, the 30-mile-long trench of the Engadine—Upper and Lower—which contains the pick of the Grisons resorts, names famous all over the world.   In the upper sector there are luxurious and sophisticated St. Moritz, which offers everything in the sport and holiday dictionary; lovely and less blatant Pontresina; Maloja, Sils, Silvaplana, Campfer, Celerina, and Samaden.   Farther down, in the lower sector, are Zuoz

D

Zernez, Tarasp, Vulpera, and, largest of them all, Schuls (Scuol), a fine and well-equipped resort for a stay of any length; while, perched on the high shelves above the main valley, are a number of tiny but charming village resorts such as Fétan, Val Sinestra, and Samnaun, set in lovely mountain scenery and offering glorious walks and minor climbs.

The Ticino

Lugano, the pride of Switzerland's sub-Alpine Italianate Canton, needs no advertisement as a lake-side paradise; but there are numerous small hill resorts in the higher valleys running down to its basin from the main chain of the Alps.

NORTHERN ITALY

Here again the Lake resorts on Maggiore, Como, and Garda are too familiar to require detailed enumeration.

The mountain resorts of the north-west corner of Italy, on and under the southern slopes of the great horseshoe bend in the Alpine chain, are, however, far less well known.

Courmayeur, the Italian counterpart of Chamonix, nestling in the shadow of Mont Blanc's stupendous southern wall, is a first-class resort, with tennis courts and all other recreational facilities (except swimming), besides being an historic climbing centre. Excursions afoot and by *teleférique* to famous view points abound, and the valleys themselves are enchanting. A mile or two above Courmayeur, in the Val Ferret, is the small climbing centre of Entrèves, and a few miles below, on the fine road which leads up from the ancient Roman city of Aosta—now sadly industrialized—Pré St. Didier offers itself as another small and unpretentious but charmingly situated resort.

To the south of the Aosta–Pré St. Didier road several narrow mountain roads penetrate into the isolated mass of the Graian Alps. Here in superb mountain and valley scenery, beneath the glaciers of the Grivola and Gran Paradiso, stand a number of small, high resorts like Valsavaranche, beloved of walkers and climbers, the best known of which is Cogne. Ceresole Reale, approached from the southern side of the massif, is a pleasant, less mountainous holiday centre.

East of Aosta, running up from the high road along the rift of the Dora Baltea valley into the southern wall of the Alps, are a number of parallel valleys of great scenic variety and beauty. Along this mountain road are to be found historic Breuil-Valtournanche* at the southern foot of the Matterhorn, and such lovely valley pleasances as Gressoney la Trinité and Champorcher. Macugnaga, the climbing centre at the southern foot of Monte Rosa, is, however, approached from Domodossola, not from the Aosta valley.

Due west of Turin, Sestriere, on a high spur of the Cottians, is northern Italy's most modern and luxurious mountain resort, particularly frequented for winter sports, but also popular in summer.

* Now known as Cervinia, the name being taken from the Italian name for the Matterhorn—Il Cervino.

The Ortler* and the Dolomites

Northern Italy's other great mountain tract to the north and north-east of the head of Lake Garda embraces the Ortler and Adamello Groups, the Brenta Dolomites and the main Dolomite region to the east of the Adige valley.

Sulden (Solda), at the heart of the Ortler's magnificent glacier scenery, lies high and at the head of a narrow road, but is an ideal centre for the walker and mountaineer. Bormio, at the southern end of the Stelvio is a pleasant valley resort.

In the Brenta, Madonna di Campiglio is as lovely as it is accessible and a veritable walker's paradise; Molveno has a pretty lake; and there are many pleasant valley resorts, such as Pinzolo and Dimaro. This is a magnificent and neglected area.

The Dolomite region proper is studded with attractive resorts, of which Cortina, offering everything known in the range of holiday and tourist attractions, has achieved world fame since the winter Olympiad of 1955–6.

Smaller, simpler, but all of them extremely attractive, San Martino di Castrozza, Ortisei, Corvara, Karersee, Misurina, to mention only a few of the high-lying centres in the area, are all delightful places in which to stay and enjoy mountain scenery and pursuits.

The great Adige valley centres of Bolzano and Merano are gateway cities rather than mountain resorts—the Interlakens of the region—but for those who prefer the larger town setting and the pleasures and comforts of the lowlands they could not be improved on; though Bolzano can be oppressively hot in high summer.

AUSTRIA

Only three major mountain roads—the Arlberg, Brenner, and Grossglockner—and the long connecting lowland highway of the Inn valley are dealt with in this book. For geographical reasons already explained, the many minor roads and beauty spots of the Salzkammergut, Karwendel, and the other ranges of the Limestone Alps have not been covered.

Along the roads described lie countless delightful holiday resorts, for the small towns along the Austrian highways have mostly a simple charm of their own and the countryside is lovely.

Innsbruck, the key to the great Alpine groups which form the long watershed south of the Inn valley, is a pearl of a city in which to stay. Igls, on the slopes to the south, is a small and charming resort for those who prefer to be near, but not in, a crowded city. All along the valley highway stand ancient and lovely towns, Landeck, Telfs, Seefels, Hall, Schwaz, Wörgl, and Kufstein.

Running south, deep into the main mass of the Alps from the Inn valley, are three lovely mountain valleys, the Oetztal, the Stubaital, and the Zillertal.

The most westerly and longest, the Oeztal, carves a way for more than

* See footnote p. 24.

30 miles into the great mountain group of the Wildspitze and Weisskugel. Along the road, which penetrates to the high climbing centres of Obergurgl and Vent, at more than 6,000 ft., are a number of delightful mountain resorts—Umhausen, Längenfeld, and Sölden.

The Stubai valley, branching off from the Brenner road above Innsbruck at Schönberg, leads to small but charming mountain resorts in Fulpmes and Neustift. Resorts along the Brenner itself are dealt with in the description of the road.

The chief places in the magnificent Zillertal are Zell am Ziller and Mayrhofen, with a number of small mountain resorts in the lateral valleys branching up into the mountains, the best known perhaps being Gerlos.

All these afford splendid mountain scenery, walking and climbing; and the usual modern amenities of cable-lifts, tennis-courts, and other holiday requirements are steadily penetrating even these high and remote valleys.

Thirty miles east of Innsbruck, and at the foot of the savage and rocky Kaisergebirge, are Kitzbühel, a world-famous resort, set among smiling meadows in a broad valley and equipped with varying degrees of sophistication, and the smaller, less-pretentious St. Johann-in-Triol. These are both low-altitude resorts, compared with those described above.

Farther east, along the road to the Glockner, are other lowland centres, like Mittersill and Bruck in the broad plain of the Pinzgau valley. The gem of this region is, however, Zell am See, with its lovely swimming and boating lake, backed by the High Tauern range and the Limestone Alps; and if the town itself is somewhat crowded, there are numerous isolated corners to be found scattered round the quieter bays of the lake.

South of the Glockner, directly at its foot, stands unique Heiligenblut; but it may be that the endless volume of traffic over the road has ruined it for all time as a stopping-place. Lienz, in the low, broad valley of the Drau (Drave) into which the road eventually emerges, is a delightful old town and a very good centre indeed from which to explore its own miniature group of Dolomites to the south and the valleys carving northwards into the Hohe Tauern, among which again are to be found numerous very attractive mountain resorts, such as Matrei, Kals, and Prägraten, to mention only the best known.

PART II

THE GREAT TRANS-ALPINE PASSES

IV

THE MONT CENIS (6,834 ft.)

France–Italy (Cottian Alps).

From Aiguebelle (1,063 ft.) to Suze (Susa) (1,624 ft.), crossing the main Alpine watershed between the Mediterranean and Adriatic: 77 miles.

Detail. Aiguebelle to Modane (3,465 ft.): 38 miles, ascent 2,400 ft.
Modane to Lanslebourg (4,587 ft.): 16 miles, ascent 1,200 ft.
Lanselbourg to Summit (6,834 ft.): 6 miles, ascent 2,250 ft.
Total Ascent: 60 miles, 5,580 ft.

Summit to Mont Cenis Hospice, Village, French customs and Italian customs at Molaretto (c. 4,000 ft.): 11 miles, descent 2.800 ft.
Italian customs to Susa (1,624 ft.): 6 miles, descent 2,400 ft.
Total descent from Summit: 17 miles, 5,250 ft.

Open: Late April to early November. Maximum gradient: 1 in 10.

A very long, beautifully engineered modern road, fast in its lower sectors, to Modane. Continuing with easy rises and bends to Termignon, thence steeply with hairpins to Lanslebourg, where the Pass proper begins. Six good wide windings without any difficulties to the summit, whence the road runs straight for some miles along the high saddle. Steep descent by numerous splendidly engineered and well-protected windings, with superbly surfaced corners, all the way down the southern slope.

Traffic heavy in summer.
Easy to moderate.

THE MONT CENIS, one of four passes at various times popular in the Hannibal wrangle, is certainly the most direct and easiest of the high passages from the plains of Central France to the northern plains of Italy. As such it ranks high among the major international trans-Alpine routes which are the chief consideration of this survey. It is, however, from considerations of beauty and grandeur, somewhat less impressive than many of the other great Alpine passes; which does not mean that it is not a lovely road to drive; and the recent engineering improvements in its lower sectors are superb, permitting rapid progress.*

The long, deeply entrenched approach from Chambéry along the Valley of the Arc—the Maurienne—is too close under the southern ramparts of the Tarentaise Alps to allow of more than a few heartening glimpses of high peak and glacier. To the south, the massive, steep, heavily wooded slopes which separate it from the Dauphiné are inclined to become monotonous and oppressive. The bottom of this very deep and narrow valley invites continual competition between the swift, glacier-grey flow

* In the spring of 1957 very heavy flood damage was done to some miles of the road in the Arc Valley below Modane; emergency repairs carried out during last year are not due for completion before the end of summer 1958.

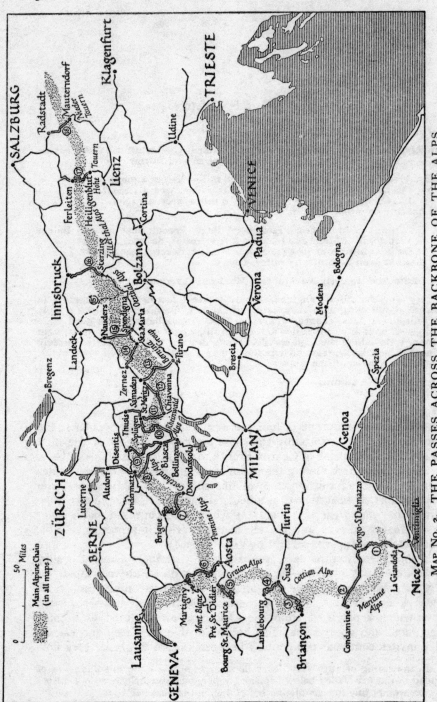

MAP No. 2.   THE PASSES ACROSS THE BACKBONE OF THE ALPS

1. Colle di Tenda
2. Col de Larche
3. Mont Cenis
5. Petit St. Bernard
6. Grand St. Bernard
7. Simplon
9. Lukmanier
10. S. Bernardino
11. Splügen
13. Bernina
14. Ofen
15. Resia (Reschen-Scheideck)
16. Brenner
17. Gross Glockner
18. Tauern

of the Arc, the double-track main line from Paris to Turin, very much in the foreground, and the road, snaking its way alongside from one narrow neck to the next. The towns along the route are unbeautiful, and one of them at least, Modane, for strategic reasons suffered almost total obliteration by the R.A.F. during the last war.

Finally, when the higher levels of the broader valley above Modane are eventually reached, the mountains immediately bounding it are bare and inclined to offer their less snowy aspects; and the fine peaks of the frontier range dividing France from Italy are tucked away at an inconvenient angle to the East, so as to be largely masked by gaunt intervening spurs.

When at last, at Lanslebourg, the pass proper addresses itself to the barrier to the south, it has already, almost insensibly, achieved a height of 4,500 ft. To reach the low col of the Mont Cenis, less than 2,000 ft. above in the watershed, it has nothing to do except to make six wide dog-legs across the pastures of a moderately inclined slope and this somehow fails to produce that feeling of achievement and elation which its more spectacular and romantic brethren arouse in the motorist's heart, though the views near the summit are very fine.

This slightly disparaging view of the Mont Cenis must, of course, be taken only in a comparative sense. There is much fine scenery along the route, and you cannot drive over even a 7,000-ft. saddle in the Alps without deriving a great deal of enjoyment and seeing many exciting things which are not visible, say, along some of the endless poplar-lined highways of Northern France. It only seems a little tantalizing to be so near so many lovely and familiar snowy mountains and yet see so little of them, considering the length of the route and the height attained. Certainly the man who avails himself of the newly instituted ferry service through the Mont Cenis Tunnel—a misnomer by the way, for it tunnels under the Col de Fréjus, some 17 miles short of the Mont Cenis proper—is doing himself an irreparable disservice.

The main landmarks on the long valley approach from Aiguebelle, at the confluence of the Arc and the Isère, to Modane are the industrialized towns of St. Jean and St. Michel de Maurienne, crowded in the narrow floor available on the banks of the Arc.

Branching off to the right at St. Michel is the long, narrow, twisting road which climbs the huge southern slope for some 2,000 ft., without much in the way of protection on the valley side, and then undulates through the pine-woods to Valloire and the fine modern Galibier road to the Dauphiné (Chapter XXIX). This gives access by the east side of the Lautaret, to Briançon and the southern passes of the Route des Alpes, as well as to the Mont Genèvre route into Italy (Chapter XIII); by its western side, to Grenoble and the plains of the lower Isère and Rhone.

Between St. Michel, Modane, and Termignon the road rises well above the true left bank of the Arc on a lofty shelf and there are some fine glimpses across the valley to the outlying peaks of the Vanoise Group of the Tarentaise Alps, with the Aiguille de Polset, the Aiguille de l'Échelle, and the Dent Parrachée, all over 11,000 ft. high, prominent among them.

Modane, whose main features are the important frontier station and its vast marshalling yards, engine-houses, and goods-sheds tucked into the floor of the valley just short of the western entrance of the 'Mont Cenis' tunnel, had to be destroyed by bombing in the interests of the interruption of vital strategic traffic between occupied France and enemy Italy. The whole thing is so narrowly compressed between the great feet of the hills that the railway could not be isolated as a separate target, and the town virtually disappeared in the resulting precision annihilation. When I last saw it, it was rising rapidly from its ashes; by now it will probably have resumed the appearance of a habitable town, and the fearful scar in a pleasant sub-Alpine valley will, I hope, have lost its livid freshness. Even then, Modane is unlikely to be much beyond the bustling railway centre it has been ever since the 8-mile tunnel, the first great railway penetration of the Alpine barrier, was opened after nine years of labour and the expenditure of 75,000,000 francs, in December 1870.

As you rise above the broadening valley level beyond Modane, the wide 3-mile *détour* by which the railway circles the town on its way to enter the tunnel mouth lying 300 ft. above it is well seen, but the tunnel itself is hidden from view below the road, which again climbs to a high shelf, with the river now hundreds of feet below. Near Bramans there is a fine view across the deep and narrow ravine to the massively tiered forts de l'Esseillon, backed by the summits of the Vanoise peaks, high above. This great double fortress shows little material change since Brockedon did one of his faithful sketches which illustrate his *Passes of the Alps*, in 1829. The Vanoise peaks still appear only intermittently above the great green ridges to the north. From them, strangely enough, the tunnel mouth is clearly visible: I recall sitting on the summit rocks of the Aiguille de Polset one sunny morning and watching through binoculars the minute worm of electric engine, sleeping- and dining-cars of the overnight Rome–Paris express crawl out of the dark pin-prick in the mountain's base and creep infinitesimally across the small green plain towards Modane station, 9,000 ft. below.

The road now climbs steadily up a series of ravines and broad valley terraces along the pleasant upper valley of the Arc, with occasional grand glimpses of the high frontier-peaks ahead to the east, and in another 11 miles reaches the small, clustering hamlet of Termignon (3,870 ft.), which, like Lanslebourg, higher up the valley, we were surprised to find in 1951 had suffered serious war damage in spite of its remote situation and the absence of any strategic target. This wanton destruction was, we learned, not from bombing but the result of systematic ruin and arson on the part of the Germans, as a reprisal for the activities of the Resistance, when they pulled out late in the War. There was, however, a defeatist and poverty-stricken air about these places, whose young men, we were told, had left them to seek their fortunes in more promising parts and whose local industries were by-passed and in a poor way. It did not seem that this part of the valley was then likely to return to prosperity, for all the rebuilding going on. There are two steep, sharp hairpins here.

Lanslebourg (4,585 ft.), 6 miles farther up the valley, stands boldly in a widening at the entrance to the highest step in its terraced floor, up which a road continues straight on to Bonneval-sur-Arc, at the foot of the fine Levanna amphitheatre, closing the re-entrant. This is the road to the great French military pass of the Col d'Iseran (Chapter XXX), the highest public mountain road in the Alps, having displaced the Stelvio by a few feet.

The Mont Cenis road, however, now abandons the valley levels abruptly, swinging off up the mountain slope to the right, and overcoming it purpose-fully but unsensationally, criss-crossing the 2,000-ft. breast of the hills between unexciting meadows and woods, in long, sweeping strides and an economic half-dozen hairpins, to reach the Col du Mont Cenis (6,834 ft.) after a steady ascent of only 6 miles.

In spite of the not unnatural suggestion that Hannibal used this most easily approached and lowest of all the western trans-Alpine crossings for his invasion of Italy with 30,000 men and 50 elephants in 219 B.C., there seems to be little convincing evidence that it was even used by the Romans. On the contrary, it seems pretty well established that they frequently crossed a number of passes, some considerably higher, which have sub-sequently remained mule-tracks, such as the Petit Mont Cenis and the Col de Clapier; it also seems fairly certain that the most regular crossings by Roman armies into Gaul took place by the Mont Genèvre, westwards from Susa, and not, as many authorities have maintained, by the Mont Cenis. Certainly descriptions of the route given by Roman writers corre-spond more closely with the features and configuration of the Mont Genèvre route, besides containing such definite references as the passage *under* the Arch of Cottius, whose remains still stand astride the Mont Genèvre route outside Susa, and not on the approach from that town to the Mont Cenis.

Brockedon suggested the interesting theory that, since the opening up of the passes was most frequently from the northern side, by invaders desirous of descending to the fertile plains of Italy, it was natural for any-one seeking a passage to follow the course of a northern river to its source and then cross the nearest col at its head; and since, exceptionally, there is no stream flowing down from the Mont Cenis saddle on the Lanslebourg side—where the Arc comes down the 'blind' main valley, which continues to Bonneval and the foot of the Levanna and the Iseran—it never occurred to anyone to prospect for a saddle at the top of a bare mountain slope just in that place.

Be that as it may, it is known for certain that Charlemagne and his successors found their way over it, and from that time onwards it became a regular and favoured crossing place in the Middle Ages.

Once again it was left to Napoleon to transform a track into an easy and safe carriage road, 30 ft. wide, well protected at its few exposed places, and engineered so as to avoid the hideous perils of the old route, which, traversing the Roche Melon side of the valley on the descent to Italy, directly under the precipices of that immense 11,000-ft. peak, was exposed

to seasonal avalanche dangers, resulting in appalling loss of life.   All this
was achieved between 1801, when the Imperial order went out for construction to begin, and 1810 by a labour force of 3,000 men, working only
during the practicable five months of the summer season, at an expenditure
of 7,500,000 francs.   The many buildings, including military barracks,
which dot the long summit plain on the south side of the pass are rich in
reminders of the Imperial mind, to which thanks for this splendid example
of an Alpine highway are due.

The finest view on the whole route is immediately before reaching the
saddle from the Lanslebourg side, shortly after the last hairpin bend.
Looking back, there is a wide prospect down the valley of the Arc, and the
Vanoise peaks are at last seen to full advantage beyond it with their snows
and glaciers from the Polset–Péclet summits to the Grande Casse (12,665
ft.) and the Grand Roc Noir.   More immediately opposite stands the tall
range of peaks separating the Arc valley from the parallel re-entrant of the
Vallon de la Rocheure, but the glaciers falling from them are all on the
reverse side to the north, so that the rocky ridges and summits present a
somewhat bare and forbidding aspect.   The fine snow peaks of the
adjoining Graian frontier range are entirely masked by the intervening
Pointe de Ronce, dominating the pass.

The road now dips a little into the remarkable summit plain (6,300 ft.)
some 5 miles long enclosed between the Pointe du Lamet and the Mont
Froid to the west.   Here stand the Hospice, hotels, barracks, and
numerous other buildings, eloquent of the days when, before the building
of the Fréjus tunnel, this was one of the busiest and strategically most
important roads in the Alps, with Lanslebourg and Susa prosperous
staging posts.   Enormous dues were collected annually, amounting to
tens of thousands of pounds a year, under the Napoleonic toll, which the
Kings of Sardinia continued to levy for years after his fall.   Here too is
the mile and a half long Cenis Lake, the source of the Cenise River, which
flows down the southern ravine to Susa and the Dora Riparia (Doire) in
the valley, forming a fine waterfall just beyond the southern lip of the plain.

The immense and abrupt descent from this point to the unseen valley
level at Susa is effected by numerous finely engineered bends and well-
protected sections on high ledges above the gorge, with the huge bulk of
the Roche Melon's rock wall dominating the upper section on the opposite
side.   This part of the journey is most impressive.   After about 5 miles
of steep descent, halfway along which stands the French customs post, the
Italian customs are reached at Molaretto.   The usual transition to
southern vegetation, walnuts, acacias, and eventually vines, in due course
announces that the plains of Italy are not far distant; and after 6 more
lovely miles the road emerges from the defile in the green valley of the
Dora at Susa, where the Mont Genèvre road comes down a deep re-
entrant to the right, passing the remains of the Arch of Cottius, already
referred to.

From Susa, the route continues pleasantly but uninterestingly downwards to the plain of Piedmont, which it enters at Rivoli, just short of Turin.

The long and crowded main road (three-lane) falls gently for more than 30 miles to reach that great industrial city and capital of Piedmont on the banks of the Po, where the Mont Cenis route ends. Following the valley of the Dora Riparia, its one great thrill is the huge Romanesque abbey of La Sagra di San Michele perched 2,000 ft. sheer above the valley-floor at San Ambrogio. Once again, Brockedon's lovely sketch made in 1829 remains a perfect portrait, and time has stood still. It is not within the scope of this book to describe cities already documented to perfection by Mr. Baedeker and others, but I hope no lover of great mountain scenery will pass through Turin without turning aside to one of the hills which ring it to the south and west—perhaps the Superga is the choice beyond compare—to look down upon it, outspread across the fertile Piedmont plain against the incomparable backcloth of the whole mighty chain of the Alps, from the Viso in the Cottians to Monte Rosa, lording it over the distant Pennines, far to the east. If any of Europe's great teeming factory cities is set more fairly than this one, I have yet to see it.

V

THE PETIT ST. BERNARD (7,178 ft.)

France (Savoy)–Italy (Aosta).

From Bourg St. Maurice (2,756 ft.) to Pré St. Didier (3,335 ft.), crossing the main
Alpine watershed between the Mediterranean and the Adriatic: 34
miles.

Detail. Bourg (2,756 ft.) to the Summit Saddle (7,178 ft.): 20 miles, ascent 4,400
ft. (French and Italian customs).

Summit to Pré St. Didier (3,335 ft.): 14 miles, descent 3,850 ft.

Open: Mid-June to late October.

Numerous good hairpin windings of medium width with gravel surface lead
to the level plain at the summit, several miles long. Steep banks of hairpins
descend the narrow ravines on the Italian side. Cobbled surface, frequently
in poor condition.

Traffic, moderate. Maximum gradient: 1 in 10.
Steep on the Italian side: on the whole, easy.

THE MOTORIST from England who has crossed France to Dijon and
then struck out south-east towards Northern Italy may well have varied the
traditional approach through Bourg, Chatillon, and Aix-les-Bains to
Chambéry by taking the direct mountain-road in miniature over the Col
du Chat, near the top of which is an excellent hotel, with lovely views over
the long, shallow basin of the Lac du Bourget towards the great hills behind
Aix and Annecy, and the distant ridges of the high Alps beyond.

Some miles beyond Chambéry, at St. Pierre d'Albigny, two of the
major routes from France to Italy diverge. The Mont Cenis road
(Chapter IV), heading south-south-east, enters the long, deep trench of
the Maurienne and ascends the valley of the Arc; the route to the Petit
St. Bernard continues for 10 miles north-eastwards along the Isère valley
to Albertville.

Thence, the road to Bourg St. Maurice and the St. Bernard follows the
deep and beautiful valley of the Isère eastwards into the mountains, keeping
for the most part to the left side (the Isère's true right bank) and, threading
a narrow, winding section, above which the slopes tower prodigiously,
emerges into a wider, more open stretch, the chief town of which is
Moutiers.

To the left rise the southern slopes of the Alps of Savoy, to the right,
across the valley, the northern wall of the Tarentaise. From Moutiers,
with its pleasant tree-lined square, a road runs across the narrow plain to
the attractive thermal station of Brides-les-Bains and, rising steeply beyond
into the valley-mouth of the Doran, climbs by a series of fine hairpins
above Bozel into the high hanging-valley which lodges the pleasant holiday
resort of Pralognan (4,500 ft.) at the foot of the Vanoise peaks.   This is a

splendid centre for walking and for the rock and glacier climbs in the Vanoise and Chasseforêt groups, whose highest peak is the impressive Grande Casse (12,665 ft.) and whose easiest high-mountain excursion is the delightful Aiguille de Polset (11,300 ft.).

In the parallel valley to the west, separated from Pralognan by a chain of rocky peaks of no great height, and also reached by a road from Moutiers, Courchevel has grown since the Second World War to be a favourite winter sports centre, whose modern hotels are also open to summer visitors.

Continuing along the left of the Isère valley from Moutiers, the main highway keeps fairly high above the broad valley floor, through the ancient villages of Centron and Aime—Axuma and Forum Claudii of the Centrones, rich in Roman inscriptions—with occasional fine glimpses of the higher mountains, from the Pralognan peaks opposite to the Mont Pourri (12,430 ft.) ahead, seen to the right above the retaining wall of the valley.

Seventeen miles from Moutiers bring you to the incredibly narrow main street of Bourg St. Maurice, a town of some 2,000 inhabitants, where the railway, which has kept company all the way from Albertville, ends and the road itself divides.

The right-hand branch continues into the upper Isère valley, which bends acutely southwards; the more important road to the Petit St. Bernard and Italy takes unobtrusively to the broad, left-hand slopes at Séez, 2 miles beyond the town, and enters an apparently minor valley, down which flows the torrent of the Recluz, on its way from the unseen St. Bernard saddle to join the Isère. At this exit from Bourg stands a famous hotel, presided over for many years by a lady with all the attributes of an empress rather than a hotelière, where generations of travellers across the Pass have broken their journey for a night or more.

For those remaining on French territory, the upper Isère road bears away into the gorges of the wild and beautiful Isère valley, whose narrow ravines and babbling cascades are deeply overshadowed by Mont Pourri's dark and rocky base on the western side and the great chain of the Ruitor–Grand Sassière–Tsanteleina range, dividing France from Italy, to the east. Beyond La Thuile the road now climbs and tunnels high in the slope of the latter to by-pass the great hydro-electric reservoir created by the completion in 1952 of the Tignes Barrage, when the plain and village of Tignes, through which the road once ran so picturesquely almost under the projecting eaves of the opposing châlets, were submerged in the interests of industry, power, and (artificial) light. Beyond this vast man-made sheet of water, 3 miles long, the valley narrows again, and the road threads its way to Val d'Isère, the chief summer and winter resort of the region, a favourite and attractive centre for holiday making, walking, and mountaineering. Here begins the actual ascent to the Col d'Iseran (Chapter XXX), a pass of comparatively modern date, now by a few feet the highest true motorable pass in Europe.

If Italy just across the intervening range is your objective, the Petit St. Bernard road, one of the historic passages of the Alps, wastes no time in gaining the necessary height to the only available saddle, 5,000 ft. above Bourg St. Maurice. Leaving the valley at Séez, a village straggling across the sunny, orchard-covered slope, it soon begins to swing up the mountain-side in a long series of hairpin turns, high above the entrance to the upper Isère valley, towards the prominent feature of the pine-crested Roche Blanche, guarding the right-hand side of the Recluz re-entrant, leading to the Col. (The old Roman road, sections of which are still visible, led directly up the torrent's right bank through St. Germain, the highest village in this subsidiary valley.) The windings of the modern road are followed by a lovely section leading through pine-woods clinging to the outer slope, with superb views opening out across the gulf of the Val d'Isère, far below, to the Iseran peaks circling its head; to the magnificent twin snow-cones of the Pourri soaring opposite; and back over Bourg along the broad and smiling corridor by which you have come from Albertville, fringed by the Vanoise summits. Beyond the pine-forest the road suddenly swings back across the slope by a short further series of hairpins and, losing the view, enters the wide upper ravine of the Recluz, along which it climbs, keeping high on the slope to the right of the torrent along wild, bare slopes to the actual pass.

This side of the pass, as far as the entrance to the summit corridor, is one of the most open and lovely in the Alps, and no greater contrast could be imagined than that between the opposing sides.

The saddle of the Petit St. Bernard—on which it used to be held that Hannibal camped with his army and his elephants during his astonishing passage of the Alps in 219 B.C., until brilliant examples of modern research were able to prove that he crossed by four completely different and widely separated passes, the Mont Cenis, the Mont Genèvre, the Col de Clapier, and the Col de la Traversette (by all standards a pretty versatile per-formance)—is less of a true saddle than a long upland plain enclosed by high mountains.

The evidence on which the discarded theory was based is interesting, even if so ruthlessly discredited. The pass, as has been seen, is easily accessible from the valley, unlike two of the others. The Roche Blanche tallies most conveniently with the white rock mentioned by Polybius. The summit-plain is about 2 miles long and a mile wide, and would be a most suitable place in which to encamp an army of at least 20,000 men with cavalry and elephants, to recuperate and reform as Hannibal is stated by Livy and Polybius to have done. On its north-eastern side there stands to this day a remarkable circle of stones about 250 yd. in circumference, the stones weighing from 200 to 600 lb., and the circle is obviously the product of an organized labour force, such as a large body of troops (or maybe elephants?) could provide, the stones being set about 10 ft. apart; known as the 'Cirque d'Annibal', this has traditionally been associated with the holding of a council of war or a religious ceremony by the great Cartha-ginian General during his halt of some days at the pass. Brockedon, the chronicler of the Alpine passes, wrote in 1829: 'the muleteers who pass the road, the people of the Hospice, the guides and the neighbouring

Bourg St. Pierre and the Vélan, on the northern approach to the Grand St. Bernard

The Bernese Oberland from near the Simplon summit

Rotary snow-plough clearing the Simplon road in winter

The new St. Gotthard road in the Schoellenen Gorge

peasantry know it only by that name.' Interesting, but inconclusive in the light of modern research.

The Hospice (7,065 ft.), a blackened building largely in ruins, was founded, like that on the Grand St. Bernard, by St. Bernard de Menthon and administered for centuries by monks of the same order. During the wars of Italy, however, in 1794, a French Division under General Dumas fought a remarkable two days' action against Austro-Sardinian troops occupying the pass, forcing the enemy's mountain positions in spite of greatly inferior numbers and a total lack of artillery, penning them into the arc of the Hospice and laying it in ruins with guns captured from them, and driving them back into the Piedmont valleys. Further damage was done by an avalanche in 1897.

At some distance from the Hospice, between it and the Stone Circle of Hannibal, stands a column 22 ft. high—the Colonne de Joux (Jovis, as in Mons Jovis on the Grand St. Bernard)—with other faint traces of a Roman temple at its feet. There is also a statue of St. Bernard.

The Pass (7,178 ft.), in itself a bare and sombre depression, is glorified by a truly stupendous surprise glimpse, away to the left, of Mont Blanc's southern face towering in the middle distance above Crammont and the mountains of the Allée Blanche. Keen walkers, with time to spare, will profit by the easy ascent, in rather over an hour, of the Belvedère (8,665 ft.) to the north-east of the pass, the view from which not only greatly enhances the splendour of Mont Blanc, with the Miage and Brenva Glaciers cascading from its huge head, but adds a wonderful prospect over the south side of the Alps to the Matterhorn and Monte Rosa in the extreme distance and, closer at hand to the south, the vast glaciers of the triple-headed Ruitor (11,430 ft.) and superb views over the Iseran amphitheatre, the snowy Pourri, and the multitudinous peaks of the Tarentaise. To the south-east Mt. Valésan (9,453 ft.) gives the advantage of additional height to a similar panorama, but is less easy and requires twice as long.

The road passes another large, fire-ravaged building, also probably destroyed during the campaign of 1794, before the end of the summit plain is reached. At a slightly lower level, on the Italian side of the water-shed and to the left of the road, lies the Lac de Verney, from which the Thuile issues to join the Dora Baltea far below, at Pré St. Didier, on its long valley course to the Po. A steep vista now opens into the ravine through which the infant river rushes headlong to the first valley level at La Thuile (the Italian one, not to be confused with the French version, also close to the foot of the pass, back in the Isère valley), rocky-sided and heavily forested below with pine and larch. A short way down the upper part of the descent stands the Italian customs house, to the right of the road, at the Cantine des Eaux Rousses (6,740 ft.).

The road now descends 1,000 ft. by numerous serpentine windings into and through the woods on the right-hand side of the rugged defile. Along-side, so deeply and steeply enclosed that only the sound of the raging waters indicates its presence, the Thuile rages through a 200-ft. chasm little more than 20 ft. wide, which it has carved through the precipitous

E

rock.   At Pont Serrant (5,415 ft.) a fine bridge leaps the torrent at a height of fully 100 ft.; beyond it the road continues its steep hairpin descent through the forest, re-crossing the river, and rapidly losing another thousand feet in height to La Thuile (4,725 ft.), which is seen from above for some time, its white houses nestling on the smooth carpet of a level, sunny, green clearing.

This savage sector of the descent and the equally fearsome though shorter gorges below La Thuile, before the main valley is reached at Pré St. Didier, were formerly held to have been responsible for the terrible losses sustained by Hannibal's army on its descent from the Alps.   The avalanches falling from the south-eastern base of Crammont and yearly destroying the old road, which till about 1750 ran on that side of the torrent, frequently leave accumulations of unmelted snow arching the raging waters.   These were formerly considered to match exactly Polybius' account of Hannibal's men and beasts of burden perishing through falling over similar accumulations or sinking through them to perish in the waters.

As has been said above, however, it is now fashionable to think that the great Carthaginian General, no doubt wishing to enjoy his Alpine tour to the full, selected a pass some 3,000 ft. higher than the Petit St. Bernard and therefore doubtless likely to be ranked as a better mountaineering record.   This is approached by a long valley route so difficult that the modern road had to be blasted out of the rock for a considerable stretch, and the route finally crosses a bare and rocky defile between towering peaks, with no obvious camping space for anything larger than a troop of boy scouts, at a height of just on 10,000 ft.   A pass so high, so remote, so barren and difficult that to this day there is only a foot-track across it; a pass highly unsuitable for tanks—but eminently suitable for elephants. But then Hannibal was one of the world's great generals, and great generals are often very odd people.

At La Thuile the road crosses the river and again plunges into a ravine, in which the Thuile is almost immediately joined by the waters of the fine Cascade du Ruitor, falling from the great glaciers of that peak, seen high above on the right.   The road, cut out of the rock high above the torrent, continues to La Balme, where it loses height by an abrupt hairpin and re-crosses the stream.

Below La Balme the valley widens for a moment, then contracts into a final savage and gloomy rift, by which the Thuile, thundering hundreds of feet below, has forced a way of escape through the final mountain barrier into the Aosta valley.   Here the road, clinging high above the torrent in the abyss, resorts to a couple of tunnels in order to find a steep way down to pleasant Pré St. Didier out in the kindly daylight of the open valley. It is all very impressive but eminently safe as you drive down in a modern car.   In 1829 Brockedon, reminding us of the toll this sector of the road has taken in bygone days, wrote:

'Fearful accidents have happened here, though the road is good and there is no appearance of danger; several crosses, the chronicles of death, are near, to solicit prayers for the repose of the souls of the unfortunate whose humble memorials are their initials and the dates of the accidents, preceded by P.I., or as is sometimes carved on the cross, *Perit Ici.*'

The views forward on this last part of the descent to Pré St. Didier, up the Courmayeur re-entrant to the immense 10,000-ft. southern wall of the Mont Blanc chain, are superb at all times of day, but perhaps best in evening lighting.

Pré St. Didier (3,350 ft.), where the Thuile gushes from the narrow St. Bernard ravine to pour into the Dora Baltea, is a pleasant little resort with thermal springs, set in the meadows sloping gently down to the main stream, and commanding a glorious view of Mont Blanc in all his majesty and some of his near neighbours. Above, the road continues up the Dora valley to Courmayeur; below, the main road down the valley leads to Aosta, Ivrea, and Turin. (These roads are briefly described in Chapter VI, the Grand St. Bernard.)

Finally, if a choice has to be made between the passes leading from France to Italy, and the most varied and splendid mountain scenery is a factor which weighs in such a choice, I have no hesitation in recommending the Petit St. Bernard as finer than the Mont Cenis or the Mont Genèvre. Though the rider must be added that if the latter pass is used purely as an appendage to the Lautaret–Galibier route from Grenoble, I would not for a moment suggest its exclusion, for the Lautaret is a 'must' no less than the Petit St. Bernard.

VI

THE GRAND ST. BERNARD (8,110 ft.)

Switzerland (Valais)–Italy (Aosta).

From Martigny (1,562 ft.) to Aosta (1,913 ft.) crossing the main Alpine watershed between the Mediterranean and the Adriatic in the Pennine Alps: 48 miles.

Detail. Martigny to Orsières (2,970 ft.): 12 miles, ascent 1,400 ft.
　　　　Orsières to Bourg St. Pierre (5,358 ft.): 8 miles, ascent 2,400 ft.
　　　　Bourg to the Summit (8,110 ft.): 8 miles, ascent 2,750 ft.
Total Ascent: 28 miles, 6,550 ft.

　　　　Level between Hospice, Swiss and Italian customs at summit.

　　　　Summit to Étroubles (4,200 ft.): 12 miles, descent 3,900 ft.
　　　　Étroubles to Aosta (1,913 ft.): 8 miles, descent 2,300 ft.
Total Descent: 20 miles, 6,200 ft.

Open: Mid-June to Mid-October.

A wide, modern road through the lower gorges to Orsières. Moderately broad straightforward road to Bourg St. Pierre. Somewhat narrow, with some sharp hairpin bends, on the final steep sector to the Hospice. The descent on the southern side is in wide, sweeping hairpin curves to St. Rhémy; then a typical mountain road of moderate width, with a final section to Aosta. Surface mainly gravel.

Moderate: easier on the southern side. Maximum gradient: 1 in 9.

THIS ANCIENT and famous passage across the Alps leaves the main Lausanne–Rhone valley–Simplon route (Chapter VII) at Martigny, the famous Roman headquarters of Octodurum, and now a pleasant staging post with excellent hotels, at the junction of several important roads.

The St. Bernard is one of the passes with no extensive or 'surprise' view at its summit, from whichever side it is approached, consisting as it does of a narrow lake-basin, frowned upon by bare and rocky ridges. I am therefore describing it from north to south, partly for conformity's sake, since the other great Swiss passes, the Simplon and the Gotthard, are being treated in that direction in this book; partly because it can in this way be more easily followed in conjunction with the description of the approach route from the west given in the Simplon chapter; and partly for a purely personal aesthetic preference.

For, fine as is the rocky, ice-fringed wall of the Grand Combin as seen lifting behind intervening crests from various points on both sides of the pass, I cannot help feeling that the lesser Mont Vélan is the true show-piece of the St. Bernard road. The wonderful glaciated face of the Combin lies hidden on its reverse (eastern) side, so magnificently seen from Verbier and better still from the continuing heights along the eastern side of the Val de Bagnes; but the northern face of the Vélan, in itself a beautifully sculptured mountain form, presents its delicately moulded snow-fields like a lovely white robe falling softly towards the Drance valley, up which the Swiss side of the pass finds its long approach. And it seems to me that the amenities are greatly enhanced by having those glittering draperies continually in sight, full ahead, as the car's bonnet points along the winding road; though there are, of course, frequent lay-bys, where you can pull in for a backward glimpse if you are coming down in the opposite direction. Only it is not quite the same thing, and I personally hate to have so lovely an object—particularly in the full afternoon light—behind my shoulder, where I cannot look at it without taking what on a road of this kind would be a suicidal risk.

The St. Bernard route from Martigny is at first also the combination of the roads to the Val de Bagnes (serving Verbier and Fionnay), to Orsières and the Swiss Val Ferret, as well as the start of alternative roads to Lac Champex, which climb at opposite ends into the high, crater-like valley cradling that favourite lake-resort. It leaves Martigny by way of the picturesque narrow main street of the Old Town and promptly climbs into the jaws of the ravine by which the Drance comes racing down to join the Rhone.

At Les Valettes (4½ miles) the first Lac Champex road climbs up to the right by numerous hairpins through Champex d'en Bas and d'en Haut. The St. Bernard road, clinging to the right-hand side of the magnificent Drance Gorge, whose yellow limestone cliffs rise sheer to the woods above, shares the narrow passage with the swift torrent, a considerable stream, and the narrow-gauge Orsières railway, which tunnels and bridges its way alongside. Hemmed in by the walls of this tremendous, narrow slit in the hills, the three wind their way steadily upwards in close company for 4 more miles to Sembrancher (2,360 ft.), where they suddenly emerge into a grassy, open plainlet.

A road diverges to the left at Sembrancher to Le Châble, where it enters the beautiful Val de Bagnes, continuing along it to Lourtier and Fionnay at the foot of the Grand Combin; beyond Fionnay, walkers can continue by the track to the Chanrion Hut of the S.A.C.* over the Col de la Fenêtre de Balme (9,140 ft.) into Italy, a fine route lately somewhat spoiled by hydro-electric constructions. At Le Chable the splendid new hairpin motor-road climbs up to the left to reach Verbier, a delightful resort at 5,500 ft. on a sunny shelf overlooking the little plain, with fine views of the Combin and, more distantly, of the Mont Blanc range, dominated from this angle by the Aiguille de Chardonnet. Verbier, whose popularity is very much on the rise, has plenty of good hotels, tennis-courts, chair-lifts to fine view-points, and a variety of walks from the short and easy to long and arduous ascents among the rocky hills behind it. The S.A.C. Cabane du Mont Fort, an hour from the top of a chair-lift, is the starting-place for good climbs on moderate peaks, as well as for the famous high-level tour across the intervening valleys of Arolla, Evolène, Anniviers, and Turtmann to the Nikolaital and Zermatt, an unrivalled four or five days' walking-tour.

* Swiss Alpine Club.

Bearing right at Sembrancher, the St. Bernard road continues across the plainlet to Orsières (2,970 ft.), beyond which, again on the right, a gently rising road leads between pleasant meadows along the open corridor of the Val Ferret, at the eastern foot of the Mont Blanc chain, to the charming small resorts of La Fouly and Ferret. Orsières itself is the starting-point not only of the second motor-road to Champex, already mentioned, but of tracks leading to the climbing huts (Cabane Orny, Julien Dupuis, and Saleinaz—for the Col and Aiguille du Tour, ascents of no great difficulty) from which innumerable glacier expeditions and climbs among the peaks at this end of the Mont Blanc group are undertaken. Beyond Ferret, a mule-track crosses the frontier by way of the 7,000-ft. Col Ferret and then descends the magnificent Italian Val Ferret to Entrèves and Courmayeur, continually skirting the foot of the gigantic flying-buttresses and hanging glaciers of the great peaks from the Mont Dolent, through the Grandes Jorasses and the Rochefort Ridge to the Dent du Géant, which plunge down this 10,000-ft. southern wall of the Alps (see also the end of this chapter, p. 73).

The St. Bernard road, however, ignoring all these attractive side-shows, crosses the Drance immediately on leaving Orsières and at once takes two long, swinging turns into a central gap in the hills to gain height. It then climbs steadily along the broad left-hand slope of the somewhat barren valley, with the Drance mostly hidden in the bottom of the cleft far below. Presently another wide bend lifts the road to the first valley-level at the fair-sized village of Liddes (4,390 ft.). Immediately the Vélan appears ahead at the far end of the long re-entrant, in all its shapely, snowy beauty, to remain the dominant feature of the landscape as the road contours unsensationally to Bourg St. Pierre (5,358 ft.), with its spacious car-park, its interesting Alpine garden, and its delightfully-named historic inn, where in the old days travellers by diligence used to spend the night— the *Hotel du déjeuner de Napoléon*. This was, of course, the route taken by Napoleon in 1800, when he successfully led the 30,000-strong army of Marengo over the Alps, in spite of serious difficulties encountered along the bleak and dangerous upper sections of the pass.

Bourg, whose church dates from the eleventh century, is situated on a knoll at the mouth of the Combe de Valsorey, down which an arm of the Drance comes plunging from the Grand Combin's glaciers above in a fine waterfall, well seen on the left on leaving the little town. A track up the steep ravine leads to the Valsorey Hut, the starting-point for the climbs of the Vélan and Combin by their least difficult routes.

Above Bourg, the Vélan, now only a mile or two distant, continues to dominate the scene, which would be somewhat monotonous and un-inspiring without that magnificent centre-piece: for of all the great passes, the Grand St. Bernard is perhaps the least picturesque, and its upper sector grim, bare, and gaunt in the extreme.

The road, often hewn out of the rock for want of other lodgement, now climbs through the wild defile of Saraise for 3 miles to the Cantine de Proz; this is the section which caused Napoleon's army its greatest difficulties. At the Cantine, the closest point to the Vélan, is a last fine view of the nearby Glacier de Proz, with its huge moraines, descending from the mountain. The road then crosses the depressing, boulder-littered pastures of the Plan de Proz till it bends away into another grim defile, the Pas de Marengo. About 3 miles farther up at about the 7,000-ft. level stand the refuge huts of Hospitalet, beyond which the Drance is crossed by a stone bridge and the road enters the dreary, aptly named Combe des Morts, up which it slashes its way in narrow windings, to come quite suddenly upon the narrow gateway into the saddle at the top of the pass (8,110 ft.).

The savage nature of the last part of this approach makes it hard to believe that in the three years 1798-9 and 1800 some hundreds of thousands of troops, Austrian and French, with their artillery and supplies, crossed this 8,000-ft. notch in the Alpine wall. (The Romans had forced its passage as early as 105 B.C. and Aosta (Augusta) was flourishing in 26 B.C.)

The actual saddle contains a sombre lake of considerable size, on the slope overlooking which are the two large stone buildings of the most famous Hospice in the world, founded in 926 by St. Bernard de Menthon and giving its name to the pass. It has also given world-wide fame to a certain breed of large dog, to study which in its habitat is—judging by the conversation of most coach-tourists on their return—the sole objective of their journey.

All these things are too well known and annotated in the guide-books to need description here. Above the lake, from whose southern (Italian) end issues the Buthier torrent, rises the hill the Romans called Mons Jovis, on which stand stone pillars and a statue of St. Bernard; the local name, Mont Joux, properly applies to the pass as well. Ahead, southwards, the saw-edged crests of various rocky ridges rising to no great height above the containing rim of the saddle give a hint of your own great elevation and of the vast gulf to be descended on the Italian side; looking back, the smooth grey southern wall of the Combin is seen, finely crowned by a rim of corniced ice.

Half a mile of gentle descent separates the Swiss and Italian frontier posts, with their black-and-white-striped barrier poles. Beyond the latter, the descent into Italy begins at once, the road losing height in wide bends for about 2 miles past the huts of La Baux to the Cantine d'Aosta and then continuing in zig-zags for some 5 miles down 2,000 ft. of the right-hand wall of the Buthier's re-entrant. A final long bend before crossing the torrent by a stone bridge brings you to St. Rhemy, charmingly set in a narrow wooded valley at about 5,300 ft.

The road continues to descend through the pines—a relief after the bare, shadeless northern side—with rare recourse to hairpin turns, till the considerable village of Étroubles (4,200 ft.) is reached in another 5 miles.

Three miles farther on, at Condemine, a lovely vista opens up to the left across the valley into the beautifully wooded Valpelline, with the snowy Dent d'Hérens rising at its far head, deep into the south side of the great mountain chain. Down this lovely valley the main arm of the Buthier brings its glacier waters, and walkers will find the road up to Ollomont and the many woodland or mountain paths to the view-points above the valley a delight.

It is well worth stopping, too, by the roadside all the way down the lower part of the St. Bernard road below Étroubles for the imposing backward glimpses to the southern faces of the Vélan and the Grand Combin, lifting higher and higher as you are more widely separated from them by height and distance. Two miles of long windings bring you from Condemine to Grignod, best seen from about a mile farther down the road, its square fifteenth-century tower, rising above white houses set on a green hillock among scattered poplar-trees, making a most attractive picture against the great skyline of the distant snow peaks.

Here, well below the 3,000-ft. level again, everything is suddenly soft and southern as you drive through a gentle landscape of walnut- and chestnut-trees, vine-clad slopes and cultivated fields tall with ripening maize.

At Variney (2,575 ft.) the motor road to the Valpelline branches off to the left, and presently, as you continue down the lush, broadening valley, the dazzling pyramid of the shapely Grivola appears ahead, high above the vale of Aosta. She is soon masked by intervening spurs, but the triple-headed Ruitor, with its fine glaciers, at once replaces her away to the right, marking the Frontier ridge between Italy and France.

As you lose height, now very gradually, and draw nearer to the main valley of the Dora, Aosta's own private mountains, the Becca di Nona and Mont Aemilius, loom dark and high in front above the town.

Aosta (1,913 ft.) is an ancient city of 9,000 inhabitants situated in the broad plain of the Dora Baltea's sub-Alpine valley at the point where the Buthier, descending from the Valpelline and the St. Bernard, falls into it.

Founded in 29 B.C., Augusta Praetoria is still rich in Roman walls and gateways, medieval fortifications and towers, historic buildings and churches, and narrow, picturesque streets radiating from a fine central square, whose arcades and stately architecture smile tolerantly on its inevitable contemporary uses as a teeming car-park and bus-station. There is plenty in Aosta to keep the sightseer busy if he decides to stay at one of its many good hotels. A word of warning, however. Shut in at the bottom of a deep valley, the place can be very hot in summer; moreover, there is a large chemical plant just to the north-west of the town, and a sulphurous haze frequently hangs motionless above the valley, capable of dimming the sun's light under the clearest sky.

Continuing southwards towards Turin, the road runs east at first, then turns south, following the Dora Baltea's fine valley through Châtillon and Ivrea, continually descending to the plain of Piedmont, into which it finally emerges 40 miles north of the great industrial city.

In the course of the lovely 17 miles to Châtillon*, which is rich in medieval castles dominating ancient towns, delightful parallel valleys open up on the left, each with its mountain road climbing northwards towards the great south wall of the Alps, which stretches unbroken from the Combin

* The adjoining village of St. Vincent is being developed as a holiday-resort.

past the Matterhorn to Monte Rosa. Each valley has its well-known resorts. The road from Châtillon leads to Valtournanche and Breuil,* historic in the first attempts on the Matterhorn, at the foot of whose fantastic, snowless southern precipice it lies; that from Pont St. Martin takes you to charmingly situated Gressonney, in the shadow of the snowy Breithorn and Monte Rosa's summits. These valleys, well equipped with holiday amenities and *telefériques*, are worth a visit for the lover of superb mountain scenery; but the roads are narrow, and the one to Breuil can at times be very trying on account of the endless stream of giant coaches carrying sightseers to and from the foot of the world-famous monolith of a mountain which lords it over Valtournanche.

Although the road to Turin is the logical fulfilment of the St. Bernard Route, Aosta is as important a road junction as Martigny on the other side of the pass. North-westwards, beyond the chemical plant, runs the beautiful high road up the Dora Baltea valley, to Pré St. Didier, 14 miles away (see Chapter V, the Little St. Bernard). Passing through rich fruit orchards, backed by lovely glimpses of the Grivola's shapely pyramid, and threading the streets of numerous picturesque villages, each crowned with its ancient princely château, the road wriggles its way into the broader upper valley through the narrow necks of rock gorges, till after a tunnel beyond Villeneuve the stupendous vision of Mont Blanc's southern elevation bursts on the eye to fill the background for the rest of the journey.

At Villeneuve and Arvier side roads break off to the left into the narrow lateral valleys leading into the heart of the Graian Alps, to the delightful resorts of Cogne, Rhêmes Notre Dame, Valsavaranche and Valgrisanche at the feet of the Grivola, Gran Paradiso, Herbetet, and a host of other fine peaks. This is ideal walking and mountaineering country.

At Pré St. Didier, set among pleasant meadows at the foot of pine-covered slopes, the road divides, the right-hand branch climbing by a series of fine, wide, modernized curves up the broad, poplar-sprinkled pastures, with the southern wall of the Alps from Mont Blanc to the Jorasses towering higher and higher ahead, to Courmayeur, the most popular and spectacular of Northern Italy's holiday hill resorts.

Here at 4,000 ft., in a narrow sub-Alpine valley backed by the gigantic wall of rock and glacier, hotels, tennis courts, cafés, and the summer villas of wealthy Italians surround and pervade the narrow alleys, deep-eaved roofs, and carved balconies of the old village, surmounted by an ancient church-tower with a crooked spire, whose clock obligingly strikes the hours twice, at a minute's interval, just in case you missed the first announcement.

This is a centre for magnificent walks and excursions, with glorious views of the Mont Blanc peaks. A narrow motor-road continues up the valley to Entrèves, serving the Val Veni and Val Ferret above—both wonderful corridors running for miles at the foot of the tremendous Alpine wall. (The track over the Col du Grand Ferret to Orsières has already been mentioned earlier in this chapter.)

* Now Cervinia: see footnote p. 50.

The innumerable climbing possibilities in the Mont Blanc Group are, of course, beyond the scope of this book.

The other branch from Pré St. Didier is in fact the southern side of the Petit St. Bernard Pass, forcing its way up steeply by sharp hairpins through the pine forests above the narrow gorges of the Thuile to the French frontier, 5,000 ft. higher up and only 14 miles away. There lies the road to Savoy and Dauphiné, and the direct way home via Albertville, Chambéry, Bourg en Bresse, and Dijon (see Chapter V).

VII

THE SIMPLON (6,594 ft.)

Switzerland (Valais) to Italy (Lombardy), crossing the main Alpine watershed between the Mediterranean and the Adriatic.

From Brigue (2,231 ft.) to Domodossola (919 ft.): 40 miles.

Detail. Brigue to Bérisal (5,080 ft.): 8 miles, ascent 2,850 ft.
Bérisal to Simplon Summit (6,594 ft.): 6 miles, ascent 1,500 ft.
Total ascent Brigue to summit: 14 miles, 4,350 ft.

Summit to Simplon Village (4,852 ft.): 6 miles, descent 1,750 ft.
Simplon Village to Gondo (2,815 ft.): 6 miles, descent 2,000 ft.
Gondo to Iselle (2,155 ft.): 3 miles, descent 650 ft.
Iselle to Domodossola (919 ft.): 11 miles, descent 1,250 ft.
Total descent Summit to Domodossola: 26 miles, descent 5,700 ft.

Open: Late April to mid-November. Maximum gradient: 1 in 11.

A long, first-class road, well graded and with easy windings, broad and (except where rebuilding is in progress) well surfaced. Several long tunnels and galleries. The lengthy sector through the Gondo Gorge is sometimes sensationally perched above the river, but always well walled and protected. Scenically most rewarding and one of the historic trans-Alpine passages.

Easy to moderate. When all the improvements are complete (1958, still in progress) will be a magnificent modern road.

THE SIMPLON is of outstanding importance among the international Alpine highways. It affords the fastest, most direct route from France, through the south-west corner of Switzerland, to Milan and all Italy beyond, crossing the main backbone of the Alps from north to south on its way.

While differing markedly in character from the St. Gotthard (Chapter VIII), it shares several of that great pass's fundamentals, in that both are north–south arteries, both link a Swiss with an Italian lake-basin, both cross the highest and most formidable sector of the Alpine barrier, and both are avoidable by putting your car on a truck at the bottom, thus missing— ostrich like—all the beauty, the splendour, and the fun. Apart from these basic characteristics, no two routes could well be more dissimilar.

For the Gotthard route rises continually and winding narrowly from the head of Lake Lucerne to its summit saddle in a series of leisurely steps, connected by steep mountain pitches, from one valley terrace to another, culminating in the 5,000-ft. level lawn of the Urserenthal, and only then faces a final pass-sector constituting a relatively minor rise. The Simplon is, by contrast, a broad, fast, level highway for 30 miles along the deep trench of the Rhone valley to Brigue at the foot of the huge barrier of the Pennine Alps. The true pass then climbs in a single unbroken assault on the stark mountain-side, to reach the 6,500-ft. saddle by which it threads its narrow way between great peaks and glaciers.

The southern sides of the two passes are also utterly dissimilar.   The
Gotthard plunges headlong down a great, open face of the mountains in a
spiral staircase of almost unrivalled daring and magnificence, hanging
always on the brink of a vast and colourful abyss.   The Simplon, by sheer
ingenuity and persistence, bores an exiguous dragon's trail through some
of the most stupendous rock-dominated gorges in the Alps, always
sombrely enclosed, overhung by thousand-foot cliffs, dauntingly far from
the narrow ribbon of the sky, for 6 miles of its grim, grey passage through
the terrifying pit worn by the brawling Diveria.

The Lake of Geneva, a 70-mile-long crescent of blue water contained

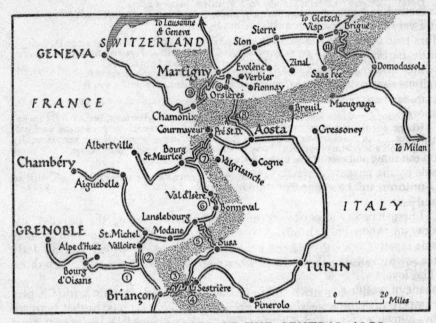

MAP No. 3.   THE PASSES OF THE CENTRAL ALPS

Passes
1. Lautaret   4. Sestrière   7. Petit St. Bernard   10. Forclaz
2. Galibier   5. Mont Cenis   8. Grand St. Bernard   11. Simplon
3. Mt. Genèvre   6. Iseran   9. Col des Montets

between the steep, rocky ridges of Savoy on its southern, French, shore
and the pleasant wooded and pasture-terraced hump-back of the Jura to
the north, is by far the largest of Switzerland's lakes; in fact, almost an
inland sea, on which the sudden mountain storms can soon lash white
horses and cause miniature breakers to tumble against its walled-up shores.

The British motorist comes down on it at Geneva by the Col de la
Faucille road across the French Jura; at Nyon by the Col de St. Cergue
extension of the same route; or, if he has come across the frontier by way
of Pontarlier and Les Joux (Vallorbe), he drops delightfully down through
Cossonnay, across the corn-fields and orchards of the smiling plateau

between the foot of the Jura and the lake-basin, on Lausanne. In clear weather the descent by this latter route offers, I think, the finest views across the basin, in which the lake at first lies concealed by the rim of the plateau, to the dark Savoy ranges beyond and the great chain of snow peaks from the Valais to Mont Blanc, lifting their distant heads above them; eastwards, too, beyond Yverdon and the blue eye of Neuchâtel, the vista of golden fields and the low, wooded hills sweeps endlessly away to the remote silver glint of the Bernese Oberland giants. On the right day and, best of all by afternoon lighting, this is an unforgettable entry into Switzerland.

Lausanne, piled up the lake-side slopes and crowned by its venerable cathedral, is a lovely city, but its steep streets and milling traffic can make it a very hot and trying point of arrival after a long day's driving over the Jura road; if a cool and peaceful break is required there is the enchanting little harbour of quiet Ouchy, with its heavily shaded water-front, its white- and red-sailed yachts, its white steamers and its swans, only five minutes away down the hill. Here, too, are good hotels for an overnight stop, far removed from the noise and bustle of the crowded city on the hill above.

From Lausanne eastwards to the head of the lake, 30 miles away at Villeneuve, the great lakeside highway runs broad and fast, sometimes high on the slope, sometimes at the water's edge, always bordered on the inland side by the terraced Lavaux vineyards, which produce the fine light wines —unfortunately they do not export particularly well—of Cully, Dézaley, and Lutry.

Long, narrow, built-up sections, with trams as an additional hazard, slow up proceedings through an almost unbroken string of famous lake-side resorts from Vevey through Clarens, townified Montreux, and Terri-tet, with charming Glion perched on a favourite balcony high above it. The lovely vistas of gardens, islets, villas, coves overhung by the green shade of weeping willows, and long lights on the limpid waters are ample compensation for occasional traffic-jams; and at Chillon there is a fine lay-by, allowing of a stroll to view the historic castle and enjoy the classic picture of the stately Dents du Midi (10,695 ft.), rising behind it and the head of the lake.

Through Villeneuve the road runs across a green plain into the jaws of the wide Rhone valley rift ahead, between the tall shoulders of the Dents du Midi on the right and the Alps of Vaud to the left, and proceeds fast and straight along it through Bex, where the Col du Pillon road drops steeply in on the left from Gstaad, Zweisimmen, and the Oberland (see Chapter XXVI), and St. Maurice to Martigny, a road junction of great importance. (This is the country of that great Swiss writer C. F. Ramuz, whose brilliant short novel *Derborance*—translated under the title *The Night the Mountain Fell*—deals wonderfully with an historic landslide in the mountains close at hand.)

At Martigny (1,543 ft.), where the Rhone valley suddenly takes a sharp right-angled bend to the north-east, a number of major and minor roads branch southwards from the Simplon route into the great hills to the right.

The most important of these is the Grand St. Bernard, which leaps over the Alpine wall 10 miles to the south into Italy by way of Aosta in the sunny valley of the Dora Baltea and on along it to Turin (Chapter VI).

Next in importance, internationally, is the road over the Col de la Forclaz (4,997 ft.)—till its recent face-lifting (in 1956) one of the narrowest and trickiest of all the passes—to Trient and then over the gentle Col des Montets (4,793 ft.) into France and so to the very foot of Mont Blanc at Chamonix (Chapter XXV).

Minor roads fan out from these main routes into the Val de Bagnes, with charming Verbier high above on its sunny shelf facing the Grand Combin, and since 1957 approached by a fine new mountain road; into the Swiss Val Ferret, where small, quiet resorts nestle at the Mont Blanc massif's north-eastern foot; and up into the nearer hills to the favourite holiday centre of Lac Champex (4,813 ft.) fringing a jewel of a lakelet, set deep—perhaps a little too deep—in a mountain crater between shady pine-woods, reflecting the distant snows of the Combin in its clear waters.

Martigny itself consists of a fine modern town, with plenty of good hotels, on the valley levels, and a most picturesque old quarter clustering on the hill-side behind it and crowned by an ancient circular fortress tower, La Batiaz, which commands a fine view over the whole neighbourhood. Martigny is an excellent overnight stopping-place for motorists who intend to cross the Simplon or either of the other passes on the morrow; though the driver who wants to take advantage of the earlier hours of the day for the passage of the Simplon may perhaps prefer to push on farther along the Rhone valley towards the actual foot of the pass. There is certainly no dearth of resting-places along the road, if he decides to do so.

This whole sector of the Rhone valley has always been subject to disaster and destruction in spring-time from tremendous rock falls and landslides, for then the dry, stormy beds of the torrents draining the southern wall suddenly turn to raging yellow infernos, carrying everything—mud, enormous boulders, and tall trees—before them into the main valley, raising the level of the Rhone with incredible speed, causing widespread havoc, and frequently, in years gone by, cutting both Simplon road and railway. As a result, the river has more recently been confined for a considerable length of its course between strong concrete dykes, giving it—till you notice the urgency of its grey glacier waters—the strangely formal look of an outsize canal.

From Martigny the road runs pleasantly along the wide valley levels between meadows and orchards, with the solid southern wall always rising near and steep to some 7,000 ft., and the jagged, cardboard-profiled limestone wedges of the Vaudois Alps—the rocky ranges from the Diablerets to the Wildstrubel—set back a little beyond vine-clad slopes to the north.

At regular intervals along this immemorial highway stand fine towns of historic as well as touristic interest—Sion, Sierre, Leuk, Turtmann, Visp—well equipped with hotels, restaurants, garages, and shops. From these centres, on either side of the valley, spring lateral roads winding their way up into the hills to serve a dozen well-known holiday areas and mountain resorts, some thousands of feet above the sun-scorched plain of the Rhone.

Sion, 16 miles from Martigny, and the capital of Valais, dominates the valley plain with its two ancient castles on the crests of opposing rocky hillocks, at whose feet nestles the modern town. The old town, the Roman Sedunum, with its castles, churches, and museums, is of considerable historic interest, and the high rocks on which the castles stand command fine views of the Rhone valley.

Southwards from Sion, the Val d'Hérens postal road swings away to the right to climb laboriously into that delightful valley past the quaint earth-pyramids of Euseigne, where the valley splits, the right-hand arm leading by mule-track along the Val des Dix by Pralong, past the new hydro-electric barrage and over the Col de Riedmatten or the Pas de Chèvres to Arolla. The main road continues upwards through the woods bordering the Borgne to the charming resort of Evolène, with its smaller sister of La Sage on a shelf above it, and on to Les Haudères, dominated by the pyramid of the Dent Blanche. There the valley divides again, the left arm continuing by a track to Ferpècle at the foot of the glacier and so to Alp Bricolla above it; the narrow road up the right-hand arm winds steeply up to Arolla, that delightful centre for walking and mountaineering at the foot of Mont Collon, accessible by jeep service since 1955.

Sierre, 10 miles farther along the Rhone valley, is an important industrial town with a large aluminium factory, and the neighbouring slopes are famous for the Fendant wines which bear the local names.

Two important lateral roads leave the valley here, one on the left at the centre of the town, leading in half an hour by wide, well-graded curves to the high green shelf, along which straggle the linked holiday and health resorts of Crans–Montana–Vermala—woefully overcrowded in the 'high season', but equipped with every form of sport and amenities for the visitor—with superb views across the deep rift at their feet to the giant peaks of the Valais opposite—Weisshorn, Rothorn, Matterhorn, and a dozen other magnificent Pennine summits.

The other tributary road leaves the Simplon route in the opposite direction about a mile after the last houses of Sierre and turns southwards to climb the mountain wall by a fine series of steep hairpins, overhanging the roofs of the town, into the narrow jaws of the lovely Val d'Anniviers. To reach the floor of that high-level and unspoilt valley at its main village, ancient and picturesque Vissoie (4,006 ft.), the road has to force its way along high ledges in the precipitous eastern wall of the Gorge of the Navisence, a foaming thread in the abyss a thousand feet below. Since 1954 the road, always just wide enough to take a medium-sized postal service, has been improved and widened at every possible point, and this is a truly magnificent drive. Beyond Vissoie the valley, one of the most beautiful in the Alps, continues to the foot of the great semicircle of peaks ranged behind Zinal (5,500 ft.) at its head. The road is good as far as

Ayer; beyond that point, where postal motor passengers bound for Zinal change to a miniature eight-seater model or a jeep, it is very narrow, very steep in places, sometimes indifferent in surface, and reversing is always necessary when a postal car is met coming in the opposite direction. This does not prevent the courageous motorist who perseveres all the way to Zinal from finding the car-park full and vehicles of all sizes and vintages tucked away under the eaves of all its châlets and hotels. But even if the car is cautiously abandoned lower down the valley, this is superb walking country in glorious scenery, and a longer or shorter stay at one of its un-sophisticated but charming resorts—St. Luc (5,390 ft.) would be my choice —is a joy for the lover of mountain paths, pine-forests, and woodland streams, set against some of the most snowy and beautiful of the great Alpine peaks. It is, of course, unnecessary to recommend Zinal and its two mountain inns to the serious climber.

From Sierre the Simplon road hurries on, poplar fringed, now close to the Rhone, now at a discreet distance, through Leuk—where the famous mule-track over the Gemmi from Kandersteg in the Oberland comes tumbling down its precipice to the north—and Turtmann to Visp. All along these 18 miles of broad and level valley there are continual glimpses of great peaks lifting their tops behind the huge retaining walls on either side.

Between Turtmann and Visp the Loetschberg Railway can be seen emerging from the Lanza Gorge, high up on the left. This main-line link was constructed in 1907–13 to shorten the journey from Berne and the North to the Simplon Tunnel, and itself involves a superbly engineered crossing of the Oberland Alps, culminating in the 9-mile-long tunnel from Kandersteg to Goppenstein, at the foot of the beautiful Loetschental. For some miles you can trace the railway's course clinging its way down the mountain-side, burrowing through avalanche galleries in the cliff face, and vaulting the deep scores of the ravines down which the mountain torrents hurtle to the valley, till it eventually joins the main Simplon line on the valley level, just before Brigue.

Visp is the railway junction for the narrow-gauge line to Zermatt, 20 miles to the south along the Nikolaital, which now opens up widely on the right, with a fine vista between the great ridges falling on the left from the Mischabel Group (the highest peaks actually on Swiss soil) and the Weisshorn–Rothorn chain on the other side. There is no motor-way as yet to Zermatt itself, but a fine road branches off into the valley and splits in two at Stalden, 5 miles along it. The left-hand branch—opened to motor traffic in 1954 and served by postal cars—leads through truly tremendous scenery up the savage gorges of the Visp and ends at the famous walking and climbing centre of Saas-Fee, superbly situated on a terrace at the foot of the immense glaciers pouring down from the Alphu-bel, Allalin, and the Mischabel Group, Dom and Taeschhorn. This is a glorious, if narrow, drive—heavily coach-laden in high summer—and will take you in some two hours to one of the grandest mountain 'close-ups' in the world. The other branch follows the Nikolaital to St. Niklaus,

The St. Gotthard windings in the Val Tremola

Looking south over Innsbruck towards the Brenner

The Gross Glockner across the Pasterze Glacier from Franz Joseph's Höhe (Glocknerstrasse)

The northern exit of the Hochtor (summit) tunnel (Glocknerstrasse)

Randa, and Taesch, and will no doubt be modernized and 'motorized' in due course; for it seems inconceivable that Zermatt—too famous to require any description here—will not in time be accessible by motor and coach traffic.

From Visp to Brigue is 6 miles, and the main highway runs through the last level plain of the Rhone valley to reach it. In front, the way is at last closed by a high mountain barrier, except where the narrower, more steeply terraced course of the youthful Rhone has carved through it a deep canyon, which carries the road to Gletsch, 28 miles farther up, at the junction of the Grimsel and Furka Passes (Chapter XXI).

Brigue is a busy railway junction and tourist-centre; it provides plenty of hotels for those who want to stay overnight before tackling the actual Simplon Pass crossing, which begins almost immediately on leaving the town.

A mile or so along the valley the great double railway tunnel, 12 miles long (the longest main-line tunnel in the world) burrows gloomily into the base of the hills, the route to Italy and the Orient. The Simplon, the fourth of the great Alpine tunnels to be completed, took from 1898 to 1901 to build and cost 87,000,000 francs. Its construction was attended by great difficulties, the pilot tunnel being continually breached by underground torrents, and no less than thirty-nine lives were lost before the problems were finally mastered and the two ends met, correct to the last centimetre. It was opened in May 1906, and carries a volume of Swiss–Italian express and goods traffic second only to the St. Gotthard's.

Here, as on the Gotthard, a motorist's shuttle service is now available. There is no doubt that it is much quicker, and if you want to miss one of the world's finest mountain roads, replete with glorious views of the Oberland and Valais peaks, you can for the modest sum of 38 francs (Swiss) have your car loaded on a truck, sit for twenty minutes in total darkness except for such light as your train compartment may provide, to emerge, the poorer by a great deal more than the fare, in Italian sunlight at Iselle on the other side of the Alps. However, I suspect that the sort of driver who prefers that blinkered method of trans-Alpine transport—except, of course, when forced by bad weather or lack of time—will not have persevered far enough in this book to be reading this paragraph.

The Simplon road has no second thoughts about attacking the huge mountain wall to the South and, forsaking the long and friendly hospitality of the Rhone valley, it gets to grips with its problem at once on leaving Brigue. That problem, put simply, is how to lift itself a vertical difference of 4,300 ft., to the fringe of the glaciers high overhead and across the only practicable saddle between them, in a distance of only 5 miles as the crow flies. In order to keep the maximum gradient down to 1 in 11, the actual length of the carriage way by which that problem was solved over a hundred years ago is four times that length in actual mileage.

How did it come into being in its present form?

The Simplon Saddle had been intermittently used as an Alpine passage from Roman times and through the Middle Ages, reaching the peak of its

F

importance as a trade route in the seventeenth century, when Gaspard de Stockalper, the greatest of all Swiss merchants, piled up a fabulous fortune by his organization of trains of mules and men incessantly moving to and fro across the pass between Milan and Lausanne. The famous three-towered castle of the Stockalper family at Brigue, now national property as an ancient monument and perhaps eventually to become the chief administrative office of the region, bears witness to this immense enterprise across the Simplon. The intermittent character of its earlier and later usage was due to the traditional hostility between the people to the north and south of the pass; and the frequent wars which flared up between them resulted in repeated and sometimes lengthy interruptions in its use.

After Stockalper's death in 1685 there followed a century during which the pass was little used. But in 1800 when Napoleon crossed the Grand St. Bernard into Italy with 30,000 men to fight his victorious Marengo campaign the difficulties of that high passage moved him to detach General Béthencourt with 1,000 pioneers to find a better crossing-place in the Simplon area, with its relatively low summit level, and to put in hand the construction of a proper road suitable for artillery transport—'pour faire passer le canon'—in future.

Thus there came into being the first of the great military roads over the Alps to enjoy the application of modern engineering science; and though Napoleon was never destined to set foot on it, the Simplon, in fact, inaugurated the series of Napoleonic roads designed to provide broad, well-graded carriage-ways, safe from the immediate perils encountered on the passage of high mountain slopes and saddles close to the line of snow and glaciation—the wrath of glacier torrents in spate, avalanches, and landslides.

The old rough track over the Simplon had led straight up the ravine of the Saltina at a gradient so steep that it is hard to credit that men and mules could move heavy loads over it. Beyond the saddle at the top, it followed a course across the green alps high above the terrific gorge of the Diveria, which cleaves the southern side of the mountains, and then descended equally precipitously some thousands of feet over a dangerous mountain-side to Iselle. The new road was planned to have an average gradient of 3·5 per cent and a width of 26 ft.

The fiat of the Emperor had gone out, and unlimited funds were thus available. After a few false starts, because the military engineers were inefficient and divided among themselves, the great civil engineer, Nicholas Céard, was called in to organize the project. Employing 30,000 men, he completed this pattern of the modern Alpine passes, in spite of the immense difficulties and set-backs, in the incredibly short space of five seasons—such work can, of course, be carried out only during the brief summer. The road was opened to artillery traffic in October 1805, and the first mail coach crossed it soon afterwards. The 40 miles from Brigue to Domodossola cost 7,500,000 francs; the cost of the whole route from the Lake of Geneva to Sesto Calende on Lago Maggiore is said to have been more than 12,000,000.

By 1849, when the Swiss postal services became Federal, all manner of coaches were using the pass freely. The Simplon had become one of the marvels of the world, romanticized in literature—Dickens' description in *Pictures from Italy* will come readily to mind—visited by hundreds of tourists and sightseers. The crossing to Italy became one of the 'done things' for holiday-makers and honeymoon couples: thousands of emigrants from Italy found their way over it to the other countries of Europe. For more than fifty years it held the popular imagination as the premier Alpine road. Then, in 1906, an event occurred which threatened to put it out of business as effectively as any rivalry of the Middle Ages between the Valaisians on the one side and the Lombards on the other. In that year the railway tunnel under the Alps from Brigue to Iselle was opened to traffic— and who would ever want to take the long journey over the top after that?

Now, fifty years later, thanks to the development of the internal-combustion engine, it is as popular as ever. A heavy stream of modern cars purrs up its gentle gradients, making short work of the 14 miles of steady ascent, and the big motor-coaches of the Swiss Postal Service daily take their full loads over it, spraying the distinctive bugle notes of their horn in salute to the great peaks which ring the summit of the pass.

Napoleon's original road from Geneva by-passed Brigue. Today the motorist leaves the town and takes a straight, tree-lined avenue towards the foot of the mountains to the south across the valley. At the imposing Napoleonic bridge across the Saltina he joins the Emperor's artillery road, which swings sharply leftwards up the slope of the Brigerberg, with the roofs and railway yards of Brigue falling away rapidly below, and the view widening every moment towards Naters at the foot of the Oberland spurs and also back along the Valais.

Gaining height, the road swings back in a wide arc past the hamlet of Ried, and presently comes back again to the edge of the Saltina ravine, in which the torrent now foams 1,500 ft. below, and traces of the old track can be seen in the depths. Continuing for a short distance high above the gorge, it reaches the Schallberg Halt, which used to be the Second Refuge (4,330 ft.), where a deep re-entrant, the Gantertal, opens up to the left with the Ganterbach rushing down its bottom to join the Saltina.

The green saddle of the pass now comes into view high overhead, only 2½ miles away as the crow flies, but still 10 miles distant by road. Leaving Schallberg, the road now clings to the left-hand slope, along which it makes a wide reach eastwards up the Gantertal past the châlets of Eisten till, at the Ganterbrücke (4,820 ft.), it crosses the stream and climbs up the steep opposite of this lateral valley in three hairpin turns, which bring you to the charming little holiday resort of Bérisal (5,080 ft.) prettily set on a spur among meadows and much beloved by artists. (It is an interesting and distinctive feature of the engineering quality of the Simplon that these are the only true hairpins on the Swiss side, and there is only one genuine sample on the Italian.)

Above Bérisal the climb continues steadily along the slope back towards the upper part of the Saltina Gorge—the Travertal. After a sharp kink into the ravine of the Durstbach, another lateral torrent crossed by a bridge, the Fourth Refuge (5,645 ft.) is reached at the glorious view-point of Rotwald.

Schallberg, which was left 3 miles back on entering the Gantertal, lies below on the opposite slope, only a stone's throw away across that deep and narrow valley. A halt is called for here, if the wide prospect over Brigue—now a toy town 2,000 ft. below—the broad Rhone valley plain, and the peaks of the Bernese Alps rising magnificently behind it, from the sharp cone of the Bietschhorn to the Nesthorn and the 13,000-ft. Aletschhorn, above the serpentine tongue of the Aletsch, the greatest glacier in the Alps, is to be enjoyed to the full. Here, too, in the opposite direction, the mighty bulk of the Fletschhorn (13,127 ft.) first looms into sight above the summit saddle to the south.

Continuing to climb high above the Travertal rift for another 3 miles, with the view over the Valais and the Oberland peaks continually broadening, the road reaches the Fifth Refuge (6,345 ft.). The wooded slopes and pleasant meadows of the lower section have now been left behind, and the rest of the approach to the saddle lies in a mountain world of polished rock, close below the glaciers falling from Monte Leone (11,670 ft.) and the Hübschhorn (10,485 ft.), the Kaltwasser and the Hohmatten. Everywhere the rocks glisten with the waters of innumerable rills carrying the melting snows down from them. The road immediately enters a wonderful section in which it curves on a ledge along the flank of a high rock amphitheatre, protected from torrent, avalanche, and stone-fall by a series of three galleries with great arched windows, built into the mountainside. These are the work of the celebrated engineer Venetz in the late nineteenth century, and did not form part of the original Napoleonic engineering feat.

The first, the Kaltwasser Gallery, defends the road from the violence of the Kaltwasserbach, which goes thundering out over the roof to the depths of the gorge in a welter of spray, as you drive under the lofty and massive vault; at the second and third, the 'Old' and St. Joseph's Galleries, there is an external by-pass for use in summer. A short rise from the end of the last gallery brings you to the summit of the pass at the Simplon Saddle, 6,594 ft. above sea-level and 14 miles from Brigue.

The saddle itself is one of the greatest surprises of the route. Instead of the stony wilderness which might be expected at the rim of a dozen glaciers, close to the feet of the great peaks which dominate it, it turns out to be a little upland valley in its own right—a place of sunny green pastures, through which the rippling brooks hurry on their swift way.

The wide views back over the Rhone's green pit and the great snowy peaks of the Aletsch backing it are now lost, as the road drops gently along the winding corridor past the huge Hospice (6,565 ft.)—intended partly as a barracks by Napoleon, but only completed after his downfall and occupied, like most of the other famous Hospices, by the Bernardine fraternity. Soon after the Hospice, the old Stockalper Hospice (6,140 ft.), with its prominent town, is passed on the right, and here, at the right season of the year, the whole floor of the valley is carpeted with red Alpine rhododendrons. Hemmed between the Monte Leone group on the left, where near the Seventh Refuge (5,855 ft.) the Hübschhorn and the bleak Breithorn are seen to advantage, and the Portjen–Weismiess–Fletschhorn chain of the Valaisian Pennines, whose other side overlooks the Saas valley, this sector of the road presents numerous fine close-ups of peaks and glaciers—among them the Rossbodengletscher, falling from the Fletschhorn down a lateral glen to the right near the sparse houses of Eggen. In 1901 the lower part of this glacier collapsed without warning, completely burying the hamlet of Seng, which used to stand where a chaos of piled earth and boulders is already overgrown by a tangle of stone pines and other vegetation. But the show-piece along the whole Upper Simplon valley is the great Eastern wall of the Fletschhorn, lifting to 13,000 ft. only 5 miles away, with its glacier pedestal reaching down almost to the valley level—nearly 6,000 ft. of rock, snow, and ice. And so, passing the 'half-way milestone', surmounted by a Gallic cock, we reach the picturesque village of Simplon Dorf (4,852 ft.), its venerable buildings and church towers, entirely built of stone, huddling for protection in that high and lonely place.

Beyond the village the road suddenly faces a blank wall of mountain to the south—the Weismiess (13,220 ft.) is now seen beyond the Fletschhorn —where all progress seems to be finally barred; but it executes a desperate left-hand wriggle back on itself and at the Inn of Gstein-Gabi (4,042 ft.) enters the head of a narrow defile which offers the only exit to the world below—the extraordinary rift the Diveria torrent (Krummbach) has bitten through the primeval granite. The Inn, by the way, boasts an inscription to the effect that Napoleon—who never actually passed this way—drank a glass of milk there.

For several miles the road now pursues a fantastic course through some of the deepest and most awesome ravines in the Alps. The 3-mile-long Gondo gorge, whose precipices tower 3,000 ft. to the narrow strip of sky caught between their tops, is longer and even more terrific than the Schoellenen rift on the Gotthard. To find a way through, the road, often in galleries hewn out of the immense rock-faces, always high above the foaming Diveria, is forced to leap like a crazy thing seeking frantically to escape destruction from one side of the narrow slit in the huge mountain masses to the other. For some this long passage of a Gustave Doré world may be too gloomy and macabre, but as a presentation of nature at her most savage and engineering skill at its courageous best this section must stand unrivalled.

In spite of the extreme contraction of the mountain walls, room was found here for the Ninth Refuge (3,514 ft.) and even a barrack building by those hardy Napoleonic builders. At the end of the 220-yd. Gondo Gallery, high above the Diveria, an inscription which reads 'AERE ITALO MDCCCV. NAP. IMP.', serves as a reminder that this amazing road was forced by Céard and his toiling thousands, often slung by ropes down the sheer face of the precipice as they worked, over 150 years ago.

Here the torrent of the Alpjenbach, thundering down the glistening rocks, is crossed by an arched bridge, which is often enveloped in a cloud of spray thrown up by the furious head of water when the snows are melting.   And so we reach Gondo (2,815 ft.), the last Swiss village in a little widening of the rift, with its prominent Stockalper tower.   Opposite, on the right, the lofty Zwischenberg valley opens up, running back deeply to the feet of the Portjengrat and Weismiess, between which the Zwischenberg Pass, a favourite mountaineer's track, climbs over a notch in the range to Saas Fee.

Between Gondo and San Marco, the first Italian village, are the Swiss and Italian customs-houses, the latter a small, solitary building, clinging grimly to the side of the gorge.

Beyond San Marco's church tower, the road, emerging at last from the vice in which it had been clamped, passes through picturesque Iselle-Villagio, and presently, just before the station of Iselle-Trasquera (2,155 ft.), the double tunnel of the Simplon Railway is seen emerging from its 9 miles of lightless, sightless transit under the Alps.   Road, river, and twin-track railway now keep company through the deep Val Divedro, which begins here and continues for 10 miles, falling steadily from Varzo and deeply carved between the mountain-sides, till the southern plain is reached after a last gallery at Crevola (1,286 ft.).

Domodossola and the end of the pass are still 13 miles away, but everything is suddenly southern and Italian, and for once there is a strong parallel between two great passes otherwise utterly different in character. For in its vegetation, its villages perched on the steep green slopes, its white campaniles, its waterfalls, its torrents, and its vines, there is an unmistakable likeness to the section of the Gotthard between Airolo and the Faido terrace, as it falls to the Levantina.   Even the railway, with its splendid spiral-tunnel between Iselle and Varzo, conspires to complete the simile, as the road continues to descend through rocky defiles towards the plains.

Beyond Varzo, with an overwhelming effect of contrast after long imprisonment between gloomy canyon walls, the fertile green plain of the Tosa opens out below, a smooth and level table which was once a lake bed and has since been covered by soil brought down by the Tosa from the mountains.   Down there, spread wide in the warm and reassuring sunlight, lies a world of villages, white church-towers, and rich orchard groves.   Looking back, there are last glimpses of the Fletschhorn, unbelievably remote and high above.   The great barrier of the Alps lies behind, and we are in the soft, warm air of the Italian plains.

A last curve to the right brings us to the marble bridge of Crevola; from Preglia, on level ground at last after 30 miles, the road runs straight as a ruler across the green floor of the Tosa plain to the white-walled houses of pleasant, unmistakably Italian Domodossola, a town of 9,000 inhabitants.

The western tip of Lago Maggiore and the lovely road through Baveno, Stresa, and Sesto Calende, and thence to Milan by the 40-mile Autostrada, lie only 20 miles ahead.

VIII

THE ST. GOTTHARD PASS (6,926 ft.)

Entirely in Switzerland (Uri–Ticino); but provides a direct through-route to Italy via Lugano or Sesto Calende.

From Altdorf (1,518 ft.) to Bellinzona (760 ft.), crossing the main Alpine watershed between the North Sea and the Adriatic: 82 miles.

Detail. Altdorf to Goeschenen (3,640 ft.): 22 miles, ascent 2,100 ft.
  Goeschenen to Hospental (4,870 ft.): 4 miles (Schoellenen Gorge), ascent 1,280 ft.
  Hospental to Summit (6,926 ft.): 7 miles, ascent 2050 ft.
Total ascent Altdorf–Summit: 33 miles, 5,400 ft.

  Summit to Airolo (3,745 ft.): 8 miles, descent 3,200 ft.
  Airolo to Faido (2,465 ft.): 13 miles, descent 1,300 ft.
  Faido to Bellinzona (760 ft.): 28 miles, descent 1,700 ft.
Total descent Summit–Bellinzona: 49 miles, 6,200 ft.

Open: Mid-May to late October. Maximum gradient: 1 in 10.

The longest of the passes, broken into three distinct and varied sections. From Altdorf to Goeschenen a somewhat narrow, old-fashioned, and sometimes indifferently surfaced valley road, rising steadily, with a few hairpins just short of Wassen and Goeschenen. Thence a wonderful new road (hairpins and gorge with tunnels) through the Schoellenen Gorge to Andermatt and on along the Urserental to Hospental. Here the true ascent to the pass begins in numerous sharp hairpin turns (entirely rebuilt and modernized 1956–7, thus eliminating a poor and difficult section). The magnificent descent of the Val Tremola slope from the summit to Airolo is a marvel of modern road engineering, the forty-eight hairpins being wide, splendidly built out, well protected, and wonderfully surfaced. From Airolo to the valley level the road is more old-fashioned again, with a narrower carriage-way, occasional banks of hairpins, but a good bitumen surface.

Traffic: Heavy in summer, sometimes excessively so at week-ends.

Long, moderate in places, easy on all the modernized sections. A magnificent drive.

THE St. Gotthard Pass, in effect linking Lucerne on the edge of Switzerland's northern plain with Lugano beyond the Alpine chain on the fringe of Italian Lombardy, is historically, politically, and economically the most significant of the Swiss passes.

This route provided the early physical cord binding Tell's country, lying to the north of the mountains, with the Ticino, warm and Italianate, to the south; and so through the centuries became the essential link and later the symbol of political Federation between the German- and Italian-speaking Cantons of the Swiss Union. There was no carriage road till comparatively recent times, the first recorded crossing in a vehicle being that of Greville in 1775; Goethe traversed it in the same year and again in 1779 and 1797.

In 1799, with the internal disruption of the Swiss Confederation through internecine strife, the area passed under French domination, and for some years suffered severely as the vital battle-ground in the campaigns between the French under Massena and the Austro-Russian alliance under the Archduke Charles and the Russian generals Korsakov and Suvarov. The fighting swayed back and forth along this incredible choice for military operations, the pass and the Schoellenen Gorge being the scene of savage fighting, in which now the French, now the Austrians held the narrow defiles. When finally Suvarov, marching with 20,000 men from Italy, forced the French back a second time after a unique four days' battle of the gorges, he came too late to save the Austrians from defeat at Zürich and the Gotthard passed for the last time under French control. It was used in 1800 by General Moncey, hastening with 23,000 men to reinforce Napoleon during his campaign in Upper Italy.

With the end of the Napoleonic wars, Switzerland regained her lost and ravaged territory, and the present carriage road was built between 1820 and 1830, a new Hospice being erected in 1834 and the Monte Prosa Hotel, now the summit caravanserai, in 1867.

The road, however, was to suffer a temporary eclipse within a comparatively short time, for between 1872 and 1882 the Swiss talent for imaginative engineering converted this difficult and daunting route into a great north–south economic artery by the construction of a main international railway line, the climax of which was the penetration of the great final mountain massif by the second (the Mont Cenis had been opened in 1871) of the famous Alpine tunnels, 9 miles long, between Goeschenen and Airolo at a level of 3,400 ft.

This double-line international rail-link, which still ranks among the world's engineering wonders—modern electrically hauled expresses traverse it at an average speed of 40 m.p.h.—opened a trade route by which the vast volume of heavy goods traffic from Germany and all northern Europe could roll in an incessant stream into Italy, saving days in transit time. So important, indeed, was the maintenance of this direct link to become to the two Fascist dictators during the Second World War that its ability to function freely was certainly one of the main considerations in the unwavering respect paid to Swiss neutrality throughout the long conflict.

Strictly speaking, then, the only sector of the Gotthard route which actually crosses the ridge of the Alpine watershed in good fresh air and daylight is the wonderful sector of motor-road over the top of the mountains from Goeschenen to Airolo; to this a purist might perhaps confine his description of the pass, arguing that the rest may be seen just as well from the windows of a speeding train.

I prefer to describe the whole lovely road route from a northern lake to a southern not only because the true significance of the Gotthard—before railways were thought of—lies in that long line of communication but also because the contention that the lower part can be seen as well from the railway just isn't true. Wonderful as it is, the railway view is restricted by the drawbacks of railway-carriage construction, however large the windows, and by the frequency of the tunnels, many of them spiral, and consequently involving bewildering changes of direction. Moreover, one sees the extraordinary ingenuity and skill of the eighty-year-old engineering feat of the railway's progress between Amsteg and Goeschenen and again, on the south side, between Airolo and Faido to far better advantage from the road; and in my view it is an inherent feature of the many wonders of the St. Gotthard Pass, and well worth seeing. Finally, like the direct main-road, the line, by travelling from Lucerne behind the Rigi ridge to Arth-Goldau and Brunnen through a broad and tame valley, misses all the enchanting scenery along the earlier shores of Lake Lucerne.

It is unnecessary to dwell at length on the beauties, familiar to hundreds of thousands of tourists, of the shores of the Lake of the Four Cantons (Vierwaldstädtersee), at whose northern tip lies Lucerne. After skirting the long, narrow arm to Küssnacht and doubling back along the green meadows of its opposite shore, close under the Rigi's steep, elongated comb, the road threads its lovely way, often close to the lake's edge, and always opposite the dark, wooded ridge of the Bürgenstock, from one charming bay to another, through narrow Weggis, Vitznau, and even narrower Gersau, with their white houses and slender, cupola'd church towers, mirrored in blue waters, to Brunnen. (Heavy traffic jams are not infrequent in the 'season' along this garland of bottle-necks—the mixed metaphor is, I think, justifiable—particularly at week-ends: as stated above, they can be avoided, at the cost of all the scenic beauty, by following the sedate and viewless railway route through Arth-Goldau.)

At Brunnen the small harbour and lake-front, with a car-park under its soldier-like trees, look out on the last and longest arm of the lake, which here bends southwards at right-angles, cradled between sterner and higher walls, dominated by the Uri-Rotstock and the small hanging glacier under its stubby crest. Almost immediately after leaving the town a side road climbs steeply to the left by a number of tight windings to Morschach, high above the lake and offering wonderful views over its basin—a digression well worth pursuing if there is an hour to spare.

The main road now enters the celebrated section of the Axenstrasse, long modernized into a wide, superbly surfaced, and fast *corniche* road, twisting and tunnelling through the great grey crags which rise sheer from the water's edge. In and out it winds, past the steamer halt at Tellsplatte —where the hero leaped ashore—and the historic chapel, along 10 miles of swift water-side enchantment to pretty Fluelen, backed by the symmetrical pyramid of the Bristenstock at the head of the lake.

After leaving the lake the road runs through the green plain of the Reuss to reach Altdorf, only 2 miles away. The paved streets and squares of this romantic old town, redolent with the Tell legend, are bordered by ancient houses, balconies, and arcades, and picturesque with innumerable fine examples of medieval Swiss architecture, well worth a halt for closer inspection.

Here the Klausen Pass (Chapter XIV) turns away leftwards into the green base of the great hills to climb over them to Linthal and Glarus;

and the Gotthard road now begins to rise steadily along the narrowing Reuss re-entrant to Amsteg. This is a relatively dull stage, encumbered with railway marshalling yards and electrical installations, while the mountain-side to the left is scarred hideously by the enormous battery of pipes plunging sheer for a thousand feet to bring the source of power to the Amsteg hydro-electric station, which supplies the railway's tractive force (though even these blemishes are dwarfed by the scale of the surrounding mountains).

At Amsteg the secluded and unspoiled Maderanertal runs up to the left into the snowy Clariden group, a walking and climbing paradise of the old-fashioned type, well off the beaten track. The Gotthard route, continuing up the deep and rapidly contracting valley, now enters the zone of pine-woods, and from here on there is something lovely or exciting to be seen at almost every twist of the steepening road, alongside which the Reuss foams down between its boulders in the green bottom of the vale.

There has been little change in the old road along this sector; it is still narrow, often running between stone walls, but as it rises between huge wooded slopes from terrace to terrace of the valley floor, each decorated with its picturesque village and church, it provides a succession of wonderful glimpses of the railway, now spanning the Reuss on tall-arched viaducts, now writhing its incredible way up the vast hill-sides, first on one side of the valley then on the other, burrowing into the dark mouths of spiral tunnels to appear again hundreds of feet higher up, crossing and re-crossing its own track on airy girder bridges, clinging its upward way on narrow ledges and leaping the tributary torrents, as they plunge to join the Reuss below, by graceful masonry arches high overhead. To follow the course of an express pounding its way up the long grade to Goeschenen and the Tunnel is a confusing task, for at one moment it is seen climbing smoothly parallel to you, only to reappear a few moments later on a different level and apparently heading in the opposite direction.

So the road mounts from meadow-level to level through Gurtnellen and Wiler till, just before Wassen, it is forced to resort to its first two or three hairpins in order to gain the necessary height. The railway has been clinging high on the right-hand wall for some time, and as you swing up to regain its level, the remarkable concrete arch by which the Susten Pass road (Chapter XXI) clears the thundering cascade of the Maienreuss comes into sight even higher up the slope. A moment later the last steep windings of the Susten tumble from the right to meet you at the entrance to the narrow main street of the ancient village of Wassen.

From Wassen to Goeschenen the road rises gently along the last high meadows of the valley, and it soon becomes clear that you are running head on into the foot of the enormous mountain barrier before you. So close are the retaining walls by now that there is only just room for road, river, and railway.

At a cottage and signpost just short of Goeschenen there is a lovely glimpse up a lateral rift which surprisingly opens up on the right, with a narrow road leading along it to the S.A.C. Hut on the Goeschenen Alp, four hours' lovely walk away, at the foot of the fine Dammastock (11,920 ft.) and its climbs. This crescent-shaped wall of blue-grey rock, often dappled with snow, and broken near its top by a necklet of hanging-glaciers, fills the head of the side valley most imposingly. It is a view worth pulling up and getting out for, but easy to miss unless you are driving slowly and looking out for it; once past the turning, the road is so narrow that it is impossible to park or turn round for some time.

Goeschenen itself clings precariously to the hill-side on a series of tiny terraces above and below the road. In the bottom of the ravine is the station with its sidings; and from the road, 30 ft. above, you look down on to the dark maw of the double-line tunnel as it bores into the vertical base of the rock only a hundred yards from the platform ends.

There is, however, little opportunity for looking, unless you have decided to stop and park, for everything here is suddenly exceedingly steep, narrow, and twisting; before you know it you are out of the village street and climbing steeply into a chaos of rubble and rock which opens up to the right. This is the entrance to the fantastic Schoellenen Gorge, an exiguous chink carved by the savage power of the descending Reuss through the immense rock screen, which towers thousands of feet to the sky, on its raging way down from the higher levels on the other side.

Into that sombre and awful crevice the road climbs courageously— accompanied at first by the single-line narrow-gauge Schoellenen railway till it is forced to burrow its onward way to Andermatt in a tunnel, high up to the left—by a series of short hairpins banked one above the other. These used to present a tricky passing problem till recently (1956) magni-ficently modernized and widened as much as the precipitous boulder-strewn débris-fan permits. At their top stands the small Schoellenen inn and its car park, from which the best view of the topless, vertical walls of this truly awe-inspiring gorge and of the Devil's Bridge, arching 100 ft. above the raging torrent in its bottom, is obtained. Here, at the right time of day the sun strikes marvellous rainbows on the haze of spray hanging between the cliffs. The ancient bridge has since 1956 been replaced for traffic purposes by a modern structure more capable of dealing with the tremendous volume of summer traffic; and the old narrow road-way, clinging and tunnelling for dear life along a ledge in the bare rock wall, has also been widened and built out for the rest of its astonishing way through the sunless ravine till at the end of the last tunnel it suddenly emerges into broad daylight again in the Urserental a mile short of Ander-matt. This whole new section is a miracle not only of natural savagery but also of engineering skill.

The historic name of the place is the 'Urnerloch'—'the Black Hole of Uri'—and it is truly a Gustave Doré setting, especially on a stormy day. This is where the decisive battle raged for four days in 1799 (see above)— surely the most improbable of the many unsuitable battle-grounds so plentifully scattered about the high peaks and passes of the Alps?

After the eerie half light of the gorge it is a positive relief to be in a broad and smiling valley between level green meadows again; and a minute or two later the long, hotel-lined main street of Andermatt—a favourite summer- and winter-sports resort (4,737 ft.)—restores a refreshing sense of normality, though alas not of architectural beauty, to the proceedings.

To the left, the Oberalp Pass lifts steeply out of the town on its way eastwards into the Rhine valley (Chapter XXII). The Gotthard road continues westwards, wide and well surfaced for a mile and a half along the level floor of the Urseren valley—that remarkable hollow more fully described in Chapters I and XXI, pp. 26-8 and 155—to the old town of Hospental. This was the medieval domain of the Langobard barons, whose dark, round tower still dominates the roofs of the little town, where the Gotthard, leaving the Furka road to continue straight ahead up the trough of the valley, swings sharply to the left into the great mountain range to the south.

The long climb towards the summit begins immediately—till recently by a short, steep terrace of five built-out hairpins forming a bewildering pattern overhead; then, for twenty minutes, the road contours up and up the ravine of the Gotthard Reuss till it eventually obtains a lodgement on the right-hand slope of the re-entrant through which the foaming torrent comes tumbling down from the watershed ahead. This sector, once unworthy of so important a route and at times, in wet and stormy weather, even dangerous, for it was regularly ground to pulp by heavy military traffic, has been entirely modernized and rebuilt during 1956-7, and its wide, swinging dog-legs can at last vie in magnificence with the spectacular marvel of the long southern side.

At Matteli there are two more sharp hairpins and a vista opens up to the left to the 10,000-ft. Pizzo Centrale at the head of the Guspistal. Above the hairpins there is a fine view back across the depths of the Urseren valley, and as the road levels out again the snowy Pizzo Lucendro is seen lifting ahead.

Contouring the mountain base more gently now for another ten minutes, with gaunt rock ridges looming opposite beyond the stream, the road crosses the Lucendro bridge and levels out suddenly along the margin of a sombre lake about ¼ mile long to reach the Gotthard Saddle (7,926 ft.), deep set between the grim rocky peaks of Monte Prosa and the Fibbia still lifting their bleak heads some 2,000 ft. above. Here stand the dark stone-built Hospice and Monte Prosa Hotel, stern buildings in a stern setting; at the lake-side close by stands a tall and elaborate winged monument to Adrien Guex, a Swiss airman who came to grief in this lonely spot. The scene is not beautiful, but it is impressive.

Immediately beyond the long, level passage of the saddle, the road dips again through a narrow, craggy ravine, losing height rapidly on the southern side of the watershed by a series of short turns to reach the head of the Val Tremola, the windings down which are the true climax of this long and varied journey. For the descent of this southern precipice is a marvel of a modern motor-way, graded, engineered, and surfaced to perfection all the way down the tremendous southern flank of the Gotthard group—a drop of 5,000 ft. of unbroken mountain-side.

The upper part of this amazing drive to the lower levels is through the precipitous re-entrant of the Val Tremola—the Valley of Fear—a steep hanging valley or score between projecting buttresses of shattered grey rock which plunge a thousand feet on either side from the base of the peaks overhead, the turf of the broad slopes below. Down this narrow, precipitous tongue of rubble and rock-outcrops the blue-grey ribbon of smooth road snakes its way in looped reaches which vary from 50 yards to ¼ mile in length, at times doubling back on themselves one above the other, then darting out across the face to find a hold on a new terrace and twisting back across the mountain face on a lower level to start a new series of banked turns far below. And all the way down, the ridgeway is protected by faced embankments and high emplacements from stonefall and landslide on the inner mountain-side, while a fine continuous parapet guards it on the outer precipice side of every hairpin curve. At the Cantoniera Val Tremola (5,564 ft.) the road enters the upper Val Levantina, down which it continues to Airolo.

There are forty-eight hairpins in all, every one of them so well graded and sited that traffic, even the great coaches, can pass on them without the slightest difficulty, and all the time, as you spiral down as if on wings, the blue-shadowed floor of the Airolo valley far down in the gulf comes wheeling gently up at you as if from another world. The valley to the right is the Val Bedretto, which falls into the Levantina at Airolo, bringing the Ticino down from its main source.

In my opinion, this section of the Gotthard in whichever direction it is driven is—as a marvel of road engineering and a driving thrill—second only to the Stelvio windings between Trafoi and the summit. Though there, of course, the magnificence of the Ortler* and its glaciers almost touching the narrow rift provides a scenic grandeur which the great green mountain slopes facing you at a greater distance beyond the depths of the Airolo valley cannot quite match—impressive though they be.

Airolo (3,750 ft.) the southern exit of the 9-mile railway tunnel whose other entrance was seen at Goeschenen some hours ago, lies in a deep green bowl at the foot of the Gotthard massif and is a fair-sized town with an important railway station and several good hotels and restaurants if it is desired to stay the night. There is a fine view up the lateral valley along which you have driven from the foot of the pass, back to the snowy 10,000-ft. peaks of Pizzo Rotondo and Lucendro dominating the Gotthard Group beyond the great slopes by which the road forces its way over the range.

This is, of course, where those who prefer to miss all those marvels to be enjoyed in driving over the top of the Alps by one of their most varied and splendid roads detrain from the car-ferry service through that blind 7-mile hole in the bowels of the earth and resume the steep road southwards. Except for the first section down to Biasca, with its wonderful companionship of writhing road, rushing river, and contortionist railway— even more marvellous in its spiral acrobatics than on the northern side,

* See footnote p. 24.

because the descending Val Levantina is narrower and steeper-sided—the rest of the journey to the lakes and plains is in truth tame by comparison with what has been missed.

There are some lovely waterfalls cascading from high up in the cliffs and green slopes along the road through Faido (2,465 ft.) to Biasca—particularly impressive being one to your right near Rodo-Fiessa, descending from Lake Tremorgio, high in the hills above, and the triple fall of the Piumogna at Faido, the capital of the Levantina. (These are all charming, small mountain resorts, with plenty of attractive excursions to be made from them.)

The rift, as you descend steeply from terrace to terrace, is narrow and deep, and the sky seems incredibly remote overhead. It seems impossible that only a little time ago you were as high up as the tops of the great wooded ridges on either side. At Biasca (970 ft.), in the first level plainlet, the Lukmanier road (Chapter XIV) comes in down the broad valley of the Brenno to the left, from Aquarossa and Olivone.

Then, suddenly, you are driving straight along the pleasant, wide, and flat Ticino valley, between lush meadows, through village after village, typically Italian in character. Everything is warm, southern, sub-Alpine; even the language is Italian in this Swiss Canton to the south of the Alpine chain. And so for 30 miles to Lugano progress is swift, and the absence of bends and terraced loops provides a strange contrast after the 50 tortuous miles from distant Wassen, away on the other side of the mountains.

True, beyond Bellinzona (760 ft.), the fine old capital of the Ticino, 12 miles south of Biasca, and where the San Bernardino road (Chapter XV) falls in from Mesocco away up the Moesa valley to the left, there is a small wooded spur barring the way to Lugano and its beautiful lake-basin. Avoiding it, the Ticino now flows broad and placid through its wide trough to the head of Lago Maggiore, a few miles away to the right. Along it lies the highway to Locarno and the other famous Maggiore lake resorts (Pallanza, Baveno, Stresa), as well as the road onwards to the southern foot of the Simplon at Domodossola.

The Lugano road continues straight ahead due south and surmounts the little ridge by what is technically the Monte Ceneri 'Pass', rising again to a modest 1,850 ft.; but you would never know it was a pass in its own right, for the broad main road curves but gently here and there to gain the few hundred feet involved and, if the road is empty, the speedometer need hardly fall below forty except for caution's sake at one or two of the less gentle sweeps up the hill-side. Down it dips again into the sunny basin of the Vedeggio valley to the north of Lugano, lined by low, wooded hills, increasingly crowded with villages and villas, past Riviera and Taverna, finally to run flat for a mile or two into that most over-populated, over-visited—and in high summer impossibly congested—of all Switzerland's famous lake-resorts. Here, at perhaps the loveliest of all lakes, where too many Cooks have spoiled the broth and not only Lunn is vile, the St. Gotthard road ends.

Southwards from Lugano the highway, in company with the railway, continues along the western fringe of the lake, crosses it presently by a causeway, and worms its way below the slopes of Monte Generoso— one of the finest lower view-points in the Alps—through the narrow neck at its southern end to Mendrisio, Chiasso, the large railway junction on the Swiss–Italian frontier, and Como (17 miles). Here you are on the edge of the plains and, by the *Autostrada*, Milan lies only 30 miles—which means little more than half an hour in that context—ahead.

An alternative road from Bellinzona to Como, by-passing Lugano altogether, leaves the Bellinzona–Lugano road a mile or two short of Lugano and bears right, past the head of the lake's western branch, to Varese (12 miles). There it strikes the northern branch of the Sesto Calende (Maggiore)–Milan *Autostrada*, providing 40 miles of speedway motoring to the capital of Lombardy.

Eastwards from Lugano the fine new Gandria highway follows the eastern arm of the lake past that most sketched of all lake-side villages to cross into Italy a mile or two farther on, winding thence over the inter- vening spurs by a miniature pass, plentifully and sharply hairpinned, especially on the Italian side, to descend charmingly on Como's lovely shore at red-roofed Menaggio.

As for Lugano's own inimitable hill roads, twisting their precipitous way high to bird's-eye views of the green unruffled lake, with ancient villages and churches perched on every shoulder and terrace of those lovely hills and unforgettable vistas into the depths at every turn in the road—stay a day or two in or about Lugano, if you can anywhere find room, and sample them all, especially at blossom time. Among short drives I myself do not know of a more exciting and repaying half-hour than the ascent to Monte Bré, either by day or when the myriad lights of Lugano, 2,000 ft. below, twinkle up on the dark velvet of a warm summer's night, like a diamond coronet.

IX

THE BRENNER PASS (4,495 ft.)

Austria to Italy. (Inn Valley to Alto Adige.)

From Innsbruck (1,885 ft.) to Vipiteno (Sterzing) (3,100 ft.), crossing the main
    Alpine watershed between the Adriatic and the Black Sea: 33 miles.

Detail. Innsbruck to the Brenner Saddle (4,495 ft.): 24 miles, ascent 2,600 ft.

    Brenner Saddle to Vipiteno (Sterzing) (3,100 ft.): 9 miles, descent
    1,400 ft.

Open: All the year round, chains sometimes necessary in winter.

  A wide, modern, and splendidly surfaced (bitumen) road from Innsbruck to
the Brenner; narrower and still somewhat old-fashioned on the Italian side, also
steeper, but generally well-surfaced. One short section at 1 in 7.

  Traffic very heavy indeed at week-ends in summer. A much frequented
road at all times.

The easiest of the genuine trans-Alpine passes, also the lowest.

T HE BRENNER is the lowest and gentlest of all the great roads which
cross the backbone of the Alpine chain. It is probably the oldest route of
all those that cross the Adriatic–Black Sea watershed, its use dating
back to beyond Roman times. The carriage road, which is still the route
followed by the present highway, was first constructed in 1772. At its
saddle, which it shares with a double-track international railway line, it is
still below the tree-level; and here, alone of the great passes, even the
railway does not resort to a tunnel to penetrate the final crest of the watershed. But, in spite of its modest elevation and this joint occupation with
other means of mechanical transport—for the most part very self-effacing—
the Brenner road is a charming two hours' drive. What it lacks in the
absence of breath-taking glimpses of giant snowy peaks it makes up for by
its picturesque progress up pleasant valleys carved deep into fine mountain
ranges, whose green slopes sweep down from imposing rocky summits,
9,000 or 10,000 ft. high, in the frontier chain dividing Austria from Italy.
And surely there is no pass which can boast more picturesque and ancient
towns at its feet and along its course?

  The importance of the Brenner has throughout the centuries rested
mainly on its provision of an easy connecting link between Austria and her
Cisalpine dependencies. No region of Europe has suffered more during
hundreds of years of incessant warfare than the Tyrol, of which it is the
main artery. From 1496, when the Emperor Maximilian acquired it by
bequest, to its final dismemberment between Austria and Italy in the 1918
peace treaty in our own times, the fine people of the Tyrol have been
subject to the ceaseless ravages of every war in which Austria was involved.
Alternately a dependency of Bavaria and Austria, and continually fought
over between them, the Tyrol was finally restored to Austria in 1812 after

The Grosse Wiessbachhorn from Edelweisspitze (Glocknerstrasse)

Lay-by on the northern descent of the Glockner road

The Lukmanier Road, looking back to Disentis in the Rhine Valley

Windings of the San Bernardino above Pian San Giacomo

Napoleon's Russian campaign, and remained part of her till, a hundred years later, the First World War again submerged it in bitter fighting.

The most famous exploit of the Tyrolese was the ambush staged by Andreas Hofer in 1809 at Mittewald, on the road from the foot of the Brenner to Brixen, when he and his men succeeded in annihilating a Franco-Bavarian army attempting to force its way over the Brenner. Every mile of this lower road, every defile, every bridge along it has been the scene of battles fought by the brave Tyrolese to gain or defend their independence.

The first mention of the Brenner is in 13 B.C., when Augustus crossed it —Innsbruck was the Roman Oenopontum—to subdue the tribes of the Tyrol, whom he civilized. The Roman peace lasted till the Marcomanni, coming from farther north, invaded Italy across the Brenner and waged a twelve years' war with Rome before she succeeded in expelling them.

In the early part of the third century the Allemani and Goths descended on Rome by the same route: degenerate Rome bought them off and they withdrew. In 452 Attila and his Huns poured southwards over the same road, and this time the Roman Empire of the West was destroyed. Fourteen years later Odoacer followed, leading the Rugii, and established himself as King of Pavia; but in 489 Theodoric came over the Brenner to evict him and found an Empire stretching from the St. Gotthard to the Black Sea. By 550 it had been disrupted by internal dissension, leaving the Lombard kings masters of the Italian portion.

There followed the wars of the Lombards and the Ostrogoths and the Franks, the wars of Charlemagne and the Lombards, and, after the demise of the Carlovingian line, endless wars on behalf of the Dukes of Bavaria, who then annexed the Tyrol till Maximilian's advent in 1496.

In all these conflicts the Brenner played a major part.

If there is a choice of ends I would elect to drive this road for the first time from south to north, climbing the shorter, steeper side from the upper Isarco (Eisack) valley; then swooping down the long, gradually widening re-entrant towards the great lateral rift of the Inn valley, with the dark, serrated heads of the Northern Limestone Alps, ranged at its farther side, drawing nearer at every mile of the lovely descent. And to make the choice still more effective, I should time my journey so that the last few miles, winding steeply down among the woods, should float me down through the late afternoon to come out above Innsbruck as the last western light lay in a level blaze on the broad valley floor beneath the dusk-dark wall of mountains opposite. For then, and as its myriad lights come out to star the deepening gloom, Innsbruck is a fairy city, set in an enchanted plain.

Affording the direct approach from the central Lombardy plain via Brescia, Lake Garda, and Trento, the southern approach to the Brenner leads from the vineyards of Bolzano (880 ft.) along the delightful valley of the lower Isarco, deep, narrow, and rich in historic castles guarding, from their perches on either steep flank, the traditional south-to-north highway from the Italian plains to Eastern Austria. Now on one side

G

now on the other of the swift-flowing river, the fine fast road squeezes its way through the gateways in the commanding hills, at times vying for passage-way with the main Italo-Austrian railway link, at others separated from it by the broad stream and its sunny meadows. Rising gradually and passing through Ponte Gardena (17 miles), where a single-span girder bridge carries the Val Gardena–Sella road eastwards across the river into the heart of the Dolomite country (see p. 234), it runs along the valley for 30 miles to Bressanone (Brixen, 1,835 ft.).

Here the broad valley route to Brunico, Dobbiaco, Lienz, and Eastern Austria through the wide and lovely Pustertal swings away to the right up the Rienz valley, while the road to the foot of the Brenner, by-passing the ancient town in its green plain—all these old places are well worth a visit and by-passes, after all, save only a few questionable minutes—bears slightly left, north-westwards towards the Alpine chain ahead.

Five miles later, at Fortezza (2,500 ft.)—Franzensfeste that was—a magnificent old fortress, one flank of which is protected by a lake, completely bars the narrow jaws of the upper Eisack valley, along which the road now climbs through Mittewald and Mauls, past picturesque castles on either hand, to emerge in a small green plain just short of Vipiteno (Sterzing still seems much more natural), where the true climb to the Brenner Pass begins.   There are fine glimpses westwards up a wide re-entrant, into which the San Giovo Pass road forks to the left of the southern walls of the snow-streaked Stubai and Oetztal Alps, over 11,000 ft. high.   The San Giovo, by the way, affords a fine alternative route from Bolzano to this point, but it is a considerable mountain pass of recent construction, 6,869 ft. high and rich in hairpins; so that the valley route described is, naturally, the traditional, the most direct, and, in point of time, far the shortest approach to the southern foot of the Brenner.

At Vipiteno (Sterzing) (3,100 ft.) there is once again a modern by-pass. Hundreds of motorists no doubt speed along it without the slightest idea that they are missing a perfect jewel of ancient architecture half a minute to the west; for ancient Sterzing's narrow main street, with its northern gate and tower, its colonnades, its carved and frescoed house-fronts, its eaves, and its ironwork is a unique example of a medieval thoroughfare in full preservation.   Please drive off the speedway into the town, park your car at the appointed place, and walk through that enchanting gateway. You will not be sorry about the quarter of an hour you may lose before getting back into the stream of the Brenner's traffic.

It is only 9 miles from the old and narrow bridge, which still spans the Isarco just north of Vipiteno, to the Brenner Saddle.   The road winds steeply up—much as it has always been for width but better surfaced, with the river now a tumbling mountain torrent beside it—bestriding the railway by a level crossing which can result in considerable traffic-jams, climbing through glades in the pine-woods, contouring meadow slopes, and wriggling between low, rocky bluffs as it rapidly gains height up the intervening 1,400 feet.

Three miles along it, at 3,500 ft., lies picturesque Colle Isarco (Gossensass) (3,495 ft.), another charming town and a favourite for summer holidays; 4 miles later, on a wide bend, stand the hotels of Terme (Brennerbad) (4,930 ft.), a pleasantly situated health resort with thermal springs, at 4,400 ft.; and 2 miles farther on, the wide, level, but entirely viewless saddle of the Brenner (4,495 ft.), with its railway station and the cluster of Italian and Austrian frontier buildings, opens up.

The Brenner, of course, carries a tremendous volume of traffic and, as at most such busy points, customs formalities are highly regimented and expeditiously executed, though there may at any time in the high season be a triple queue of cars and coaches lined up outside the customs houses.

The northern side of the pass consists of the 24-mile descent of a long, straight re-entrant, the valley of the Sill, during which the road, falling from green level to green level between the containing slopes, loses 2,600 ft. of height. The upper sectors of the valley are narrow and, shortly after leaving the pass, the road curves high above a small, deep-set green lake. Presently, as the easily graded road wanders down between smiling meadows and through pretty villages—Steinach with its frescoed houses and Matrei—the view ahead widens and the upper heights of the Northern Range, still distant beyond the unseen Inn valley, fill the broadening window in the hills, not to be lost again till their full stature is revealed from the last descent to Innsbruck's valley level.

At Schönberg (3,310 ft.) the road from the Stubaital comes discreetly in on the left from Fulpmes, Neustift, and Ranalt (4,130 ft.) 12 miles away at its lovely head, where the snowy peaks and glaciers of the Zuckerhütl and its 11,000-ft. neighbours provide fine but unsensational climbing and numerous easy glacier routes for experienced mountain-walkers, from one famous Club Hut to another. A very different and far stiffer proposition is the challenge afforded by the savage rock-teeth of the Kalkkogel range, lifting half-way along the valley on its western side. This is a beautifully quiet and unspoiled fold in the great hills; but if you decide to drive up it in search of mountain adventure among the paths and peaks rising at its far end, remember that the bus route ends at Neustift, beyond which there are 4 miles of mountain road, adequate but extremely narrow, before, at the little inn of Ranalt, it peters out altogether and the mule-tracks to the Huts begin.

Below Schönberg the Brenner road broadens into a fine modern motorway and falls in beautifully graded curves, well protected by border fences and walls, with red cat's-eyes in each marginal stone—a very pretty effect at night—through the woods which clothe the left-hand slopes of the rapidly widening re-entrant. River and railway, now on the other side of the valley, lie far below; and ahead the crests of the Limestone Range, from the broad and stolid Hafelekar to the solitary splinter of 'Frau Hitt' and the Brandjoch beyond, rise higher and nearer beyond the Inn valley, still hidden from view. It is a long, continually snaking descent, and one is just beginning to wonder what can have become of Innsbruck when, suddenly, the road emerges on to the final slope above the broad valley-plain, and there below you, athwart its river, lies the lovely city, filling the whole level basin at the feet of the splendid mountain-wall beyond. Here, by a gentle touch of irony, lies the Brenner's only hairpin bend, only a hundred feet above the level of the countless spires and towers and roof-tops of one of the most beautiful and magnificently situated cities in Europe. Near as you are to journey's end, it is worth pulling in to the right of the road directly after the bend and enjoying the prospect; especially if you are one of those who like to record the best moments of your voyaging with a camera.

As for Innsbruck itself (1,885 ft.), with its old colonnades, churches, and towers, its monuments and balconies, its broad, modern shopping streets, its concert halls and theatres, its swift-flowing river spanned by bridges old and new, all backed by the splendid mountain range which towers immediately above them all, the established guide-books are the proper mentors. But if you love the wider mountain scene, do not forget the splendid provision of cable-railways to the heights of the Hafelekar and Patscherkofel, with their superb views over hill and vale; and if you do not care to go so far or so high afield, at least drive yourself or, if tired of motoring, take the old-fashioned funicular up to the Hungerburg shelf, to look down on the clustered city spread like a map across the plain below, and out beyond into the gentle green re-entrant, dominated by the distant rock-pyramid of the Serles, down which the Brenner road has brought you from its historic saddle.

Up on that delightful shelf, only a thousand feet above the busy streets, there are two charming restaurants from whose windows and terraces the diner, as he consumes a first-class meal, can watch the lights flicker into chains of diamonds in the deepening gloom below, as the summer dusk fades out on the wooded slopes and the faint glow dies from the topmost rocks far away to the south. It is a very pleasant way of spending an Innsbruck evening, and in high summer it will be much cooler up there than in the hotel dining-room or any of the restaurants bordering the hot, paved streets of the town.

X

THE GROSSGLOCKNERSTRASSE (HOCHTOR)
(8,212 ft.)

Entirely in Austria (Hohe Tauern Group)

From Bruck im Pinzgau (2,480 ft.) to Heiligenblut (4,268 ft.), crossing the main
Alpine watershed between the Adriatic and the Black Sea: 30 miles.

Detail.   Bruck to Ferleiten (3,775 ft.): 9 miles, ascent 1,300 ft.
Ferleiten to Fuschertörl (7,966 ft.): 8 miles, ascent 4,200 ft.
Fuschertörl to Fuscherlacke (7,422 ft.): 2 miles, descent 550 ft.
Fuscherlacke to Summit (Hochtor Tunnel) (8,212) ft.): 2 miles, ascent
790 ft.
Total ascent Bruck to Summit: 21 miles, ascent 5,700 ft.

Summit to Guttal Control (6,100 ft.): 4 miles, descent 2,100 ft.
Guttal to Kasereck (6,310 ft.): 1 mile, ascent 200 ft.
Kasereck to Heiligenblut (4,268 ft.): 4 miles, descent 1,900 ft.
Total descent Summit to Heiligenblut: 9 miles, 4,000 ft.

Spur Roads:

(1) Fuschertörl Junction (7,966 ft.) to Edelweisspitze (8,428 ft.): 1 mile,
ascent }450 ft.
descent }

(2) Guttal Control and Junction (6,100 ft.) to Franz Joseph's Höhe (7,655
ft.): 5 miles, ascent }1,550 ft.
descent }

Open: late June to late October.   Maximum gradient: 1 in 8.

A superb road of the most modern construction, first built in 1935, but continually under modernization and improvement to meet the ever-increasing
flow of traffic (over 200,000 vehicles in 1956).   The whole conception, matching
the surrounding scenery, is magnificent: but the finest view-points are at the
end of the two spur roads, not along the pass itself.   To miss the glacier prospect
at Franz Joseph's Höhe would be to miss the finest thing of its kind in Europe,
possibly in the world.   Edelweisspitze is not quite such a 'must be', but the
panoramic view over the plain to the north and to the Bavarian Limestone Range
is glorious, and is not seen at all from the lower level at Fuschertörl; in any case,
the *détour* is one of only five (very exciting) minutes.   The ascent of the pass on
both sides is steep and very long, especially from Ferleiten to Fuschertörl on the
northern side.   Boiling here is a frequent occurrence, but there are plentiful
lay-bys and provisions of water: in descending it is advisable to use the gears
to the utmost possible extent to avoid overheating brake-drums.

The opening of the pass provided the long-felt need for a first-class road
passage of the high Alps somewhere between the Brenner to the west and the
difficult Tauern–Katschberg to the east, thus saving a huge *détour* by the valleys.

Traffic: Heavy at all times, excessively so in the high season.   Very heavy
coach traffic, sight-seeing from all the surrounding resorts.

Apart from its great length and the heavy traffic, presents no difficulty whatever to the driver, on account of its splendid grading, surfacing, and engineering.

Note: This is a toll-road.   Tickets are obtained at the controls at either end.
Charge: Single journey, 20 schillings per passenger.   Minimum for a private
car 60 schillings.

I T MAY seem strange to many readers that, with all the length,
magnificence, modernity, and variety of scenery provided by this truly
stupendous mountain road, I have remained faithful to the ancient and

historic Stelvio as my choice for King of the Alpine Passes.   These things are in the end a matter of personal taste, association of ideas, first loves, and last loves.   I would therefore not dare to argue with anyone who put forward a strong preference for the Glocknerstrasse in an attempt to award imperial honours.

There is, however, one factor which weighs strongly with me in my comparative assessment of the two roads.   While both are true and very lofty passes across the main Alpine backbone—the Glockner is only 830 ft. lower than the Stelvio—the main glories of the more modern road lie not in the pass itself but in a somewhat complicated system of offshoots and accessories.   For the actual Alpine passage achieved by the Glockner road at the tunnel under the bare and unlovely Hochtor Saddle—the true pass road from Heiligenblut on the south side to Ferleiten at its northern foot, including the crossing of the subsidiary Fuschertörl ridge before the last tremendous drop to the valley level on the northern side—cannot, I think, compare with the Stelvio as a pass.   Wonderfully engineered as it is, rising hugely out of abysmal green depths on either side to bare, grim, stony heights, with magnificent views of the lower snow peaks of the Hohe Tauern range at the Fuschertörl car-park, it would still have nothing to match the Stelvio wall and its unbelievable windings set against the majesty of the Ortler's* snowy dome and the vast cataclysms of ice cascading into the ravine below the edge of the clinging, writhing road.

To achieve something like the Stelvio's magnificence of view, at close range, of glacier, rock rib, and snow peak—and again the beauty of the Ortler and the Grossglockner respectively, with their satellite peaks and glacier entourage, must be assessed by the beholder according to his individual preference—the Glocknerstrasse has had to throw out an arm some 5 miles long on its southern approach, from about half-way up the climb to the true pass.   This long offshoot, contouring a huge slope and finally winding steeply up the last thousand feet, leads to a superb view-point above the long and level Pasterze Glacier, with the spire of the Grossglockner, Austria's highest peak at 12,460 ft., almost directly opposite, at the Franz Joseph's Höhe—a dead end at a height only 600 ft. less than that of the pass itself at the Hochtor, some miles back along the road.   The whole of this spur road has to be retraced, with a loss of some 1,600 ft. in altitude, to the junction with the main pass at Guttal.

Similarly, after crossing the Hochtor at the true mountain divide and descending 300 ft. to the Fuschertörl (describing the route once again from south to north), the road throws out another much shorter, steeper spur northwards to the Edelweissspitze—almost 300 ft. higher than the Hochtor tunnel—in order to encompass the truly glorious view northwards, towards the valley levels of Zell, with its lake at the foot of the stony ranges bounding Austria and Germany, and to improve out of all measure the Fuschertör view of the Hohe Tauern snows close at hand across the gulf of the Ferleiten ravine.   This spur—I am not complaining—has to be descended again in order to rejoin the true course of the pass at the Fuschertörl.

* See footnote p. 24.

The point I have perhaps laboured a little is that there is something artificial and strictly irrelevant about the finest moments of this wonderful Glockner road—an element of superb but conscious showmanship, adorning and pointing a pass which, if it had stuck to its primary job of crossing the mountain range at its most accessible point, would have run a comparatively undistinguished course so far as scenic beauty is concerned; while the Stelvio, in linking the two opposite valley levels by the only practicable route, naturally encompasses its scenic glory without the necessity—or indeed the opportunity—for any side-shows or elaborations on its constricted way.

After these qualifications let it be said at once that the Glocknerstrasse is magnificently daring in conception, superb in execution, and positively staggering in its furnishings—view-points, rest and refreshment places, roadside lay-bys, and, at the culminating vantage points, coach- and car-parks the size of football grounds, hewn out of the living rock, with all the necessary appointments for the needs of hundreds of travellers and sight-seers at a time. Nothing less would have been sufficient. For Austria, in building this mammoth causeway across her highest mountain range, intended it to be just as much of a national achievement, attracting the world's tourism, as Switzerland's famous railway to the glacier world at Jungfraujoch. And Austria has succeeded. Each summer thousands of cars and huge coaches churn their way up to those immense heights carrying tens of thousands of passengers to look down upon glacier ice and up at nearby snowy peaks and rocky spires, perhaps for the first time in their lives. In 1956 the figures were more than 150,000 cars, 50,000 motor cycles, and 10,000 coaches in the three and a half months the road is open.

Friends of mine who have driven the road in the high season of July and August have told me on their return that they really saw nothing of the road or its surrounding scenery because they were so busy dealing with bonnet-to-tail conditions and the incessant swoop of huge coaches bearing down in the opposite direction—likening the ordeal to that of a fine summer day on the Brighton road. Indeed, so heavily is the traffic mounting, that the task of widening and improving, where possible, is continually in hand; and when we visited the Franz Joseph's Höhe in September 1956 the work of extending the already fantastic car-parks, high above the glacier, was in full swing, with hordes of workers, tip lorries, and bull-dozers, so that by the opening of the 1957 season that high platform might be capable of receiving all the massed phalanxes of cars and coaches which had already outgrown their capacity.

All these lavish appointments, of course, cost vast sums of money, and it is not surprising that the passage of the Glockner road is subject to a toll. The charge is reasonable enough, amounting to about £1 for a car with four passengers; a levy which is fully justified. There is nothing new in this—the Mont Cenis, a hundred years ago, and others of the great passes in their early days, were toll-roads, bringing enormous sums into imperial coffers which had laid out initially the great cost of their construction. But somehow, I must confess, the entry into and exit from a mountain pass through a kind of imaginary turnstile for cars and the presentation of tickets for punching at check points on the way does something to lower its status as an essential transmontane artery in the eyes of one who has driven all the other great links, ancient and modern, without once being subjected to demands for 'tickets, please'. That is, perhaps, one of the reasons why I still cannot help regarding this marvellous road rather as a glorious piece of window-dressing—for which I am none the less immensely grateful—than one of the honest-to-goodness Alpine crossings. I expect to be told that I am at fault.

The history of this gigantic undertaking begins in 1924, when the need for a new road from the northern to the southern lowlands of Austria, in the light of the growing motor traffic, was officially recognized.   There was nothing between the Brenner and the awkward, steep, and excessively difficult Katschberg Pass, far to the east, to take the growing through-traffic from Germany to the valleys of the Drave (Drau) and Save, and beyond them southwards and eastwards.   A road over Austria's highest mountain group, the Hohe Tauern, linking the plain in which lies the charming Lake of Zell and the broad corridor of the Pinzgau valley with Lienz in the Drave valley 30 miles to the south would not only be at the right point between the two existing roads but would also provide the shortest and scenically finest through-route.   The difficulties of so long and high a passage would obviously be immense and the cost prodigious, but in spite of Austria's comparatively straitened finances, the courageous decision was taken to survey the ground and push on with the construction of the best road available funds could support as swiftly as possible. Eleven years were to elapse before this far-sighted and imaginative project came to final fruition, with the triumphant and ceremonial opening of the completed road on August 4th, 1935.

The engineering was throughout in the hands of the great Austrian expert Professor Ingenieur F. Wallack, who has recorded the story of the intervening years in a detailed and fascinating book.*   It is a thrilling tale of courage and perseverance in the face of every kind of difficulty and frustration over long years of stupendous effort.   In the face of divided counsel, parochial friction, shortage of funds, the brevity of the season during which work could be maintained on the high, exposed sections, bitter weather and the ravages of winter snows and storms, the work went on, section by section and yard by yard.

Several alternative routes were debated, favoured and rejected for the ultimate passage of the watershed.   Long after the approach roads in the lower valley sections were firmly established, heated controversy raged as to which of three routes should carry the road over the top.   Eventually the alternatives were reduced to two, and the final fight lay between the merits of the present route by a summit tunnel under the Hochtor Saddle (8,212 ft.), some miles from the Grossglockner and its glaciers, and an even more sensational, more direct and much higher assault on the main snow-range by way of the Obere Pfandlscharte (9,000 ft.).   This spectacular

* *Die Grossglockner-Hochalpenstrasse* (Springer Verlag, Vienna, 1949).

road would have been an engineering miracle which would probably have matched or even outclassed the Stelvio road in the most obdurately prejudiced eyes; it would, moreover, have been a true Glockner Pass, obviating the long spur road on the southern side, which would then have formed the legitimate continuation of a single road *descending* on the Franz Joseph's Höhe from the actual saddle, high above. But it was not to be— and Professor Wallack's disappointment comes through clearly enough. As so often, finance was to have the final word. The more ambitious project would have cost three times as much as the only less ambitious; and there just wasn't the money. So, in April 1934, the final choice fell on the actual route now taken by the road, over the 8,212-ft. Hochtor, 8 miles east of the Grossglockner.

The rest of the story is that of the heroic struggle to get the road and the tunnel completed by the scheduled due date, in face of unexpected difficulties and set-backs which might well have broken the hearts of everyone engaged on the project. That the road was opened to the advertised hour speaks volumes for the courage, ingenuity, and indefatigable endurance of all concerned, from the brilliant engineer in charge to the humblest member of a labour force of several hundred men. The motto which inspired them all through the long, hard years of the road's emergence from a blue-printed dream to a unique Alpine highway is boldly and simply enshrined in the pediment above the north entrance to the Hochtor Tunnel:

'In te Domine Speravi'.

I do not think there is any markedly right or wrong way of driving the Glocknerstrasse. To be consistent, I suppose, I ought to recommend the north-to-south transit because in that direction the finest view of all, that of the Grossglockner itself from the Franz Joseph's Höhe, is the climax to a long and gradual approach. But this does not seem to me to hold any particular virtue in the case of this particular road, which, as has already been stressed, is at its least interesting at the actual pass, where the view is somewhat bleak and limited, and which lies almost mid-way between the two scenic high-lights, both off the main road, both at the end of long climbs from the opposing valley levels, at Edelweisspitze and the Franz Joseph's Höhe respectively.

Moreover, this road is so long and there is so much to look at and to photograph along it, that I am not at all sure whether the best way to enjoy it to the full is not to spread it over two days, especially if the weather is playing tricks and there is heavy cloud on the tops of the surrounding mountains. This gives one a second chance of seeing the wonderful mountain scenery, which is, after all, the *raison d'être* of the whole expedition; to drive the road in a dense fog, when the clouds envelop it, or even with the neighbouring peaks and ridges obscured from view, must be a very disappointing and, at worst, a trying and tedious experience. And if it is decided to take two bites at the cherry a very convenient way of breaking up the journey is to come up from the southern side in the afternoon, stopping the night at either the Glocknerhaus or the hotel on the Franz Joseph's Höhe itself—always remembering that the one is 7,000, the other 8,000 ft. up, in the thin atmosphere of high altitudes, where the cold air from the nearby glacier can strike pretty chilly even on a summer's night—and continuing over the rest of the road next morning, to reach the northern foot by lunch time or early afternoon of the second day. It should not be forgotten that in fine weather cloud often builds up on the high mountains in the middle hours of the day and the peaks are normally at their clearest in the early morning and the evening.

I therefore propose to describe the road from the south, starting at its true point of departure from the lowland levels of the pretty Drau valley at Lienz, where the high roads come in from Klagenfurt and Villach to the east and from the Austro-Italian frontier at Sillian to the west, bringing the traffic from the Brenner, from Bolzano, Merano, and the Arlberg, and from Lake Garda and the Dolomites, to the foot of the main Alpine chain, some 20 miles south of the great wall of the Hohe Tauern.

Lienz itself is a delightful, ancient, and typically Austrian town, set in a wide green plain, backed to the south by the rocky towers of its own private group of miniature Dolomites. To the north, narrow, pine-clad valleys carve deep into the foothills of the Tauern, and to reach one of them, the beautiful valley of the Möll, the road to the Glockner soon swings away, a little east of Lienz at a point on the Villach Road where an attractive-looking Motel has been sited, to surmount a steep spur—the Iselsberg —by a series of wide hairpin reaches. Here, in late 1956, men were hard at work converting an average mountain road into a highway fit to rank as an approach to the great pass ahead, widening the straightaways, resiting and building out the corners; these operations are no doubt complete by now, and the miniature subsidiary 'pass' well worthy of its huge neighbour to the north.

From Iselsberg the road drops down by wide curves, with glimpses of the snow ranges ahead, to the junction of the two arms of the Möll valley, the wider of them leading away eastwards to Spittal. At Winklern it begins the gentle and very pretty ascent of the narrower arm, through picturesque Mörtschach and Döllach, with the great dark shields of the pine-forests sweeping up from the velvety meadows on either side of the stream to the green crests towering overhead. After some 10 miles the gradient steepens appreciably and Heiligenblut comes into view on its green spur ahead, backed by dark, conical peaks over which the tip of the Grossglockner lifts its sharp, snowy spearhead into the remote sky. The 25 miles of this delightful approach from Lienz can be comfortably covered inside the hour.

Heiligenblut, in spite of all the efforts of commercialism and touristic fame to spoil it, remains a unique and charming village, narrowly perched at the gateway to the great mountains, its lovely tall church dominating the huddled châlet roofs, its unusually slender spire lifting proudly yet humbly as a kind of human recognition and reflection of the great snow-spire so serenely poised many thousands of feet directly above it.

The car-parks may be wedged with cars and coaches, children and *portiers* may besiege you touting with offers of accommodation, the cafés and restaurants may be packed to overflowing; but I defy anyone to come back unimpressed from his visit to the cool, high-vaulted shrine which houses the relic of the Holy Blood which St. Briccius brought back to give the place its name six centuries ago, and to that little terraced acre of the dead above the valley's edge where the rude forefathers of a mountain hamlet lie buried. And, if a smile be needed to temper a deeper emotion, there, in the crypt, is the little grinning negro boy whose China head and shoulders keep watch over the offertory-box, bowing his thanks with greater or less enthusiasm according to the weight of the coin inserted.

Here at Heiligenblut, turning back on itself up the slope at the entrance to the village, the Glockner road proper begins. Should you wish to break your journey, so as to give yourself plenty of time for the pass and all its accessories next day, and yet do not relish an overnight stay as high up as the Glocknerhaus or the Franz Joseph's Haus, the village offers hotel accommodation and rooms for the night in plenty, with a busy little *Touristenbureau* to advise you. But it should be remembered that in the high season the place will probably be packed to overflowing, and a telephone call beforehand may avoid disappointments and dilemmas.

The first section of the road was in existence for some way up the mountain-side before the mooting of the project for a road to replace the mule-track over the Hochtor. The project had no choice but to incorporate, adapt, and improve the existing road as far as it went, for there was nowhere else on this huge breast of the mountains where a road could go. The first leg is very steep, and immediately after a classic view back and down on to the village roofs, with the Glockner rising behind, there is a compulsory halt at the toll-house, where you purchase the ticket which will permit you to drive the whole length or merely shorter sectors—for instance, Franz Joseph's Höhe and back, or the summit and back with a visit to the Höhe thrown in—of the road.

From the toll-house the road continues to wind steeply by terraced hair-pin turns up the abrupt green feet of the hills, with the Möll valley falling away deeper and deeper at every turn and the view back along it towards the distant Dolomites of Lienz widening every minute. There are lay-bys in plenty and frequent *Wasserdiensts*—faucets or conduits for the distressed driver whose car elects to boil—here as on all the steeply graded sections of the route. Surface and roadside protection are throughout impeccable.

Surmounting the first great shoulder barring its way, at the Kasereck, the road presently dips steeply for about half a mile into a wide re-entrant in the bottom of which, at the Tauernbrücke, it crosses the roaring mountain torrent of the Tauernbach descending from the right; then mounts again to Guttal (6,310 ft.), where at the first Control the road divides—the spur to Franz Joseph's Höhe and its wonderful glacier view going straight on, the true pass ascending to the right towards the Hochtor Saddle. The spur-road continues—to take it first—now mainly contouring the immense flanks of the mountains, steadily rising, past handsome view-point lay-bys

—Gipperalpe, Schobereck, Schmidlwand, Schöneck, and Schönwand. The slopes are by now bare, the trees are left behind, the Möll valley's floor is blue and abysmally far below, and the fine rocky heads of the Schober Group, occasionally flecked with snow, rise close beyond it, dark and ruggedly impressive. All this time the Glockner peaks are out of sight, hidden by great stony spurs of the mountain-side up which the road labours and curves its way, with fine torrents dashing down at intervals from the heights above.

Then, at a height of about 6,500 ft., the tongue of the great Pasterze Glacier comes into sight, squeezing its way down between huge stony ridges overhead, and in about three-quarters of an hour from Heiligenblut (8 miles)—if you are driving sensibly and as such a road requires—you reach the Glocknerhaus (6,985 ft.), sheltering close under the great black spurs, overlooking the two small dams which have been built to harness the flow from the little lake in the narrow bowl below the glacier's lower lip.

This solid old stone building had weathered the mountain storms for many decades before ever the road pushed its insolent way up to the very rim of the glaciers. It was put there as a refuge and shelter house by the Austrian Alpine Club in the later years of the last century and retains its Club Hut character—pains are taken to explain that it is not a hotel—to this day. Accommodation consists of the usual small, plain pine-boarded cabins and bunks, with blankets and sheet, to be found in this type of mountain shelter-house, and costs about 8 shillings (sterling) per head;* the catering downstairs in the big double-windowed living-room is excellent, and a first-class hot meal can be obtained at all times, at reasonable prices. Should you want to see the ineffable spectacle of the dawn on the Glockner's spire and graceful shoulders from your window or, better still, drive the remaining ten minutes of the road up to the Franz Joseph's Höhe and witness the coming of day over the much more extended glacier scene unfolded there, someone will call you in good time by arrangement the night before. There are no frills about the Glocknerhaus; but it is clean, inexpensive, and they feed you well. Our bill for four people was about £6.

As you stand outside the Glocknerhaus, looking up at the bare ridge masking the Glockner and its snowy neighbours around the corner, the Franz Joseph's Haus at the top of the road, just a thousand feet higher, stands silhouetted, its roof jutting from the profile of the mountain face. It is a modern luxury hotel, with all comforts, set at nearly 8,000 ft., high above the glacier and commanding the superb view denied to the old Club Hut below. Unless the extra thousand feet of altitude affects your ability to sleep (nobody with heart trouble should, of course, contemplate either of these high perches; but then they should perhaps not be on the Glockner road at all) a night spent there will certainly be more comfortable and hotel-standard, with h. and c. and all mod. cons., than at the Glocknerhaus. It will, however, cost about twice as much, or perhaps a little more.

* Less, of course, if you are a member of the Austrian, or an affiliated, Mountaineering Club.

This last stretch of the spur-road from Haus to Höhe bites into a dark and deep re-entrant, crossing the Pfandlscharte torrent in its farthest recess at the Nassfeldbrücke, then ascends the far wall by three or four tiers of hairpins and finally contours high above the ravine, with magnificent views back over the Mölltal and the Schober peaks. Then, suddenly, you turn the last corner and swing into the huge smooth car-parks of the Franz Joseph's Höhe—a vast terrace, hewn out of the dark rock of the mountain-side, high above the flat, straight, crevassed course of the largest Austrian glacier—the Pasterze—with the long, snowy-crested, rock-buttressed wall of the Glockner peaks, from the Schwerteck through the Grossglockner itself (12,460 ft.) and the Glocknerwand to the spot-lessly white Eiskogel, all rising sheer and close from its farther shore. It is at all times a sudden revelation of breath-taking magnificence; to see it when the rosy fingers of dawn are charming it back to life out of the night is an unforgettable experience; once reserved for hardy mountaineers, now available to, at least, the imaginative motorist.

Beyond the car-parks a good path cut into the rock and at points tunnelling through it, provides an almost level walk, contouring above the glacier for about an hour, to the Hoffmann's Hütte Club Hut, from which the ascent of the Grossglockner by the route known as the Hoffmannsweg is undertaken. Arrangements for a guide can be made from Heiligenblut, the Glocknerhaus, the Franz Joseph's Haus, or the Hut. The climb, which is not difficult in good snow-conditions, leads across the level glacier and then for four hours steeply up the snow-slopes to the capacious Hut on the Adlersruhe (11,370 ft.), from which the summit is reached in only an hour and a half's further ascent of a fine snow ridge. The views from Hut and summit alike are mag-nificent, and both are usually very crowded in fine spells during the summer.

Below the car-parks at the Franz Joseph's Höhe a long terrace gives access to a block of modern lavatories sufficient to accommodate a football crowd. A short approach road leads up to the fine modern hotel already described. All the traffic and bustle of this amazing place does not seem to disturb the marmots living in the rocks between the terrace and the glacier; whole families of them, accepting the motor age more or less philosophically, can be seen scampering in and out of their holes, close to the din of the incessant constructional work.

It will thus be seen that the halt at the Höhe can provide entertainment for anything from a few minutes' glance at a lovely high-mountain view to a protracted stay, during which the fit and active can undertake one of the numerous glacier or mountain expeditions in the Hohe Tauern Group, to whose heart the road has brought them. All this is, however, a scintillating side-show.

Motorists bound for the pass and the valleys at the northern side of the watershed must turn their backs on the Glockner and its neighbouring peaks and retrace the 4 miles of descent to the Guttal road-junction, losing 1,600 ft. of altitude in the process. The lovely views out over the Mölltal's blue depths to the rocky Dolomite spires away in the distance beyond Lienz, now facing one all the way down, are ample compensation.

At Guttal, where tickets are inspected, the main route to the Pass is rejoined and the road immediately gets to grips with the huge turfy shoulder of the main range bulking 2,000 ft. up to the unprepossessing rock comb surmounting the Hochtor Saddle, which is the true Pass. The great green spur is as spacious as it is lofty, and the road goes swinging its way up it in wide, easy, looping patterns—the grey-blue ribbon of the broad carriage-way tracing bewildering designs against the yellowy-green turf. Through Tauerneck and Fallbichl it climbs past occasional water-falls, amid a wild and barren landscape. Half-way up to the summit of the pass stands the Wallackhaus Restaurant, commemorating the builder of the road and commanding from the top of its knoll, as does this whole sector of the road, grand unrestricted views across the unseen Mölltal, now fallen far below, to the dark and rugged heads of the Schober Group. It takes 5 miles and about a quarter of an hour from the Guttal junction to regain a height equal to that of the Franz Joseph's Höhe; a minute or two later the highest point on the pass, or its byways, is reached at the park outside the southern entrance to the Hochtor Tunnel, 8,212 ft. above sea-level.

There is no new prospect to detain one here, unless one wishes to take a last opportunity to look southwards. A completely different scene awaits one at the northern end of the 300-yd.-long tunnel, electrically lit and furnished with railed-off footways on either side.

Here, with the unmelted snow-shields sweeping down to the edge of the road even in summer, a wide, bleak, upland basin of smooth greenish-grey rock opens up, contained on the left by sharp-edged ridges and bounded on the more distant right by the snow-streaked crests of the Goldberg–Sonnblick range (11,000 ft.). Before and below you, the road, utterly different now in character, clings its way down the steep slope with hardly a deviation—a thin, taut, white, kinky thread stretched downwards into the forbidding cauldron for 4 miles, till it reaches the farther retaining rim a thousand feet lower down. There it is forced to writhe its way out to reach the tiny buildings on the Fuschertörl ridge by a wide loop, which takes it far westwards along the near side of the spur and doubles sharply back again, hidden by the intervening comb, on the other. The only major swerve in the long descent is about half-way down, where an intractable wrinkle on intervening rock has forced it to side-slip into the Mittertor tunnel—pinhole size from this distance and elevation—from whose farther side it emerges to take a line a little lower down the mountain face.

This long, grim stretch from the Hochtor tunnel exit, through the Mittertor and on to the Fuschertörl, is not beautiful; it might perhaps be accused of a certain stark monotony. But I wonder whether anyone who traverses it can fail to be conscious, here more than anywhere else on the road, of the faith, the fervour, the human toil and sweat which forced the passage of that fearsome wilderness of stone in the teeth of the mountain's menace and fronting the fury of the winter winds. That inscription above the south portal sums it all up with touching and appropriate brevity—

'In thee, O Lord have I trusted.'

The descent from the pass to the Fuschertörl does not take more than a quarter of an hour, during which there is not much, and certainly nothing new, to look at. Then the road doubles back suddenly around the base of the Fuschertörl spur, literally almost touching itself in the process, another enormous flat parking space opens up, with the restaurant buildings on a hillock crest above it; and opposite, across a narrow, deep abyss to the north, the snowy domes and pyramids of the Baerenköpfe–Grosse Wiessbachhorn range of the Hohe Tauern (11,700 ft.) leap up against the blue. All of a sudden, after drab, formless imprisonment, everything is beauty, form, splendour, and colour. The mountain prospect from Fuschertörl is second only to that from the Franz Joseph's Höhe, and so different in texture that many may find it the more beautiful, if the less exalted.

But, lovely as is the terrace facing the snows at Fuschertörl, on the brink of the vast drop to the northern plains, the men who planned and built the road were not satisfied with this hard-won lodgement on the mountain rim, giving direct access at last to the Hochtor Saddle above, 4 miles to the south, over which the pass must go. A small, sharp conical peak, the Edelweissspitze (8,500 ft.), lifted its dark head 600 ft. above the Fuscher gateway, directly to the north, only a stone's throw away in the opposite direction. From its narrow summit the view was far more extensive. Not only would the Grosse Wiessbachhorn's stately white pyramid soar more grandly above the ravine when seen from a belvedere just so much higher up; not only would there be a glimpse sheer downwards on to the amazing pattern of the roofs and roadworks at Fuschertörl and the looped windings down into the northern depths below it; not only would there be a complete survey of the stony slopes above, with the whole length of the onward road slashing up them, first to the Mittertor tunnel, then on to where it disappeared into the summit tunnel at the Hochtor, a tiny dark dot below the crest of the pass, 4 miles away and on the same level as the beholders. Besides all these good things, the Edelweissspitze commanded a unique treasure which, although so near at hand, would otherwise be denied to users of a road which merely climbed onwards to the pass by way of the Fuschertörl gateway. This was the immense panorama northwards, beyond the lower spurs of the Wiessbachhorn, the Hohe Tenn, and the plummeting depths of the Salzach ravine and valley below them, opening out on the distant Pinzgau plain, the blue eye of the Lake of Zell serenely set in it, and away and away to the cloud-topped, stony barrier ranges of Lofer and the Steinernes Meer, floating in the haze of the Austro-German border, 25 miles away.

So, yet another spur-road was thrown out, little more than a mile long, demolishing the abrupt mountain-side in six marvellous windings, steeply banked one above the other, to the small flat platform which has replaced what was once the rough summit of the sharp little peak. It would be a very great pity to take the line that 'there has been a lot of this pass already, let's give this "extra" a miss'.   In my view there was a touch of genius about the addition of this brief side-show, involving ten minutes each way and, wisely, barred to coaches.   If the weather is anything like fine, the clouds and the traffic not too thick, go and see for yourself.

From Fuschertörl to Ferleiten at the northern end of the Glockner road is a drop of 4,200 ft., breath-takingly accomplished in the space of a wonderful 8 miles.   It is simply a question of carving a way down a colossal mountain flank into the deep, green-carpeted floor of the Salzach valley, first by a bewildering pattern of wide windings down a turfy, boulder-littered shoulder, then contouring great buttresses and deep ravines carrying rushing torrents and cascades, linked by vaulting bridges and sections of hairpin turns where progress is barred by jutting cliffs—down, down, and always steeply down.   Each feature of the descent has its picturesque and appropriate name and also its own particular lay-by—Hexenküche (Witches' Kitchen), the Unter-Nassfeldbrücke, Hochmais, Lärcheck, Piffkar, Mitteralm, Piffalpe, and Pfierselgraben; each built-out corner is marked with its number.   Just before reaching the bottom of this continuous descent of about three-quarters of an hour there is a lovely and well-named waterfall—the Schleierwasserfall (Cascade of the Veils) and a minute or two later the unlovely Ferleiten Tollgate, at which, as well as at Fusch, 3 miles farther down the road, there is an inspection of tickets. And here the Glocknerstrasse proper—42 miles of it, if all the spur roads are traversed as well as the main pass—comes to an end.

Four miles below Fusch, the narrow Salzach valley—a lovely contrast of leafy shade, flowery meadows, and the tumbling waters of the stream, to welcome you back from high and barren places—opens gently out into the broad green plain of the Pinzgau corridor.   Out in the middle of it lies the sunny town of Bruck; and there the Glockner route strikes across the high roads which run west to Innsbruck, east to St. Johann and Salzburg, and continues the great Alpine link northwards, by Zell and its charming but over-populated lake, to a variety of passes which lead through gaps in the wall of the 'Stony Mountains' to Germany.

By any standard, the Grossglockner Hochalpenstrasse is a masterpiece among mountain roads, a message I hope I have contrived to convey. Austria is justly proud of it, and Austria spares no pains to publicize and popularize this tremendous show piece in its front window.   Where prospects please so abundantly, man and his contraptions can at times display themselves in their viler aspects.   I, personally, having driven the road most comfortably for the first time in early September, would not dream of returning to it in the high summer season between, say, July 15th and August 20th of any year.   For, amid so much wonder and delight—

> What is this life, if full of care
> We have no time to stand and stare?

Nor does an endless procession of forty-seater coaches particularly improve a mountain paradise.

PART III
THE LESSER TRANS-ALPINE PASSES

XI

THE COLLE DI TENDA (COL DE TENDE) (4,331 ft.)

France–Italy (Alpes Maritimes).

From La Giandola (1,059 ft.) to Borgo S. Dalmazzo (2,103 ft.), crossing the main
Alpine watershed between the Mediterranean and the Adriatic: 26
miles.

Detail La Giandola to Tende (2,674 ft.) (French customs): 12 miles, ascent,
1,600 ft.
Tende to the Tunnel (4,331 ft.): 6 miles, ascent, 1,700 ft.
Total ascent to summit in Tunnel: 18 miles, 3,300 ft.

Tunnel to Limone by-pass (Italian customs) (3,285 ft.): 6 miles, descent
950 ft.
Limone to Borgo S. Dalmazzo (2,103 ft.): 11 miles, descent 1,250 ft.
Total descent Summit to Borgo S. Dalmazzo: 17 miles, 2,200 ft.

Open: Usually all the year round: occasionally blocked for short periods by
snow in winter.

The Colle di Tenda (4,331 ft.) is the southernmost road-crossing of the Alpine
Chain, and runs across the Alpes Maritimes watershed from the French Riviera
to the plain of Piedmont.   A modern bitumen-surfaced road, with easy and well-
protected hairpin bends and a tunnel over 2 miles long beneath the saddle, it
presents no difficulty for the motorist.   One of the easiest passes: traffic in
summer can be heavy.   Maximum gradient: 1 in 11.

THE COLLE DI TENDA (4,331 ft.) affords the direct route across the
mountains from Nice and other Riviera resorts to the Piedmont plain and
Turin.

From Nice the picturesque approach road with many sharp hairpin
bends runs by a series of minor Cols, through Sospel (25 miles), to La
Giandola (37 miles) at the true foot of the pass.   This is a very pretty
drive, surmounting two small 'passes', the Col de Nice (1,247 ft.) and the
much more considerable windings of the Col de Braus (3,281 ft.), from
which there is a fine view, before reaching Sospel (1,145 ft.) with its old
bridge and church.

Two more small saddles, the Col de Perus (2,165 ft.) and the Col de
Brouis (2,887 ft.) separate Sospel from La Giandola (1,059 ft.), where the
steady, moderately graded ascent of 12 miles to the Colle di Tenda tunnel
begins, passing Fontan through the gorge of St. Dalmas-de-Tende, on the
way.   At Tende (Tenda) (2,674 ft.), a pleasant town with remains of old
fortifications, are the French customs.

The ascent continues through Viève (3,078 ft.) to the 2½-mile-long
tunnel, lit by electricity, which passes under the true Colle di Tenda

(6,263 ft.), the old road to which diverges to the left and climbs up in sixty-nine windings between fortified heights to the watershed.   Four miles beyond the Italian mouth of the tunnel are the Italian customs, near Limone (3,285 ft.), which the road by-passes.   The road then descends steadily for another 12 miles to Borgo S. Dalmazzo (2,103 ft.) at the edge of the Piedmont Plain and the eastern foot of the Col de Larche route from Barcelonnette and Briançon (see next chapter).

XII

THE COL DE LARCHE (6,545 ft.)

France–Italy (Maritime Alps).

From La Condamine (4,291 ft.) to Vinadio (2,986 ft.), crossing the main Alpine watershed between the Mediterranean and the Adriatic: 32 miles.

Detail. La Condamine to Larche (5,565 ft.) (French customs): 8 miles, ascent 1,350 ft.
Larche to the Summit (6,545 ft.): 4 miles, ascent 1,000 ft.
Total ascent to the Summit: 12 miles, 2,250 ft.

Summit to Argentera (6,550 ft.) (Italian customs): 4 miles, descent 1,000 ft.
Argentera to Vinadio (2,986 ft.): 16 miles, descent 3,550 ft.
Total descent Summit to Vinadio: 20 miles, 3,550 ft.

Open: Late April to mid-November. Maximum gradient: 1 in 12.

A good but narrow road, with no great difficulty (gravel surface). Scenically very attractive.

Traffic is usually very light, the route being much neglected in spite of its ease and attractions.

THE COL DE LARCHE or Colle della Maddalena (6,545 ft.), though the road is narrow, provides the easiest passage of the main Alpine chain between the Colle di Tenda to its south and the Mont Genèvre to the north. As a result it was in frequent use from the sixteenth century to the Napoleonic wars, when it became the '*Route Imperiale d'Espagne en Italie*'—for the swift passage of various armies. It is, however, little used nowadays as a main motor-route, chiefly because to approach to its western end entails considerable mileages of mountain passes and valley roads—a feature, however, which did not prevent it being the scene of bitter frontier fighting at the end of the Second World War.

The road leaves the Col de Vars route from Guillestre to Barcelonnette (p. 206) at the junction of the Ubaye and Ubayette just after La Condamine–Châtelard (4,291 ft.), and rises by a wide hairpin below shattered rocks—sometimes in dangerous condition—to the hamlet of Meyronnes (4 miles) with a ruined castle. This ascent, the *Montée de la Rochaille*, is dominated by the savage rock-crest of the Pitchouent opposite and the picturesque village of St. Ours.

Three more miles of winding road, over unstable slopes, lead to the French customs post at Larche (5,565 ft.), which was held by a German garrison and destroyed by them in the evacuation of 1945. The road then rises, gently at first and then more steeply, over rich pasturages, with two hairpins after the last hamlet, Maisonméane, to the Col itself (6,545 ft.), 3 miles beyond the customs and 10 from the start of the road in the Ubaye valley. Just before it is reached, the wide valley of the Lauzanier opens to the south and there is a small chapel standing isolated in a meadow.

The Col de Larche is the point for French and Italian pedestrian customs examination, and is sometimes known as the Colle della Maddalena or de l'Argentera. At the saddle a fine prospect opens ahead, over the Lac de la Madeleine, to the Punta d'Argentera and Monte Matto.

The long 41-mile descent into Italy to Coni (Cuneo) (1,762 ft.), follows the beautiful valley of the Stura di Demonte to the Piedmont plain. It begins by skirting the lake on the right and then falls by six big hairpins to the Italian road-customs point at Argentera (4½ miles).

The next 20 miles to Demonte, the chief place in the valley, where it falls into the plain, are most attractive, the road threading its way through numerous rock barriers between picturesque Berezio and Ponte Bernardo; it then passes through a fine Dolomite amphitheatre (de la Madone) with its multi-coloured limestone crags and stunted forest.

At Planche a fine zone of chestnut-trees begins and, 3 miles farther on, the road passes the strong-point of Vinadio (2,926 ft.), beyond which another 6 miles of delightful scenery bring the road to Demonte (2,550 ft.), in a wide basin.

Ten miles lower down, at Borgo San Dalmazzo (2,083 ft.), the valley debouches into the Piedmont plain, and here it meets the main road and railway from Turin to Nice.

Turning left, Cuneo is reached in another 5 miles by a modern viaduct by-pass; if the right-hand road is taken it will bring you back into France by the Colle di Tenda road, which leads to Nice and the Riviera in some 50 miles (see previous Chapter).

XIII

THE COL DU MONT GENÈVRE (6,100 ft.)

France–Italy (Cottian Alps).

From Briançon (4,396 ft.) to Suze (Susa) (1,624 ft.): 39 miles.

Detail. Briançon to the Col du Mont Genèvre (6,100 ft.), in the main Alpine watershed between the Mediterranean and Adriatic: 7 miles, ascent 1,700 ft.

From the Col to Cesana (4,458 ft.): 12 miles, descent 1,550 ft.
    Cesana to Oulx (3,532 ft.): 5 miles, descent 900 ft.
    Oulx to Susa (1,624 ft.): 15 miles, descent 1,900 ft.
Total descent from the Col to Susa: 32 miles, 4,350 ft.

Open: Usually all the year round, chains sometimes necessary in winter.

A well-engineered and graded ascent in six wide hairpins from Briançon to the Col. Long, winding descent through ravines and valleys on the Italian side. Width, moderate. Surface: good, but gravel on the Italian side, sometimes in poor condition.

Traffic: generally light.
Easy. Maximum gradient: 1 in 10.

THE MONT GENÈVRE pass, No. 3 in the list of true road passages of the Alpine backbone, is interesting as one of the several passes at times suggested as Hannibal's route from Gaul to the northern plains of Italy. Dismissed by scholars as not fitting in with the descriptions given in Livy and Polybius, it none the less possesses many advantages which would have made it an ideal crossing place for his large army equipped with a cumbersome armoured brigade of elephants. It is easy of approach by the river valley of the Durance from south-eastern France and the plain of the Rhone; it is of moderate height, with by no means difficult approaches on either side, and it has been known as a convenient gap in the mountain barrier since time immemorial. It certainly was regularly used later by Roman armies on their way to the Gallic provinces, as witness the Arch of Cottius to the west of Susa, astride the Mont Genèvre approach route. Moreover, it provided a direct route from Turin (Augusta Taurinorum) to Grenoble (Gratianopolis) by way of Briançon (Brigantium) and the Lautaret (Collis de Altareto).

In spite of its relatively easy link between France and Italy, the Mont Genèvre is not, in modern times, numbered among the great trans-Alpine traffic routes; the main reason being that, in order to approach its western foot at Briançon, it is necessary first to cross the much higher passes of the Lautaret or Galibier, or else to make a very long *détour* south and then turn north-west again by immensely long valley routes. It is, however, the obvious route by which to cross the Alps from the lower Rhone valley, between, say, Valence and Avignon, to Turin and any destination

in the north-east corner of Italy.   But, for the reasons given, it is unlikely
that the Mont Genèvre will ever compete with the Mont Cenis, just to its
north, for popular favour as the direct one-pass route between eastern
France and the plain of Lombardy.

From Briançon (see Chapter XXIX, the Lautaret and Galibier) the
Mont Genèvre road swings in a business-like half-dozen wide curves up
the great wooded slope of the Cottian Alps to the east of the town and
overcomes a modest height differential of 1,700 ft. in a matter of seven
miles before crossing the wide meadow-slopes dominated on the north,
across the frontier, by the heavily fortified Mont Chaberton to reach the
broad and gentle saddle between the Signal du Chenaillet and the Serre
Thibaud.   Just before the Col, overlooking the Vale of Briançon and the
Durance basin, and connected with the lower levels by the inevitable
aerial ropeway, has risen, of recent years, the considerable winter sports
centre of Mont Genèvre, equipped with modern hotels and ski-lifts to all
the surrounding slopes.

The chief attraction of the ascent from Briançon to the top of the pass
is the continually broadening view back, westwards, across the wide basin
of the Durance, beyond Briançon, with its huddled roofs and fortifications,
to the south-eastern wall of the Dauphiné Massif, culminating in the rocky,
glacier-streaked, triple-summited Pelvoux, well over 12,000 ft. high.
The short sector from Briançon to the saddle is thus scenically the most
interesting part of the journey.   On the continuation through the gentle
corridor at the top and thence down the long valley-trough for some
30 miles to Susa and the junction with the Mont Cenis route at that
picturesque old town of churches, the prospects are definitely more
constricted.   For which reason, the connoisseur's preference, with anticipation delaying the climax of the fine vistas on the Briançon side, might
perhaps be for an East–West passage, climbing from the plain at Turin to
earn his greatest reward at the end of what is perhaps not more than two
hours' pretty drive into the heart of the hills.

However, pursuing the eastward direction in which I have started this
description, we come to the French customs and the actual Col directly
beyond the village (6,100 ft.).   Here stands a tall obelisk, with inscriptions
in several languages, commemorating the opening of the present carriage
road in 1807.   It records that this is another of the great Napoleonic
military roads, decreed in 1802 with a far-seeing eye; for, when at the
beginning of 1814 his other two great routes, the Simplon and Mont
Cenis, had fallen into enemy hands and were finally denied him, it was by
the Mont Genèvre alone that the great strategist kept open the lines of
communication with his army of Italy, and by the Mont Genèvre he safely
withdrew its 40,000 men when retreat was at last forced on him.

Napoleon was probably not unaware that almost every northern invader
of the Italian plains had used this least difficult of routes across the
Cottian Alps.   In the reverse direction Caesar, during his conquest of
Gaul, took only eight days from Rome to Geneva by this road.   Charlemagne and Charles VIII are known to have entered Italy by it, the latter

at the head of a considerable army supported by 600 pieces of artillery. And, more recently, when in 1918 the Austrian and German armies invaded Italy, it was by the Mont Genèvre that French reinforcements were flung at short notice into the line of resistance.

From the Col the road descends the upper course of the Piccola Dora to Claviere, another well-equipped winter sports centre only a mile below the pass (Italian customs), and contours a precipitous slope high above the foaming torrent. It then descends rapidly through an avalanche-tunnel and past barracks, swinging down in a wide hairpin and crossing the Dora to reach Cesana Torinese (4,429 ft.), 5 miles from the Col, with its fine forests of pines. Here the Piccola meets the main stream of the Dora Riparia, and the little market town, set in a small, grassy basin, hugs both banks below the pine-clad slopes.

At Cesana an alternative and slightly longer route to Turin branches off to the right by way of the Colle di Sestriere (6,660 ft.), to reach which it climbs 1,000 feet in some 7 miles, with a couple of hairpins after a passage cut in the rock, and thence by a long descent by the Chisone gorges and valley to Pinerolo, 45 miles farther on (1,234 ft.), at the edge of the Piedmont plain. Sestriere (6,660 ft.), Italy's most fashionable and modern winter-sports resort, commands sweeping views over the western side of the frontier range, and the road is much more interesting scenically than the direct and enclosed descent of the true Mont Genèvre road to Susa.

This falls away steadily for the next 6 miles, passing through the gorge of Soubras, where sections of the road are carved out of rock, and then across some lovely meadows, shaded by walnut-trees, to the village of Oulx (3,500 ft.), at the junction of the Dora valley and the lateral valley of Bardonnechia. The main Modane–Turin railway line is seen coming down from the southern exit of the so-called Mont Cenis tunnel at Bardonnechia (4,125 ft.)—the tunnel is actually beneath the Col de Fréjus, 17 miles to the west of the Mont Cenis—and accompanies the road for the rest of the way, except for one short section near Susa.

From Oulx to Susa (1,625 ft.) the road provides a straightforward descent of the deep valley of the Dora for 15 miles, with a couple of final windings just above the picturesque town, a little before entering which stands the Arch of Cottius.

The route onwards to Turin (42 miles) through Bussoleno and Rivoli, following the broad, straight valley of the lower Dora, is described in the chapter on the Mont Cenis Pass (Chapter IV).

XIV

THE LUKMANIER PASS (6,289 ft.)

Entirely in Switzerland (Rhine Valley–Ticino).

From Disentis (3,772 ft.) to Olivone (2,945 ft.), crossing the main Alpine water-shed between the North Sea and the Adriatic: 25 miles.

Detail. Disentis to Lukmanier Pass (6,289 ft.): 12 miles, total ascent 2,500 ft.
Lukmanier Pass to Olivone (2,945 ft.): 13 miles, total descent 3,300 ft.

Open: Early June ot early November.   Maximum gradient: 1 in 11.

A good, finely engineered, mountain road of moderate width, with frequent tunnels on the ascent, but no wealth of hairpin windings.   Wide curves, followed by banked hairpins on the upper part of the descent on the southern side, continuing in a long, twisting section of typical valley road.

An easy pass to drive, with only moderate traffic normally.   Gravel-surfaced, but plans for rebuilding and modernization have recently been announced. Postal Motor Route.

FAR TO the east of the four great passes which cross the Pennine Alps between the Mont Cenis and the Gotthard, lies the Lukmanier, the Lucus Magnus or big forest of the Romans, the lowest of the gaps in the main chain of the Alps between the Mont Blanc group and the Maloja Gap at the head of the Engadine, reaching the moderate altitude of 6,290 ft. One of the easier passages, it has been a favourite route since the foundation of the monastery at Disentis by St. Sigisbert in A.D. 700; so much did it come to be used in the succeeding centuries that half a dozen minor chapels and hospices were founded along it by the parent monastery for the succour and shelter of travellers using it.   Among its most devoted patrons were the Carlovingian Emperors, and it is known that Charlemagne in 747, Pepin the Short in 754, Charles the Great twice in 781 and 801, Lothar in 824, and finally Charles the Fat in 875 all crossed by the Lukmanier route.   It seems highly probable, too, that the Saracen hordes, who in about 940 burst into the Rhine valley, burning the monastery at Disentis, ravaging the whole bishopric of Chur, and penetrating as far as St. Gallen, were users of it for less peaceful purposes.   By 965 Otto I had driven the invader out and restored order and safety to the Alpine roads, and it is known that he crossed into Italy by it, as did Frederick Barbarossa on several occasions 200 years later.   But in about 1200, with the rise to favour of the St. Gotthard as the most direct passage from the northern to the southern side of the Alps, the Lukmanier lost its importance and the hospices along it fell into disuse and disrepair.   It was not till the late nineteenth century, when for a short time a furious battle raged between its claims and those of the St. Gotthard for the main railway route across the Alps, that the Lukmanier Gap came into prominence again.   The

St. Gotthard won; but the Lukmanier earned a consolation prize in the
construction between 1871 and 1877 of the excellent road—if not particularly exciting from the scenic point of view—which is the shortest
link between the upper Rhine valley and Milan.

The most interesting part of the road is actually the first section by which
it leaves the main valley of the Vorder Rhein and obtains a foothold in that
of the Middle or Medel Rhein, which comes pouring down from the watershed due south. The river has worn deep gorges through the lateral
range, and the road penetrates them—first a broader, glacier-worn trough,
then a very narrow rift carved by the incessant pounding of water—by a
series of ten tunnels high to the right of the stream. This brilliant piece
of engineering lifts the road some 800 ft. to the upper valley floor of
Platta, where the valley again opens to a broader ice-worn U and progress
upwards is steady between meadows and wooded slopes at the foot of
finely polished rocks. The road gains height gradually without any need
for hairpin turns, crossing and recrossing the river, passing the wayside
chapels of Curaglia (4,370 ft.) and Platta (4,528 ft.), a scattered village,
with a fine fall of the torrent where the Medel peaks begin to show to
advantage, to Santa Maria (6,043 ft.) in the Val Cristallina, the last and
most important village on this side of the pass. Here stands the old
hospice—for, unlike most of the other passes, the Lukmanier Saddle boasts
no buildings, but only a cross, many centuries old, and some colossal
boulders. The crest of the pass is reached by a steady, almost straight
climb; and, for all its moderate elevation, this is in fact the true Alpine
watershed between the Rhine and the Po, into which, by way of the
Ticino, the Brenno torrent, rising here to the right on the southern side
of the saddle, eventually empties its waters. The slaty 10,500-ft. summit
of the Scopi dominates the saddle on the left, the 9,000-ft. Piz dell' Uomo
on the right.

All the way up through Curaglia and Platta there are charming vistas
back over Disentis and its monastery, across the main Rhine valley, and at
Acla, the last high hamlet inhabited all the year round, near a fine fall of
the Medel Rhine, the Fumatsch, there is a splendid view of the distant
pyramid of the Tödi (10,000 ft.)—'the King of the Lesser Mountains'—
soaring in the background. At St. Gion and St. Gall there are ancient
chapels and hospices among the rock-strewn meadows.

The descent is unsensational, curving from one wooded valley-terrace
to another. Crossing avalanche-tracks and muddy streams from the
yellow Piz Corva (9,840 ft.), it reaches Casaccia (5,967 ft.)—not to be
confused with the similarly named village in the Val Bregaglia below the
Maloja Pass (Chapter XVI)—the highest of the old hospices on the
southern side. Soon after the village, the view to the south opens up
finely, with the snowy peaks of the Adula Range and particularly the
imposing 12,500-ft. Rheinwaldhorn dominating the scene, seen at its best
above the old hospice of Camperio, where the road emerges from pine-
forests, which give way to pastures and lower vegetation. The usual exit-
gorges are wanting here, but to overcome the considerable fall to the main

valley, the road resorts to long windings, crossing the Brenno at Camperio (4,028 ft.) and reaching away to the foot of the mountains on the opposite side and back again in a great hairpin, which is not only the longest on this pass but on any of the Swiss Alpine passes. Resuming its southward course, the road drops from a lofty terrace to the considerable town of Olivone (2,930 ft.) in the Val Blenio, with a splendid surprise view over the upper part of that fertile southern basin, overshadowed by the stark granite pyramid of the Sosto (7,277 ft.) backed by numerous 10,000-ft. peaks forming a range which runs south-westwards parallel with the valley.

Chestnuts, fig-trees, and vines are soon the order of the day, and from Olivone, generally reckoned as the true southern foot of the Lukmanier, the road continues down the smiling, luxuriating Val Blenio through Aquila, Dangio, Torre, and Acquarossa on its way to Biasca (970 ft.), where it joins the main Gotthard route to the Ticino, Bellinzona, and Lugano (Chapter VIII). Only the last sector of the long valley is unattractive, marred by the débris of landslides which overwhelmed its villages as long ago as the sixteenth century, but whose scars still show unhealed on the great mountain-sides.

XV

THE SAN BERNARDINO (6,768 ft.) AND SPLÜGEN (6,930 ft.)

(For separate detail, see below pp. 127 and 128)

THE PLEASANT posting town of Thusis (2,369 ft.) commanding the wide valley of the Hinter Rhein, is more fully described in the chapter dealing with the approach routes from Chur and the Rhine valley to the Julier and Albula Passes into the Engadine (Chapter XXIII).

Its main importance is, however, due to the passes of the Splügen and San Bernardino, whose joint northern approach starts just beyond the end of the main street. These fine and interesting carriage roads, more particularly the lofty Splügen (6,930 ft.), were constructed between 1820 and 1832; and for several decades they carried a heavy volume of passenger and trade traffic between the Rhine valley basin and Northern Italy. To the Splügen, descending more directly on Chiavenna and the head of Lake Como, fell the lion's share; but the San Bernardino, which parts from it at the high village of Splügen itself and takes a more westerly course through the Misox valley to join the extreme end of the Gotthard route at Bellinzona, was also much frequented. In 1882 more than 20,000 people crossed the Splügen, and 5,000 the San Bernardino. Eclipsed eventually by the advantages of the Gotthard railway route, both roads fell into comparative disuse, till within the last thirty years the development of the Swiss Postal Motor Services renewed interest in them as convenient and scenically attractive alternative crossings for the motorist from the Rhine valley basin into Italy.

One of the major natural attractions of the route is the series of remarkable gorges into which the road climbs immediately after leaving Thusis. These have been bored through the primeval rock by the furious onslaught of the Hinter Rhein's swift waters, descending from the great glaciers of the Rheinwald group, 10 miles away and 10,000 ft. above. As early as 1473, Thusis and two neighbouring communes had pooled their resources to build a passable carriage way through the gorges to connect with the traditional tracks over the passes, which had both been in use since Roman days. The modern road is a marvel of engineering, for the great rocky crags tower up almost perpendicular, with the ruined fortress of Hohenratien and the chapel of St. Alban crowning the left-hand bastion, and the Rhine gushing out in furious spate below. This first gorge is known as the 'Verlorene Loch'—freely rendered, 'The Chasm of the Lost'—and the road assaults the right-hand slope most courageously to penetrate the gloomy rift.

The short, rock-girt ravine is immediately followed by a small open bowl in whose meadows lies the hamlet of Rongellen. The valley then narrows rapidly again and the road bores into the dark and fantastic gorge of the Via Mala—sufficiently sombre and awe-inspiring to merit so sinister a name. Here, between cliffs of grey rock towering thousands of feet to the sky, the Rhine has carved a deep and gloomy passage, often not more than a yard wide, down which it thunders terrifically in a series of foaming cascades and whirlpools. Threading its way high above, the road is forced to cross and recross the chasm; this it does on modern bridges which have replaced the old stone arches; but the loftiest of them has been left to lend a most picturesque effect to this tremendous mani-festation of nature's irresistible forces. For all its grim and daunting character, the scene is one of great and impressive beauty, with the hamlet of St. Ambriesch, occupied only in summer, perched high up on a rocky plateau above the second bridge.

A third bridge at Rania (2,903 ft.) brings the road out of the enclosing jaws of the ravine into the pleasant contrast of meadows and pines which clothe the broad and gentle second step of the valley, the little plain of Schams. Its chief village is Zillis (3,060 ft.), whose tiny church contains some remarkable thirteenth-century roof paintings.

The road presently crosses the Rhine by another bridge at the thermal baths of Bogn, with the hamlet of Clugin—where another picturesque old church houses fourteenth-century frescoes—on the other side of the river, and soon reaches the remarkable little township of Andeer (3,210 ft.), still bearing every mark of its importance as a staging and trading post in the days of the prime importance of the Splügen and San Bernardino. Here the remarkable external wall-designs on the Padrun house and the frescoes of the Conrad House are well worth inspection.

Beyond Andeer, at the Stone Bridge, the Averser Rhine comes down from the long re-entrant of Avers on the left to meet the Hinter Rhein in a cloud of spray. The long, high Alpine valley—the Aversertal—leads up to Cresta Avers (6,440 ft.), the highest Swiss village inhabited all the year round, and beyond Cresta a famous and beautiful walker's track ascends the Jufern Alp and crosses a saddle from which it descends to join the mule-track of the Septimer Pass on its way from Bivio, on the Julier road, into the Val Bregaglia at Casaccia (Chapter XXIII).

The road to the passes now penetrates the lesser and far less intimidating Roffla Gorge (3,559 ft.), after which the valley widens again and the road runs level with the swift-flowing Rhine on its right. Directly after the little Rheinwaldthörli tunnel ('The Little Rheinwald Gate') the village of Sufers (4,670 ft.), several times destroyed by fire, is seen on the other side of the river, where the old road used to run and still affords a good track for walkers.

The road continues to rise through pines and firs till at Rütenen the snowy summits of the Rheinwald Mountains, the Guggernüll, the Eins-horn, and the pyramid-shaped Piz Tambo suddenly lift into view. At the next little ridge, which is reached after crossing to the right (true left) of the Rhine, Splügen (4,790 ft.), in its high, bare valley, rather like a minor Urserental, comes into sight, with the white road running to it and beyond it as straight as a ruled line.   Equally straight is the line of the Splügen Pass road running at right-angles to the south, and here parting at last formally from the San Bernardino.

Splügen, like Andeer, bears marks of its importance in the great trading and coaching days: its stately and patrician residences, bedecked with fine wrought-iron work, and its huge old warehouses and sumptor-houses, now fallen into disuse.   Overlooking it on the north stands the fine rocky peak of the 10,000-ft. Kalkberg or Teurihorn.

1. THE SPLÜGEN PASS (6,930 ft.)

Switzerland–Italy (Grisons–Bregaglia).

From Splügen (4,790 ft.) to Chiavenna (1,083 ft.), crossing the main watershed between the North Sea and the Adriatic: 25 miles.

Detail.   (Thusis to Splügen, see detail of San Bernardino Pass, below, this chapter.)
        Splügen to the summit of the Pass (6,930 ft.): 5 miles, ascent 2,150 ft.
        (Swiss customs at summit: Italian customs at Monte Spluga—1 m.)

        Splügen Pass to Campodolcino (3,618 ft.): 11 miles, descent 3,300 ft.
        Campodolcino to Chiavenna (1,083 ft.): 9 miles, descent 2,500 ft.
Total descent from summit to Chiavenna: 20 miles, 5,800 ft.

Open: Early June to mid-October.   Maximum gradient: 1 in 11.

A high and splendidly engineered road of good width, particularly notable for its banked hairpin 'staircases' on the Italian side, from the top of the pass to Campodolcino.   Long, winding descent thence to the Val Bregaglia (Valley of the Mera, see also Maloja Pass, Chapter XVI) at San Giacomo; normal valley road the rest of the way to Chiavenna.   Not of outstanding scenic interest compared with some of its neighbours.

Traffic mostly moderate.   Moderately easy and interesting to drive.   Postal Motor Route.

Leaving the San Bernardino to run its straight westward course along the main valley, the Splügen road also runs briefly straight to the foot of the southern slope, which it then ascends after passing through a rock-gallery, in half a dozen banked-up hairpins.   It then follows the stream in the bottom of the high re-entrant falling from the Splügen watershed which appears high above, between the glacier of Piz Tambo (10,748 ft.) and the slightly lower Surettahorn.   To overcome the last steep slope to the narrow corridor of the pass—with continual glimpses back to the Splügen valley far below and only 4 miles distant—it requires six very short hairpins indeed, followed by the same number of rather longer ones. A quarter of a mile after the last hairpin bend, beyond another gallery, lies the Splügen Pass, with its frontier hospice, at an altitude of 6,930 ft., and, after threading the narrow defile for ½ mile you are looking down the south slope into Italy.

A few windings lead down to the village of Monte Spluga (6,246 ft.), where, at the beginning of the mile-long Stuetta Reservoir, stands the Italian customs house.

The road skirts the east bank of the artificial lake and falls continually down the broad slope below the glaciated Cima di Val Loga (9,850 ft.) and Piz Terri, with numerous short sections of bold windings—there is a particularly steep bank of ten just after the fine 650-ft. Pianazzo waterfall— and through galleries to Campodolcino (3,618 ft.) in the narrow, steep-sided valley of the Liro, already 3,300 ft. below the level of the pass, now 13 miles behind you.

From here onwards you drop steadily into the warmth and foliage of the south, following the long, straight declivity of the Liro valley, past San Giacomo, to where it debouches into the deeply enclosed plain of Chiavenna at the foot of the Maloja road (Chapter XVI). This drop in 20 miles from 7,000 ft. at the pass to the level of Como's lake at the very foot of the great mountain wall, is a tremendous transition from the Alpine to the temperate. It would not be surprising if, as the traveller draws up in the old square outside a famous posting inn, a momentary feeling akin to claustrophobia and suffocation afflicted him. If so, it will soon be dispelled as, refreshed by a rest and a good meal, he drives on by the enchanted, narrow, twisting road southwards to Como along the west shore of the loveliest of lakes.

2. THE SAN BERNARDINO PASS (6,768 ft.)

Entirely in Switzerland (Grisons–Ticino: Adula Alps).

From Thusis (2,369 ft.) to Bellinzona (760 ft.), crossing the main watershed between the North Sea and the Adriatic: 62 miles.

Detail. Thusis to Splügen (4,790 ft.): 16 miles, ascent 2,400 ft.
    Splügen to the Pass Summit (6,768 ft.): 12 miles, ascent 2,000 ft.
Total ascent Splügen to San Bernardino Pass: 28 miles, 4,400 ft.

    Summit to San Bernardino Village (5,270 ft.): 5 miles, descent 1,500 ft.
    San Bernardino to Mesocco (2,495 ft.): 9 miles, descent 2,800 ft.
    Mesocco to Bellinzona (760 ft.): 20 miles, descent 1,700 ft.
Total descent summit to Bellinzona: 34 miles, descent 6,000 ft.

Open: Late May to late October. Maximum gradient: 1 in 11.

A good secondary pass rising from the high plain of the Splügen Valley to the summit of the pass in a bank of sharp hairpin bends. Long and gentle descent on the Ticino side, curving down to meet the valley levels at Mesocco; thence a long, normal valley road descending to Bellinzona.

Traffic: Not usually very heavy. Postal Motor Route.

Having bidden farewell at the village of Splügen (4,790 ft.) to the Splügen Pass road and its windings into the steep hills of the south, the San Bernardino continues on its westerly way along the almost level floor of the Hinter Rhein valley, soon reaching the village of Medels, all that is left, thanks to the ravages of avalanches, of a much larger habitation, and Nufenen, at the foot of the craggy Guggernüll and Einshorn. Six miles from Splügen lies Hinterrhein (5,330 ft.), the highest village in the Val Rhein, which terminates a short distance ahead against the 12,000-ft. peaks and glaciers of the Adula or Rheinwald Group, rising close by to the west.

Silvaplana, in the Upper Engadine, on the northern approach to the Maloja Pass

Splügen, the junction of the San Bernardino and Splügen passes

The southern windings of the Maloja Pass

The road now turns due south and crosses the Rhein by a triple-arched bridge, after which it at last starts in earnest on the final ascent to the pass, still 6 miles and 1,400 ft. above. To reach the narrow break in the watershed overhead, it climbs a steep, wooded slope, falling from the 8,000-ft. Mittaghorn in a veritable staircase of sixteen short hairpins, banked directly one above the other. As it goes up, there are fine glimpses of the Rheinwald peaks and, particularly, looking back to the north, of the Kirchalphorn–Schwarzhorn chain, backing the Hinter Rhein valley. Crossing the stream after the top of the windings, the road traverses a bleak valley and soon reaches the tilted saddle of the pass, between Piz Uccello (8,911 ft.) on the east and Piz Moësola (9,521 ft.) on the west.

Here, by the little lake of Moësola, stands the small hospice where, in the fifteenth century, St. Bernard of Siena preached the gospel and so bequeathed his name to the pass. For walkers with time to spare there is a glorious view from a prominent boulder three-quarters of an hour to the north-west of the hospice, the way to which is well marked.

The road now follows the left bank of the Moësa, issuing from the lake, and descends in short windings, with fine views of the rocky peaks dominating the Ticino side and their glaciers. Still lower down, a fine bridge spans the river and a long curve brings the road down to the pleasant summer-resort of San Bernardino (5,270 ft.), which has long been a favourite holiday haunt for Italian visitors. Here are excellent hotels and charming woodland walks of half an hour to the Belvedère and the pretty little Lago d'Osso (5,400 ft.), as well as attractive longer excursions and climbs, including Piz Ucello's sharp tooth, already seen above the pass.

After a short rise, the road descends the upper Val Mesocco in a number of hairpins, losing height rapidly and recrossing the Moësa at the Inn of San Giacomo (3,845 ft.). It continues to fall steeply past Cebbia, on the left, to Mesocco (2,495 ft.), where the electric railway to Bellinzona begins. On a rock below the town—another considerable resort—stands the magnificent four-towered ruin of Misox, which has given its name to the whole district.

The pass proper ends here. For the rest of the way to Bellinzona (760 ft.)—another 20 miles—the route follows the bottom of the lovely Italianate Val Mesocco, joined later from the right by the almost parallel Val Calanca. These two long valleys of the Misox thrust their twin wedges deep into the southern flank of the Rheinwald Alps from the broad Ticino basin below; the Val Mesocco from the San Bernardino saddle to the confluence of the Moësa and Ticino at Bellinzona being more than 20 miles in length.

These last miles from Mesocco downwards are of great and varied beauty, as the road descends continually crossing and recrossing the river. The valley is deep and steep-sided, its slopes are covered in luxuriating southern foliage, its heights are crowned by romantic ruins, the clear Moësa stream goes babbling down over its stones, and lesser torrents everywhere come tumbling to meet it. The road falls steadily through

I

one pretty village and town after another—Soazza, Grono, Roveredo, the capital of the valley—close-built in the sunny meadows around their slender white campaniles, among the surrounding vineyards and orchards. By the time the wide Bellinzona basin and the Ticino road at the foot of the Gotthard are reached, at a level of about 800 ft., the great green hills of the south seem to tower overhead to a prodigious height.

XVI

THE MALOJA PASS (5,960 ft.)

Switzerland–Italy (Grisons–Lake Como).

From St. Moritz (Engadine) (5,900 ft.) to Chiavenna (1,083 ft.), crossing the main Alpine watershed between the Black Sea and the Adriatic: 32 miles.

Detail. St. Moritz to the Maloja Pass (5,960 ft.): 12 miles, ascent 50 ft.

    Maloja Pass to Castasegna (2,263 ft.) (Swiss and Italian customs): 13 miles, descent 2,700 ft.

    Castasegna to Chiavenna (1,083 ft.): 7 miles, descent 1,200 ft.

Total descent from the summit to Chiavenna: 20 miles, 4,900 ft.

Open: Usually all the year round, chains sometimes necessary in winter.

From St. Moritz to Maloja, good valley road of moderate width, almost level, with some sharp corners along the Lake of Sils. Beautiful lake-side and mountain views all along this sector. From the Saddle a finely engineered descent of 1,800 ft. in a dozen built-out, well-surfaced hairpin turns, to reach the level of the upper Mera Valley (Val Bregaglia). Thence a long, steady valley descent with very narrow village streets and many tortuous sections. Gentle windings below Promontogno to the level of the Italian plain before Chiavenna.

Traffic: Heavy in summer, very heavy at week-ends.

A very easy pass, the actual pass sector being extremely brief. Postal Motor Route. Maximum gradient: 1 in 11.

I T IS difficult to know where, on the Swiss side, to start a description of the Maloja road. As has already been mentioned, it shares with the Umbrail the distinction of being unilateral, but it is a distinction with a big difference. For the Umbrail is only a spare 'leg' of the Stelvio, by which you either climb from an alternative starting-point in Santa Maria to join that pass or branch off from it to descend to that point. Whereas the Maloja is a highly important through route, affording a direct connection between western Austria and the plains of Italy by way of Switzerland's south-east corner. It is unilateral only in the sense that, owing to an extraordinary freak of geological formation at the point it uses to breach the Alpine watershed, its southern side alone provides the normal characteristic of a steep mountain slope, and a very short one at that, to be overcome by engineering ingenuity; the northern side is a high valley, so nearly level that the road runs more or less straight through it, without any sensible climb, and certainly without a single hairpin bend, for its last 10 miles, till at the 'summit' of the pass it spills suddenly over a steep precipice on the southern, Italian, side. This gives rise to some difficulty in deciding where the Swiss 'side' of the pass begins. The long, steady rise over 30 miles from the far end of the Lower Engadine by a series of gentle slopes only lifts the road by 2,000 ft. from beyond Schuls at the north-eastern end of this long, and at many points picturesque, mountain corridor to where it abruptly terminates at Maloja.

Into the Engadine, moreover, at various points fall a number of minor passes bringing roads up from the Rhine valley basin over the rocky north-western containing wall of the valley—the Flüela, the Albula, and the Julier (Chapter XXIII). Each of these might in a sense be regarded as a more or less direct link between Italy and the lowlands of the Rhine Basin, Constance, and Liechtenstein, by making use of a longer or shorter sector of the Engadine road between Bevers and Maloja. Similarly, the long road over the Ofen Pass on the opposite side of the valley, which traverses the Swiss National Park from Münster in the Val Mustair to Zernez in the Engadine, might be considered a link between Merano and Chiavenna, across the Maloja Gap—if the driver were timid and oblivious enough to wish to avoid the much shorter and direct passage of the Stelvio. And even the Bernina Pass, which tumbles into the Engadine on the same side, could be used as an attractive day's round trip from Como back to Como by way of Maloja.

Since all except one of the passes named reaches the level floor of the Engadine below (north-eastwards of) St. Moritz, and their user therefore has to converge on that resort, it is perhaps right to confine a true description of the Maloja Pass's northern side to the short, level, and lovely 6 miles from St. Moritz to the sudden end of the Engadine at the Maloja Kulm. St. Moritz itself is so famous that it needs no description here.

Leaving its narrow main street—a thing I, for one, am usually glad to do, provided I have had time to sample its one glory, coffee or chocolate with whipped cream and an inimitable, beguiling choice of *confiseries* at Hanselmann's expensive *Conditorei*—the road passes the Segantini Museum on the right and looks down on St. Moritz Bad fringing the head of the lake below to the left.

A short belt of pine-wood leads to the small but lovely lake of Campfer, at whose far end among more pine-woods—they sweep up magnificently on either side of this stretch of the Engadine to the foot of the fine rock peaks above—nestles Silvaplana. On quiet mornings there is a charming picture here of the village and its sheltering pines reflected in the still jewel-green of the lake and the rocky blunt 10,000-ft. snow-streaked head of La Margna behind it.

Silvaplana, where the Julier road comes sweeping down from the right, has recently added to its long-standing fame as a member of the chain of Engadine holiday resorts, offering everything the visitor can want in summer or in winter. Just beyond the large and busy garage at the Maloja end of the little main street, some 30 yd. from the road, in among a small outcrop of rock on a steep grassy slope, a family of marmots has muscled-in on the tourist racket. Two of these shy creatures, usually visible only in the early morning on the high rim of remote glaciers, and famous for their alarm system of whistling signals, given by sentries on the approach of human or other danger, took up their abode here in 1952, close by the hurly-burly of the busy main road, with car and coach traffic passing bonnet to tail all the long, hot, busy summer days. Now a whole family of immensely fat, sleek marmots occupies the colony, and every car or coach passing that way pulls up to allow its passengers to call on them. Sometimes at week-ends there will be a queue of ten or twenty cars and coaches drawn up at the foot of the slope.   And there, within a few yards of all the bustle, the slamming of doors, the revving of engines, and the whining of gears, the unbashful marmot family holds court, coming right out of their burrows to accept an endless feast of carrots and other delicacies from the hands of children and grown-ups alike.   Not unnaturally, they are about the roundest, largest marmots ever seen anywhere; and the only thing that still sends them scuttling like lightning into the darkness of the tunnels behind them is a sudden clumsy movement of the proffering hand or a child's voice raised in excitement at close range.

The road now continues close to the shore of the Lake of Silvaplana till it reaches Sils Baseglia, where a turning branches off to the left to cross the valley to the popular resort of Sils Maria, a mile away on the other side, under the steep slopes of Piz Corvatsch.   Presently there are lovely views up the re-entrant of the Fextal, a pretty mountain valley running at right-angles to the Engadine, from Sils towards the foot of the fine crescent of the Tremoggia group, with the snow-clad mountains and the dark pine slopes below them, reflected in the green waters of the lake.   If there is time to spare, the narrow road beyond Sils Maria up the Fextal's green meadows and fine glacier scenery is worth a couple of hours enjoyable diversion: this is lovely walker's valley with charming small hotels.

The long, low saddle joining the summits of Corvatsch and Rosatsch in the direction of St. Moritz is the Fuorcla Surlej, one of the classic 'close-up' view-points in the Alps, the inn on which is crowded every night in summer by mountain-walkers who have climbed its 9,000-ft. eyrie by the excellent paths from Silvaplana or Sils, an undertaking requiring four to five hours.   Sunset and sunrise on the great 13,000-ft. Bernina peaks and glaciers, which the saddle entirely masks from the Engadine but which tower above it at only a stone's throw on the southern side, are unforget-table experiences.

The Maloja road now cuts a way through the rock of a wooded promontory projecting into the Lake of Sils, the longest of the five Engadine lakes, and continues to hug its shore to Maloja.   The little pine-clad headland (only minutes from a parked car) is a favourite picnic spot and commands a lovely view back across the lake to the village of Isola, set on a green flat at the foot of dense pine-woods, above which the long, graceful ridges of Piz Corvatsch (11,350 ft.) sweep to their snow-crowned apex.

At the southern end of the Lake of Sils the hotels and châlets of Maloja (5,950 ft.) confront you, a low green hummock in a narrow neck between the slopes rising abruptly on either hand.   Down it the infant Inn comes bubbling into the lake.   Hidden away in the pine-woods to the south lies the lovely Lake of Cavloccio, an hour's easy walk away, and paths lead to the more distant Forno Glacier, with its fine rock peaks, a climber's paradise, and across the frontier ridges by the Muretto and other passes into Italy, descending on the valley of the Adda.

As you approach the village there is nothing to suggest that you are about to cross the backbone of the Alps or are on the very watershed between the Mediterranean and the Black Sea. It is well worth while to swing right-handed into the Maloja Pass car-park and get out to study this unique phenomenon in geological conformation.

For here, some thousand years ago, the southern side of the Alps suddenly caved in, and the waters draining the peaks of the Bondasca and Bergell, instead of flowing as previously northwards into the basin of the Inn, were diverted southwards to pour into the Italian lakes.

The car-park stands at the very rim of this astonishing cataclysm. The precipitous wall, curving between the huge rocky ranges lifting to the sky close on either side, has come in time to be densely forested with pine and larch. It plunges straight down at your feet, and the next thing you see beyond the dense curtain of the pines below is the stream foaming its twisting way down the green bottom of the first step in the long sub-Alpine Mera valley, and Casaccia, a huddle of toy houses about a toy church, 2,000 ft. below.

Down this sheer and narrow escarpment the Maloja road swings back and forth in a dozen splendidly engineered, beautifully graded hairpin turns, well surfaced and of comfortable width. In ten minutes from the cool upper air of the Engadine you are in the deep trench of a sun-drenched Italianate valley at a level of 4,000 ft., with the great pedestals of the Bergell rock-ranges sweeping high overhead to the south and only slightly less savage ribs and ridges to your right.

There are altogether four terraces in the 20 miles of the valley down to Chiavenna in its narrow plain at 1,000 ft. From one white-walled village to another, each with its picturesque narrow, heavily guttered, main street, the road runs straight between fences and meadows, then winds its way sharply down between rocks or through miniature gorges to the next level below. As on the north side of the Grimsel, it is rather like being lowered by a series of locks from one level to another of a long descending waterway, only here the level sections are longer and the loss of height between them less severe.

Each of the euphonious Italian names marks another terrace in the descent. Casaccia, Vicosoprano, Stampa, Promontogno, Castasegna—of the Val Bregaglia—whose Italian identity the Swiss are prone to hide under the collective name of the Bergell. All the way down the valley there are clear traces—to be seen best along the mule-track not far from the main road used by walkers—of the old Roman road from Clavenna over the Maloja saddle into the territory of the Rhaetii beyond.

And so we come, between white-washed stone walls and southern foliage, first to Vicosoprano and then to Promontogno (2,685 ft.), clustering at the junction of the wild Bondasca and the Mera in a little green plainlet. Here the grand Bondasca ravine bites deep and steep into the mountain mass to the south, crowned by the splendidly savage rock spires of the Cacciabella, Sciora, and Bondasca peaks, a crescent of shattered rock and hanging glacier whose greatest glories are the Cengalo (11,070 ft.) and the stupendous smooth north-east face of Piz Badile (10,853 ft.), one of the last great climbing problems in the Alps to be solved, as recently as 1938. The mountain-walker in search of sublime scenery will want to pause at Promontogno and walk all the lovely three hours' length of the Bondasca's steep rift, to the Sciora Hut (7,057 ft.) at the feet of these great precipices.

The motorist who has less time to spare, but who still would wish to see that splendid circle of peaks to fuller advantage than from so screened and undercut a view-point as the bottom of the valley, will either drive in a quarter of an hour up the narrow road which winds up the opposite slope of the Mera valley or walk up in an hour, either from Stampa or Promontogno, through the shade of the famous chestnut groves to Soglio (3,570 ft.), the historic Bregaglia home of the de Salis family in the Middle Ages, and perhaps the most perfectly situated village in the Alps—certainly the most photographed.

The little road is just broad enough for one fair-sized vehicle, and it is as well to make sure before embarking on it that the downward Postal Motor is not due; for it has the right of way, and a good deal of tedious shunting in reverse can be avoided by waiting a quarter of an hour.

The de Salis home in the picturesque square is now an excellent hotel (Pension Willy), and some of the ancient rooms are still on show in their original state. Here Maria Rainer Rilke lived and died, and the register is bright with famous names. A stroll through the white-walled village street—at least 15 ft. wide—with its wrought-iron balconies and scarlet geraniums, leads in a few minutes to gentle grassy slopes from which the huddle of grey roofs about the slenderest of white church towers, set against the marvellous background of the valley below and the Bondasca Gorge with the sharp spires towering above, is seen at its lovely best.

Below Promontogno the main road winds pleasantly down between pines to the Italian frontier just beyond Castasegna (2,263 ft.). To the right of the road soon afterwards lies a gigantic boulder-strewn area to mark where in 1618 a vast sector of the mountain-side broke off to engulf under its piled-up débris the village of Piuro. Only a solitary church-tower stands now to mark the site. From there it is only 4 miles among fruit-trees and maize-fields to the ancient town of Chiavenna (1,083 ft.), lying spread out at the foot of great mountain walls. To the left, the broad levels of the Adda plain open up towards the head of Como; to the right is a misty hint of the deep gorges through which the Splügen road finds its way through the towering main mountain masses of the Rheinwald Alps to the north.

Everything is suddenly soft and sleepy and southern as you drive into Chiavenna with an odd feeling that you have not crossed the Alps at all, but only fallen over the edge of some high tableland among the great peaks still close behind you.

XVII

THE BERNINA PASS (7,644 ft.)

Switzerland–Italy (Engadine–Adda Valley and Lake of Como).

From Samaden (5,670 ft.) to Tirano (1,405 ft.), crossing the main Alpine watershed between the Black Sea and the Adriatic: 36 miles.

Detail.   Samaden to Pontresina (5,910 ft.): 5 miles, ascent 250 ft.
Pontresina to Bernina Pass (7,644 ft.): 10 miles, ascent 1,750 ft.
Total ascent Samaden to the Pass: 15 miles, 2,000 ft.

Bernina Pass to Poschiavo (3,317 ft.): 11 miles, descent 4,300 ft.
Poschiavo to Campocologno (1,814 ft.) (Swiss and Italian customs): 9 miles, descent 1,500 ft.
Campocologno to Tirano (1,405 ft.): 1 mile, descent 400 ft.
Total descent from the Pass to Tirano: 21 miles, 6,200 ft.

Open: Mid-May to late October.   Maximum gradient: 1 in 10.

After the slight straightforward ascent to Pontresina, the road climbs steeply by a series of hairpins (famous view and lay-by at the Montebello Corner) to Bernina Häuser high in a stony valley, up which the route continues easily for some miles by a wide modern road with few bends, to the Hospice and the Pass, beyond it through a tunnel.   The upper part of the huge descent on the southern side (over 6,000 ft.) is at first uncomfortably narrow and somewhat exposed, then continues to fall steeply in numerous somewhat broader windings for more than 10 miles to Poschiavo, where the valley level is at last reached.   Rather narrow and tortuous valley road through the long series of defiles thence to Tirano.

Traffic can be heavy at times in the season (coach trips), though this is, exceptionally, not a Postal Motor Route.
Easy on the northern side, one or two moderately difficult sectors on the upper part of the southern descent, which require special care.   Scenically very attractive indeed.

H AVING DESCRIBED the Maloja route from its high end in Switzerland downwards into Italy at Chiavenna and related it loosely to the main road which runs south-westwards, the lovely length of the Engadine from Nauders on the Austrian frontier to the Maloja escarpment, it is, I think, logical to take the Bernina Pass in the same direction—that is from the Engadine downwards into Italy.

Unlike the Maloja road, however, the Bernina has to climb out of the Engadine over a saddle some 1,700 ft. above the level of the high valley-plain before it can think about its long, continuous, and sometimes steep descent of some 20 miles and 6,000 ft. to Italian soil.   And in the short half-hour of ascent from Samaden in the wide main valley to the hospice at 7,644 ft. it exhibits all the characteristics of a true pass that the sister road lacks and at the same time packs into the relative short ascent some truly magnificent mountain scenery.

The road leaves the main Schuls–Süs–Zernez–St. Moritz–Maloja highway at Samaden (5,670 ft.), which, like every Engadine village along the road, has a wealth of the ancient houses typical of the district, with lovely wrought-iron balconies, window lattices, quaintly eaved roofs, and often frescoed walls.

From Samaden the road crosses the Inn and runs level straight across the enclosed plain formed by the junction of the Berninabach re-entrant and main Inn valley, then rises gently between pine-clad slopes to the long, straggling resort of Pontresina (5,910 ft.), whose plentiful hotels, tennis courts, bandstands in the wood, chair-lifts, and funiculars provide everything for the visitor from charming, short, shady walks in lovely scenery to moderate and, if desired, serious expeditions in the great Bernina group, which takes peculiar pains to hide itself at this stage behind high intervening spurs.

Approaching Pontresina, there is a lovely glimpse between them up the heavily wooded Roseg valley to the beautifully white circlet of the Sella-Glüschaint peaks (11,000 ft.). A mile or so after the end of the village, just before the road begins to climb in earnest through the pine-woods ahead, a side road branches off to the right to Morteratsch (6,260 ft.), below in the valley, and there is a fine vignette of Piz Palü's three icy buttresses lifting mightily to 13,000 ft.

The Inn at Morteratsch, a few minutes along the dead-end of the side road, is worth a visit for two purposes only. If the traveller has not previously seen the dirty snout of a great glacier close at hand he can walk from the inn to the foot of the Morteratsch Glacier in half an hour and there visit the blue ice-cave in its 300-ft.-thick base from which the stream issues in muddy urgency. Incomparably better, in my opinion, is the climb by a steep zig-zag path to the wooded spur of Chünetta (6,876 ft.)— also half an hour from the Inn—which commands a splendid view up the glacier's morained and crevassed surface to the great peaks ranged at its head. Whereas the one expedition yields a combination of the strange, the ugly, and the wonderful in nature, the other not only mitigates the ugliness but also adds an Alpine view of supreme grandeur and beauty. In either case the explorer will be glad of the refreshments available on his return.

The Bernina road now swings in three pairs of wide hairpin turns through the tall pines—at one point crossing, on the level, the electric railway, with which it shares the ascent—till, at the famous Montebello Corner (6,500 ft.), it rises clear of the screening forest and suddenly reveals the dazzling view over the great Bernina peaks which is the road's supreme glory. This is, to my mind, in composition and texture, the finest and most beautiful view, at close quarters, over the peaks and glaciers of a great group of snow mountains to be had from any road in the Alps.

It is, of course, a matter of individual choice. Others may think the huge lift of the Ortler—much closer at hand—from the Stelvio more impressive; the Glocknerstrasse allows you to look down also at closer range on a wide stretch of glacier stream with the great peaks confronting you across it, in a more detailed and impressive way; the more distant views of the Oberland Peaks lifting above the Aletsch tongue from the

Simplon and of the wonderful surge of the Finsteraarhorn and its great neighbours seen from the Furka's window may appeal more to another. For me, the perfect proportions of this semicircle of mighty peaks, all reaching to the 13,000-ft. level or near it, all unusually snowy-breasted because of their northerly aspect, some soft and undulating in contour, the Bernina herself sharp-ridged and knife-edged, with the great expanse of the riven icefall and tongue of the Morteratsch perfectly centralized below, and all in middle distance, where they stand up without undue foreshortening, give this glorious prospect pride of place for sheer beauty of form and texture.

There is a lay-by for three or four cars at Montebello. It is almost as difficult to get into it on a fine summer morning—this view is at its very best in the earlier part of the day—as it has now become to find a parking-place in central London at any time of the day or night. Once in it, very few cars seem to have an owner for the next half-hour. The amount of camera film exposed here in a good summer would no doubt stretch from Pontresina to Poschiavo at the other end of the pass.

A couple more hairpins bring the road to the top of the great bluff it has been ascending and finally, above the tree level, into a long and arid rift between high, stony slopes, with the torrent brawling down alongside the road and the Bernina railway's pylons and overhead wires strangely inconspicuous on so large a canvas.

At Bernina Häuser (6,720 ft.) a couple of lonely stone buildings and a railway halt, the Val de Foin, noted for its flowers and its marmots, bends away to the left, while on the opposing side rises the steep path leading up in three hours to the Diavolezza Hut (9,760 ft.), famous not only as a climber's refuge but also as a view-point for ordinary mortals.* Innumerable mountain-walkers spend the night there in order to witness the magnificent spectacle of sunrise on Piz Palü (12,835 ft.), towering overhead across the narrow basin of the Pers Glacier; and many make their first acquaintance here with the delights of glacier expeditions next day by completing, under guidance, the easy 'Diavolezza Tour', which brings them down the Pers and Morteratsch glaciers in five wonderful hours to the Morteratsch Hotel.

Above Bernina Häuser the road curves gently upwards towards the hospice at the saddle ahead. On the right the Cambrena Glacier, pouring down from the fine pyramid of the same name (11,834 ft.), is suddenly revealed, and the icy summit ridges of Palu lift their uppermost slopes to advantage over the high intervening ridges.

The road skirts the dark waters of the Lago Nero and Lago Bianco (7,316 ft.) and reaches the old Bernina Hospice (7,400 ft.), a grim and rather weather-beaten building in bare and forbidding surroundings. Here the road and railway diverge, the latter curving away to the right to make the crossing of the saddle at the green Alp Grüm (6,850 ft.), closer to the mountain wall and the foot of the Palü Glacier streaming down from the great peak's reverse side. The road makes a more business-like climb

---

* A cable railway, opened in 1957, now does away with the expenditure of the slightest effort.

in a couple of short bends to a tunnel a few yards beyond which, on the
southern side (at 7,649 ft.), is the summit of the pass.

From the rim of the green saddle opposite the summit inn there is a
superb downward glimpse into the blue-green depths of the Vale of
Poschiavo, soft and southern in the sunshine, with the eye of the little lake
of Le Prese glinting up from 6,000 ft. below, and the windings of the road
at various levels on its long descent into this impressive abyss. The
whole prospect is serenely backed by the huge velvety green walls of the
Italian frontier range culminating in the bold rock peak of the Pizzo di
Sena (10,000 ft.). To the right under the western retaining wall is the
green terrace of Alp Grüm—three-quarters of an hour's walk by mule-
track—with the railway buildings and hotel dwarfed by the tongue of the
Palü Glacier and, farther round, by the magnificently iced upper precipices
of Palü itself, lifting over the rocky Cambrena ridges.

Up this great green southern wall of the mountains for hundreds of
years the mule-trains maintained an endless traffic in the famous Valtellina wines from the Adda valley below, a cask on either side of each
mule, with all the hazards and excitements of the smuggler's craft thrown
in. And so since time immemorial the Bernina has had a second name—
the Wine Pass. Now the splendidly engineered electric railway built in
1907–10 at a cost of 15,000,000 francs carries the traffic from Tirano to the
Engadine 'over the hump' in a couple of hours.

The carriageway on the southern side of the pass is still narrow and at
places exposed, particularly in its upper section, as it twists its steep way
down to the first village La Rösa (6,162 ft.). Lower down, the curves are
wider, as the road crosses and recrosses a broader slope, passing San Carlo
(3,590 ft.), swinging endlessly down towards the remote valley-levels, whose
reluctance to come up and meet you eventually becomes a little tedious.

But at long last you straighten out on a welcome strip of level ground,
in the narrow bottom of this immense rift in the hills, and find yourself
entering Poschiavo, the busy capital of Puschlav (3,315 ft.), beyond which
the road runs for ½ mile along the rim of the blue and charming lakelet of
Le Prese, whose picturesque village lies ahead at its southern end (3,165 ft.).

There is a sudden further contraction in the valley bed here, and for a
while the road drops steeply past picturesque Brusio (2,560 ft.), through a
narrow, rock-bound gorge, through which it vies with the foaming torrent
and the single line of the railway for passage-room. Then in a widening,
but still closely imprisoned between the huge mountain walls, you come
to the Italian frontier and both customs houses at Campocologno (1,814 ft.).

Beyond, the road still falls rapidly, between every variety of southern
foliage, with the sun-drenched breadth of the Adda valley appearing
between the jaws of the defile, at right-angles ahead, and in another mile
or so you emerge into the full heat and light of Italy at Madonna di Tirano
(1,436 ft.), a typical white-walled Italian town with an interesting church.

Tirano stands astride the long Valtellina road, half-way between the
head of Lake Como and the foot of the Stelvio at Bormio—23 miles to the
north-east.

Turning right-handed into the broad Adda valley, you are on the fast main road which runs straight and almost level but hot and dusty between maize-fields and fruit orchards, with the vineyards everywhere terraced up the slopes of the great containing hills, to Sondrio (16 miles) and Colico (41 miles) and so to Chiavenna or Como, according to which way you turn there.

A mile or two after leaving Tirano and just before Tresenda a turning on the left leads down southwards to the Adda, which it crosses by an imposing bridge, to swing uncompromisingly up the foot of the opposite mountains in a long walled ascent to the north-east. This is the road which by way of the minor Aprica (3,875 ft.) and Tonale (6,181 ft.) passes affords an attractive link with Edolo, Ponte di Legno, Dimaro, Madonna, and the Brenta Dolomites (Chapter XXXIII).   Used in conjunction with this route, the Bernina Pass is thus the most direct route from the Engadine and adjacent districts of South-eastern Switzerland to Bolzano and the Dolomites.

XVIII

THE OFEN PASS (7,070 ft.) AND THE UMBRAIL (8,212 ft.)

Entirely in Switzerland (Engadine (Grisons)–Münstertal (Val Müstair), traversing the Swiss National Park).

From Zernez (Lower Engadine) (4,836 ft.) to Santa Maria (4,547 ft.), crossing the main Alpine watershed between the Black Sea and the Adriatic: 22 miles.

Detail. Zernez to Ofen Pass (7,070 ft.): total ascent 14 miles, 2,250 ft.

Ofen Pass to Santa Maria (4,547 ft.): total descent 8 miles, 2,500 ft.

Usually open all the year round, but chains sometimes needed.

In spite of its altitude, a mild and not particularly interesting road, passing through fine but slightly monotonous scenery. It rises fairly steeply from Zernez, with some windings, into the long Fuorn Valley of the Swiss National Park, along which it undulates gently for several miles. A few final curves lead to the broad grassy saddle, with a well-known distant view of the Ortler. On the south side it curves unsensationally down into the pleasant Val Müstair (Münstertal).

Traffic not generally unduly heavy, but much frequented by coach traffic in the season. Maximum gradient: 1 in 11.
Postal Motor Route.

ANOTHER PASS leaving the Engadine to the south demands some description, for three reasons. First, it crosses the true Adriatic-Black Sea watershed, and must therefore rank as one of the genuine trans-Alpine passes; secondly, in conjunction with the Umbrail, it provides a useful link between the Engadine and the Stelvio, 30 miles to the east, and so with Merano, Bolzano, and the Dolomites; and lastly it traverses the Swiss National Park, an area of 160 square miles set aside in 1909 for game reserves and flower sanctuaries, and a particular pride and joy to the Swiss.

These considerations apart, the Ofen (Il Fuorn, 'the Kiln'—so called from the numerous derelict smelting furnaces still visible to commemorate a considerable iron-mining industry carried on along its route in medieval times) is in spite of its altitude one of the least exciting of all the passes. For, romantic and unspoiled as are the long valleys and rocky ridges which form the National Park, the 25 miles of road runs through vast areas of splendid woods of larch, spruce, and fir, overlooked by the screes and faces of unimportant rock peaks, none of them especially distinguished for their individual beauty. There is consequently a certain monotony about the heavily wooded scene, the green alps high above and the inevitable containing-walls topped by similar limestone crests; perhaps it could all be best described as a surfeit of what would be sheer beauty on a local morning walk.

As a pass, the Ofen's qualities are in truth sadly lacking.

Starting at a level of 4,828 ft. at Zernez in the high trough of the Lower Engadine, it eventually reaches an elevation of 7,070 ft. at the wide, open saddle which is here the Adriatic–Black Sea watershed. This modest rise is achieved gradually over a distance of some 15 miles, and the final lift to the summit hardly demands anything in the nature of a curve.

From Zernez the road rises steadily to a first crest of over 6,000 ft. at the Gorge of Ova Spin, with a fine view over the Spöl valley, then drops a few hundred feet through the long basin of Ova del Fuorn. At Punt la Drossa it begins to rise again and gradually climbs for another 3 miles past the Ofenberg Inn at Il Fuorn (5,919 ft.)—where starts a lovely five hours' round on foot, by easy paths, across the wide Buffalora Alp, to Munt La Schera (8,450 ft.), a splendid viewpoint—to the broad summit saddle.

Here there is an attractive view forward along the wide Val Müstair— the Münstertal—with a fine but distant glimpse of the 12,798-ft. Ortler lifting its snowy dome high above the intervening ranges beyond the valley.

The drop on the eastern side of the pass is much steeper, and several wide curves and a few narrower hairpin sections are necessary to bring the road down to the level of the Müstair valley's pleasant pastures, through which the road descends straight, passing through Tschierv and Valchava, to the main village, Santa Maria (4,555 ft.).

The downward continuation of the Ofen route lies along the valley to the Swiss–Italian frontier at Müstair (Münster) (4,094 ft.) 3 miles away, whence the road continues through Tubre (Taubers) (4,042 ft.) to join the main Arlberg–Merano highway in the upper valley of the infant Adige, at Sluderno (Schluderns) (3,095 ft.). There the left-hand turn leads westwards to Hochfinstermünz (Reschen–Scheideck Pass, Chapter XIX), Landeck, and the Arlberg Pass (see Chapter XXVII); the right-hand, eastwards down the lovely Adige valley, bounded on the north by the snowy Zillertal Alps, past Spondigna (2,903 ft.)—where the Stelvio road comes in over the top of the Ortler* Range to the south—to Merano, Bolzano, and the Dolomites.

THE UMBRAIL PASS (8,212 ft.)

Switzerland–Italy (Grisons–Alto Adige).

From Santa Maria (4,547 ft.) (Val Müstair) to the junction with the Stelvio Pass, near its summit, at 8,000 ft.: 9 miles.

Detail. Santa Maria to the Umbrail Pass (8,212 ft.) (Swiss and Italian customs): Total ascent 8 miles, 3,650 ft.

Umbrail Pass to junction with Stelvio (8,160 ft.): Total descent 1 mile, 60 ft.

Open: Mid June to late October. Maximum gradient: 1 in 11.

The highest of the Swiss motor-roads. A finely engineered but none too broad road, with a gravel surface, ascending in an unbroken series of thirty-six hairpins, often built out one above the other, to the Umbrail summit. The road is rather a Swiss ' leg ' to the Stelvio Pass (all in Italy) than a true pass in its own

* See footnote p. 24.

right, and falls gently into the latter only a mile or so beyond the saddle of the Umbrail.   (For the continuation either north or south see Chapter XXVIII, The Stelvio.)

Traffic can be fairly heavy in the season (coach-trips and Postal Motor Route). Moderately difficult: could worry an inexperienced driver.

At Santa Maria, however, you can branch off to the right by the Umbrail road, which provides a steep link with the Stelvio Pass to the east; the summit of that wonderful road (Chapter XXVIII) can thus be reached more directly from the Engadine over the Ofen–Umbrail route than by taking the Bernina Pass (Chapter XVII) into the depths of the Adda valley and then approaching the Stelvio from its true southern foot at Bormio.

The Umbrail, though the highest saddle reached by any of the Swiss roads, is thus not a true pass in its own right, but simply a unilateral link ascending from Santa Maria in Swiss territory to a height of 8,212 ft. on the Italian frontier, where it feeds through a narrow col into the southern side of the Stelvio Pass, about 900 ft. below its summit.   Constructed in 1889–91 to replace a historically frequented sumpter-track to Bormio, this fine road follows the deep Muranza Ravine and overcomes a vertical difference of nearly 4,000 ft. in only 5 miles as the crow flies; this it achieves by means of no less than thirty-six finely engineered hairpin turns, almost without respite.   This Swiss avenue of access to the glorious summit view of the Stelvio has been greatly popularized in recent years by the national Postal Motor Services, which traverse it daily in summer. On the last part of the ascent, fine views of the Monte Cristallo (11,360 ft.) glaciers and the Geisterspitze (11,405 ft.) in the Ortler Group are gradually revealed ahead, and the Col itself lies close under Piz Umbrail (9,951 ft.), an imposing rock mass, towering up on the right.   Directly after the 'pass', and with scarcely any loss of height, the road joins the southern approach to the Stelvio at the hut of the Fourth Cantoniera, on Italian soil (Chapter XXVIII).   Here too, at ' Stelvio ', are the Italian customs: the Swiss are at Santa Maria.

XIX

THE RESIA (RESCHEN–SCHEIDECK) PASS
(4,947 ft.)

Austria–Italy (Arlberg–Inn Valley–Alto Adige).

Landeck (Inn Valley) (2,670 ft.) to Spondigna (Spondinig) (Upper Adige Valley) (2,903 ft.), crossing the main Alpine watershed between the Black Sea and the Adriatic: 48 miles.

Detail.   Landeck to Prutz (2,840 ft.): 7 miles, ascent 150 ft.
　　　　Prutz to Hochfinstermünz (3,730 ft.): 16 miles, ascent 900 ft.
　　　　Hochfinstermünz to Nauders (4,480 ft.): 5 miles, 750 ft.
　　　　Nauders to Reschen–Scheideck (Resia Pass) (4,947 ft.): 3 miles, ascent 450 ft.
Total ascent Landeck to Resia Pass: 31 miles, 2,300 ft.

　　　　Resia Pass to St. Valentin (4,820 ft.): 6 miles, descent 100 ft.
　　　　St. Valentin to Mals (3,435 ft.): 6 miles, descent 1,400 ft.
　　　　Mals to Spondigna (2,903 ft.): 5 miles, descent 550 ft.
Total descent Resia Pass to Spondigna: 17 miles, 2,050 ft.

Open: Usually all the year round, chains sometimes necessary in winter.

One of the lowest and easiest international trans-Alpine passes, and a time-saving alternative from the Arlberg to Bolzano, short-circuiting the Inn Valley–Brenner route.   A long series of striking gorges on the north side, and fine views of the distant Ortler group on the southern descent.

Traffic not normally very heavy.   An easy road to drive.   Maximum gradient: 1 in 9.

T HE RESIA PASS (4,947 ft.), exploiting the deep gap carved by the Inn between the Rhaetian (Grisons) and Oetztal groups of high peaks and glaciers, affords one of the easiest of all the passages from one side of the main Alpine chain to the other.   It is the obvious through-route for the motorist who has crossed the Arlberg into Austria from eastern Switzerland and who is making for Bolzano, the Dolomites, or Lake Garda in a hurry, purposely avoiding the attractions of Innsbruck, 30 miles to the east, and the slightly longer journey over the Brenner.   It is not one of the passes to be taken for the sake of high mountain views such as are associated with the great roads which surmount lofty saddles in the mountain backbone; but is, in its milder way, scenically attractive, mainly for its views into the deep cleft of the Inn Gorges, which it follows.   And it is an excellent alternative to the Brenner.

Leaving Landeck (2,670 ft.) at the eastern foot of the Arlberg, the road immediately dives into the mountain wall to the south and follows the narrow defile, through which the Inn comes racing down from the Engadine, for $7\frac{1}{2}$ miles to Prutz (2,840 ft.).   On the way it crosses the famous bridge of Pontlatz, where the levies of Tyrol twice annihilated the Bavarian invaders in 1703 and 1809, two famous victories now commemorated by a monument.

he Montebello Lay-by on the Bernina Pass, with Morteratsch Glacier and Bernina Peaks

Looking back from the Umbrail windings, over Santa Maria in the Müntertal to the Ofen Saddle beyond

Nauders, on the Resia Pass, with the distant Ortler

Half-tunnels on the Bernese side of the Susten, near the summit

At Prutz, lying at the entrance of the Kaunertal, which opens to the east, the road recrosses the Inn and continues up the Inn valley past Ried, with its castle of Sigmundsried; crosses the river again at Bruggen; and, in another 12 miles, reaches the picturesque double village of Pfunds (3,185 ft.), which consists of Stuben on the high road and Pfunds on the other bank of the Inn.

About 1½ miles farther on, the road again crosses the river, by the Cajetan Brücke, and forces its way along the left-hand wall of the gorge, into which it is blasted at several points, and by way of three tunnels and some avalanche galleries, reaches Hochfinstermünz (3,730 ft.). This is the most interesting sector of the road. The gradual nature of the ascent will be noted, for in the 23 miles from Landeck to this point the road has risen only a little over 1,000 ft.

Hochfinstermünz, with its cluster of houses and inns clinging to the hill-side, provides the most picturesque of all the views down into the narrow rift of the Inn Gorge. Five hundred feet below, at the river level, lies Altfinstermünz, with its ancient tower and a bridge across the swiftly moving stream.

The road here finally leaves the Inn valley and ascends the side valley of the Stille Bach, reaching Nauders (4,480 ft.), in a long bend, after 4½ miles. At this point the high-road to the Engadine via Martinsbruck goes off to the right, climbing a few hundred feet to the dividing ridge, from which there is a fine view over the Lower Engadine valley and peaks. Nauders is a large village with an ancient castle; and from the cemetery, on a hill about five minutes east of the road, there is a good distant view of the Ortler (12,800 ft.).*

The gradual ascent of the Stille Bach now continues for another 3 miles till, at the Reschen-Scheideck (4,947 ft.), the culminating point of the pass is reached, at the watershed between the Inn and the Adige, which flows eastwards from its nearby source. Both customs houses are near the frontier.

The village of Resia (Reschen) (4,890 ft.), close to the small green Reschen See, lies 1½ miles farther on; and, a little beyond it, a fine distant view opens up ahead of the whole Ortler chain, from the remote Cevedale, through the pyramid of the Königspitze (now Gran Zebru), to the Ortler itself on the right; and this remains with one all the way down to San Valentino (St. Valentin), 6 miles farther on.

Two miles from Resia lies the ancient Graun, with the Mittersee beyond, along which the road continues for 4 miles to San Valentino (St. Valentin) (4,820 ft.), where yet another lake, the Haidersee, begins. Beyond the lake a rather monotonous descent of some 6 miles, with the Ortler, how-ever, still a splendid object ahead, leads past Burgeis, the castle of Fürsten-burg, and the Benedictine abbey of Marienberg, on a hill to the right, to the ancient hamlet of Malles (Mals) (3,435 ft.), dating from Roman days.

Here a road goes off to the right up the Münstertal (Val Müstair), leading by way of Laatsch and Taufers (Tubre) to the Swiss frontier at

* See footnote p. 24.

K

Münster (Müstair) and on to Santa Maria, $1\frac{1}{2}$ miles beyond Münster; it is there that the Umbrail Pass, climbing east to join the Stelvio road, and the Ofen Pass, rising northwards towards the Engadine, both begin (see Chapter XVIII).

The Resia road now continues to fall gently into the broadening valley of the upper Adige by way of Sluderno (Schluderns) (3,095 ft.), at the mouth of the fine Matschertal, which carves northwards into the Oetztal snows and whose head is dominated by the 12,290-ft. Weisskugel. Three miles farther on, and 5 from Malles, the pass ends at Spondigna (Spondinig) (2,903 ft.), from which important road junction the Adige valley high-road continues eastwards, in 30 miles, to Merano; while the lesser road crossing the bridge over the Adige to the right is the quiet start of that most sensational of all the Alpine passes, the Stelvio, 17 miles to the south (see Chapter XXVIII).

XX

THE TAUERN (5,700 ft.)–KATSCHBERG (5,384 ft.)
ROUTE

Entirely in Austria (Enns Valley to Drau (Drave) Valley; Salzburg to Carinthia).

From Radstadt (2,725 ft.) **to Spittal** (1,732 ft.) **across the main Alpine watershed of the Niedere Tauern, the most easterly group of the Alpine chain, rising to nearly 10,000 ft.: 55 miles.**

Detail. Radstadt to Unter-Tauern (3,294 ft.): 7 miles, ascent 550 ft.
   Unter-Tauern to the Tauern Pass (5,700 ft.): 6 miles, ascent 2,400 ft.
Total ascent Radstadt to Tauern Pass: 13 miles, 2,950 ft.

Total descent Tauern Pass to Mauterndorf (3,681 ft.): 10 miles, 2,000 ft.
   Mauterndorf to St. Michael (3,504 ft.) (Valley road): 6 miles, level.

Total ascent St. Michael to the Katschberg Pass (5,384 ft.): 4 miles, 1,900 ft.
   Katschberg Pass to Gmünd-in-Kärnten (2,400 ft.): 6 miles, descent 3,000 ft.
   Gmünd to Spittal (1,732 ft.): 8 miles, descent 650 ft.

Total descent Katschberg Pass to Spittal: 22 miles, 3,650 ft.

Open: Kept open if possible, but often obstructed by snow from mid-November to mid-May.
   Both passes, notorious for extremely steep gradients, are under long-term reconstruction, but many sections remain abnormally steep (1 in 7 is not unusual, and there are still some at 1 in 5: the famous 1 in 3½ sector has been eliminated). The surface is still mainly gravel, but the roads are both fairly wide, and there are no sharp hairpin bends. Not one of the easiest routes to drive and, with the advent of the Grossglockner road, no longer a link which has to be taken to save a *détour* of vast mileage. The scenery is fine, but not outstandingly so.

   Traffic is, for obvious reasons, not very heavy at any time.

A CHAPTER IS devoted to this lesser-known combination of two rather difficult passes mainly in order to give a complete survey of all the roads of more than 5,000 ft. which cross the true Alpine backbone (see map 2, p. 56).

   Before the Grossglockner road came into being in 1937 there was no such crossing between the Brenner and this (till recently excessively steep and difficult) route, a great hiatus of 100 miles. There was an alternative, *under* the mountains, by putting a car on the railway and proceeding through the Tauern tunnel between Bad Gastein and Obervellach, and then joining the Katschberg route at Spittal; but this meant considerable delay, and gave little pleasure to those who enjoy mountain motoring rather than 'trucking'. So the motorist unwilling to resort to artificial aids, who wanted to drive from the Salzburg area to the Dolomites or anywhere east of Lienz in the Klagenfurt region (Carinthia) and on to North-eastern Italy or Jugoslavia, had either to betake himself westwards all the way to Innsbruck, then down over the Brenner and then all the way east again, a roundabout journey of quite 150 miles; or he had to brave the terrors of

the Katschberg, with its notorious gravel sector at 1 in 3½.   Now there is
the Grossglockner, and the Katschberg's journey is no longer necessary.

Rebuilding and modernization, which will continue gradually over the
years, have already eliminated much of the ordeal; but the road still
remains very steep—frequently 1 in 10, 1 in 7 less often, and once 1 in 5—
and among the most difficult of the Alpine crossings.

From Radstadt (2,725 ft.) in the Enns valley the Tauern Pass ascends
the side-valley of the Taurach, with fine backward views over the 8,050-ft.
Bischofsmütze and neighbouring peaks, to Unter-Tauern (7 miles, 3,295
ft.).   There it enters the Tauernklamm, with its magnificent waterfalls,
one of them 460 ft. in height, and in a steep climb of 7 miles reaches the
Radstädter Tauern Pass (5,700 ft.), from which there is very little to be
seen.   A slightly less steep descent brings the road, in 9 more miles,
through the village of Tweng (4,090 ft.), to Mauterndorf (3,681 ft.), a
small market town and summer resort in the Taurach Tal.

Six miles of valley-road lead to St. Michael (3,504 ft.) in the Murtal
at the foot of the Katschberg road, which immediately crosses the Mur,
rises sharply, and surmounts the 5,384-ft. saddle ahead in 4 extremely
severe miles of gruelling ascent.   The pass, which offers no view of
particular quality, is the boundary between Salzburg and Carinthia.   The
descent down the pretty Liesertal from Rennweg (3,743 ft.) is at 1 in 5
from the summit to that village (4 miles), and much at 1 in 7 below it,
through Gmünd-in-Kärnten (6 miles, 2,400 ft.) to Spittal (1,732 ft.).
This pleasant town stands on the main Drau valley road from Klagenfurt,
the Wörthersee, and Villach—that delightful holiday region of the
Carinthian Lakes—to Lienz, the Italian frontier at Sillian (p. 106) and
the northern entrance to the Dolomites from Dobbiaco in the Pusteral
(Chapter XXXII, p. 232).

At Gmünd-in-Kärnten, on the descent from the Katschberg, a turning
across the bridge on the left leads in 5 miles to Millstatt (1,905 ft.), the
famous lake-side resort on the Millstätter See, considered by many to be
the most beautiful of all Austria's Carinthian lakes, also, of course, easily
reached from Villach.

PART IV

THE SWISS INTERNAL PASSES

XXI

A TRIO OF GREAT ROADS: THE SUSTEN-FURKA-GRIMSEL ROUND

O NE OF the finest days of motoring over high Alpine roads, always through the heart of superb mountain scenery and often in close company with famous peaks and glaciers, can be obtained by linking these three passes in a long day's round. The three great Swiss roads have, of course, their independent function as internal arteries, which afford vital connecting links between the Bernese lowlands to the north and the Valais lowlands to the west, on the one hand, and the Rhine valley in Eastern Switzerland and the Ticino to the south, on the other. The motorist in search of the appropriate through-route will be able to select his individual pass or combination of passes easily enough. For the benefit of the visitor to any of the Bernese Oberland resorts who may wish to enjoy a day's incomparable mountain driving without any further destination in mind—a day that can equally well be taken, though in a different sequence, by anyone spending his holiday on the shores of the Lake of Lucerne—it is proposed to describe these wonderful routes, two of them venerable carriage roads, the other among the most modern examples of magnificent motor highways, as a combined operation starting and finishing at Interlaken.

1. THE SUSTEN PASS (7,300 ft.)

Entirely in Switzerland (Bernese Oberland–Uri).

From Innertkirchen (2,067 ft.) to Wassen (3,018 ft.): 30 miles.

Detail. Innertkirchen to Gadmen (3,960 ft.): 9 miles, ascent 1,900 ft.
Gadmen to Steingletscher (6,120 ft.): 5 miles, ascent 2,150 ft.
Steingletscher to Summit Tunnel (7,300 ft.): 3 miles, ascent 1,200 ft.
Total ascent Innertkirchen to Summit: 17 miles, ascent 5,250 ft.

Total descent Summit Tunnel to Wassen (3,018 ft.): 13 miles, descent 4,300 ft.

Open: Early June to late October. Maximum gradient: 1 in 12.

A magnificent modern mountain highway, starting with a long section of easy valley road, then overcoming a sheer mountain wall by a dozen superb hairpins (some built out on steel girders) with a beautifully surfaced, well-protected and drained carriage way 18–30 ft. wide throughout. Frequent lay-bys along the tunnelled section above the hairpins to the Steingletscher car-park. Further broad windings to the summit tunnel 400 yd. long (car-park at summit). After a short, steep bank of equally fine hairpins, the road descends the long Maienreuss Valley, gently contouring the slope for 10 miles till just above Wassen, where, by a splendid and ingenious engineering feat, it forces

151

its way, in two spiral tunnels linked by a magnificent concrete arch, through the constricted gorge of the Maienreuss and over its final cascade. A few hairpins bring the road steeply down to the lower Gotthard route at the main street of Wassen.

Traffic very heavy in the season (coaches and Postal Motors); but the road can take it. Comfortable and easy to drive. Scenically glorious and superb as an engineering feat.

The Susten Saddle, separating the Bernese Oberland from the Canton of Uri, lies between the Titlis group and the higher peaks of the Reuss–Rhone–Glacier watershed, at a height of 7,420 ft. Till after the Second World War, the only means of crossing it was a long minor road declining into a mule-track, beloved of mountain-walkers, who thus enjoyed a monopoly of the glorious and varied scenery hidden away in and above the Gadmental.

During the War the Swiss Postal Department, ever imaginative in throwing open the beauties of their country to increasing numbers of visitors and travellers, pushed forward the construction of a daringly conceived and superbly appointed motor-way—one is almost tempted to use the inappropriate word speedway, for it is a triumph of grading, surfacing, cornering, and safety-protection, with a normal width of 30 ft., allowing the huge coaches of today to pass without difficulty, even on the marvellously engineered hairpins of the precipitous Gadmen side.

This latest addition to the great network of the major Swiss passes took eight years to build and cost 32,000,000 Swiss francs—the 400-yd. tunnel by which it pierces the ultimate crest, which the old mule-track surmounts, alone absorbing 1,750,000 fr.—was opened for traffic from the Uri (Gotthard) side to the summit in 1946, the more difficult and spectacular Gadmen side being thrown open and the pass thus completed in the following year. Apart from its engineering wonders and its great scenic beauty, the new road affords a valuable short cut between Interlaken and Andermatt on the Gotthard road, whence the easy passage of the Oberalp Pass leads directly over into the Rhine basin. It is thus now possible for the through-traveller, pressed for time, to save valuable hours in travelling from the Bernese Oberland to the Engadine, by-passing entirely the old Grimsel–Furka road, which dictates the crossing of two major saddles of some 7,000 ft., with a steep descent between them, before reaching Andermatt and the Oberalp.

The pleasant road along the pretty shores of Lake Brienz and through the wide floor of the Haslital from Interlaken to Meiringen and then over the low wooded ridge to Innertkirchen through which the Aar cuts its famous gorge, traversed on foot by thousands of tourists every year, is probably too familiar to require description.

Innertkirchen is a charming village, with good hotels, lying in a green circular plainlet completely enclosed by great wooded ridges soaring overhead. To the right the deep Urbachtal curves away to the Gauli Hut and glacier and the eastern wall of the great Oberland massif, with only a mule-track penetrating it. Ahead lies the great rift into which the Grimsel road ascends; and to the left is the broader opening of one of the most smiling valleys in the Bernese Alps, the Gadmental.

Into this the Susten turns left at the Innertkirchen cross-roads and for some miles wanders charmingly upwards through corn-fields, pasturages, and wooded meadows, always close under the huge rock-ramparts of the Gadmerflüh and Titlis range (10,620 ft.), rising sheer to the northern (left-hand) side of the road, till the village of Gadmen (3,960 ft.), with its old brown châlets, is reached. (This unspoiled valley, so recently groomed for stardom, is full of lovely old timbered and balconied buildings.)

Then, suddenly, the valley contracts and the way is barred by an immense, almost vertical, buttress of the hills, apparently putting an end to all hope of progress, and the marvels of the Susten road begin.

This wall, the base of the 9,500-ft. Uratstock and appropriately known as Hölle (Hell), is some 3,000 ft. high, and is overcome, with bewildering and courageous ingenuity, in a dozen hairpin turns, all clinging by their eyebrows to the precipitous rock face, yet all easy, spacious, and perfectly graded, though at least one of them is built out from the implacable wall on steel girders projecting over the abyss.

As you swing up the mountain-side on this prodigious, smooth, spiral staircase, glorious views open up in the direction from which you have come, with the long green carpet of the Gadmental far below in the foreground and, rising magnificently behind the Innertkirchen bowl, the lovely summits of the Wetterhörner (12,250 ft.) three clean-cut snow peaks crowning enormous precipitous plinths of rock thousands of feet high, dominating the valleys at their feet.

A moment later, however, as the last gallant hairpin finally overcomes the crest of the huge buttress, at a height now of nearly 6,000 ft., the interest shifts violently ahead and across the narrow hanging-valley, along the left-hand side of which the road now clings and climbs straight on and up, at the very edge of the precipice, occasionally tunnelling through projecting cliffs to find a way forward.

For now, as you rise easily along this broad, paved balcony in the hills, with frequent lay-bys, whose little grassy lawns enable you to get out and enjoy it all to the full, you are faced, at close range across a stony chasm piled with grey moraine rubble, by the shattered icefall of the Stein glacier, pouring from between the gracefully curved snowy saddles and sharp peaks of the lovely Susten peaks—Sustenhorn (11,520 ft.) and Gwächten-horn (11,245 ft.).

From here on to the tunnel at the summit it is all mountain magic, with a dress-circle view; and the local name of Hell has given way to an equally appropriate 'Himmelrank'—Heaven.

A couple of wide turns bring you to the Steingletscher Hotel and car-park (6,120 ft.), from which walkers may take paths down to the base of the glacier in the hollow below and climbers start out on the great variety of ascents offered by the Susten group or the rock peaks closer at hand.

A few more hairpins swing the road up in ten minutes to a point at 7,300 ft., just below the Susten Saddle, which boasts another car-park and a small refreshment hut and shop.   From here it is a ten-minutes' stroll by the last few yards of the old mule-track to the pass proper above the road tunnel on a narrow, turfy saddle between frowning rock slopes (7,420 ft.).

The Susten snows are by now cut off by intervening spurs, but the pass has a magnificent downward prospect on the Uri side to the east, where the whole length of the curving valley of the Maienreuss is revealed, with the road contouring its downward way across the great curtain of reddish-yellow rock which falls from the Spannörter (10,500 ft.), the well-known rock peaks so familiar from Engelberg on their other side. The view is closed by another immense screen of rock, this time bluish-grey, on the far side of the Gotthard valley ahead.

Except for four tight hairpins immediately below the summit, banked sharply one above the other, the whole 10-mile descent of the Maiental to just above Wassen at the foot of the pass in the Gotthard valley is achieved without a single further turn, and the whole road is protected on the outer side by concrete pillars and a three-rail steel fence.   As you lose height there are fine glimpses back to the five rocky spires of the dark Fünffingerstock, but in summer this side of the range is, by contrast with the splendour on the Gadmen side, dour and almost completely snowless.

On the descent, several pretty villages and church towers are passed by the side of the stream, down below in the valley, which is for the most part quite broad and gentle.   But just before its lower exit into the main Gotthard valley, running at right-angles below at Wassen, the valley narrows prodigiously and suddenly seems to have no outlet.   It is here that the Susten exhibits its last and almost its greatest marvel of engineering skill, for the gateway through which the Maienreuss forces a passage is a mere crack in the towering cliffs blocking all egress.   Down this the torrent roars and leaps in a series of foaming falls and cataracts, with the opposing walls only a few feet apart.

There was not even room for half a road in this awesome defile.   So the problem was solved by taking the 30-ft. motor way through a spiral tunnel in the living rock of one side.   As it emerges, still losing height, it leaps the raging cascade by a slender concrete arch 50 ft. above the torrent and bores its way downward on the other side in another sharply curving tunnel to emerge in the Gotthard valley almost overhanging the huddled grey roofs of Wassen.   A couple more steeply terraced hairpins and the Susten joins the old Gotthard road at the entrance to the village. There is apparently nothing a modern road cannot do if it (and the Swiss genius for engineering sets its mind to it.

The motorist now turns right, through Wassen, and proceeds by the sector of the Gotthard road, already described in Chapter VIII, p. 90, through Goeschenen, and the Schoellenen Gorge, to Andermatt and Hospental in the remarkable high plain of the Urseren valley, where the Furka road properly begins.

2. THE FURKA PASS (7,976 ft.)

Entirely in Switzerland (Urserental–Upper Valais).

From Andermatt (4,737 ft.) to Gletsch (5,777 ft.), crossing the subsidiary water-shed between the Mediterranean and the North Sea: 20 miles.

Detail. Andermatt to Realp (5,060 ft.): 6 miles, ascent 350 ft.
Realp to Furka Pass and Hospice (7,976 ft.): 8 miles, ascent 2,900 ft.
Total ascent Andermatt to Furka Pass: 14 miles, ascent 3,250 ft.

Summit to Belvedère (7,545 ft.): 1 mile, descent 450 ft.
Belvedère to Gletsch (5,777 ft.): 5 miles, descent 1,750 ft.
Total descent summit to Gletsch: 6 miles, descent 2,200 ft.

Open: Mid-June to late October.   Maximum gradient: 1 in 10.

A fine, historic, old-fashioned mountain-road of moderate width. Heavy seasonable traffic leads to frequent deterioration of the gravel and bitumen surfaces, and repairs to one sector or another are almost continuous. From Realp numerous easy hairpins loop their way up a broad, turfy shoulder to the Galenstock Inn (6,595 ft.). The road then continues high up on the north (right-hand) slope of the bare Furka Ravine all the way to the summit.   A short, straight descent, with magnificent views of the Oberland peaks and Glaciers, to Furka Belvedère, is followed by half a dozen sharply hairpinned dog-legs down a sheer 1,000-ft. wall of rock: these are somewhat exposed in places.   At the foot, the road doubles back on itself and contours easily along the opposing slope to Gletsch in the flat bowl of the Rhone Valley below, finally dropping into the village by three or four sharp, steep hairpins. Postal Motor Route.

Traffic always heavy in summer, and the moderate width of the road can make the journey somewhat trying in the popular middle hours of the day.
A moderately easy road to drive, with a few exposed sectors which might worry an inexperienced driver. Scenically magnificent on its western side, where the road almost touches the Rhone Glacier's icefall and the great Oberland peaks dominate the bowl of Gletsch. In clear weather the distant Valais giants are also seen to advantage.

I have purposely taken the Susten–Furka–Grimsel round in the order named because it seems to me that, if I were going to advise anyone who had never driven over any of them and who wanted to take them singly, or in conjunction with other routes, for the first time, I should still counsel the same approach to each.

Certainly, I would say that the Furka summit view as you come to it from the Andermatt–Urserental side is one of the greatest of all the 'surprise' views which should be earned by the long, enclosed cling to the slope up the intervening range from the valley-level to the sudden sublime moment of revelation. The approach by the steep, short Gletsch side, wonderful as it is, unfolds that great spectacle of ridge and glacier and rift, dominated by the Finsteraarhorn, piecemeal and to its detriment. After all, you will still see all the separate components equally well, at leisure, on the downward way, after the impact of the completed master-canvas when the curtain is swiftly drawn on it at the summit; it is, in my view, infinitely better than first watching all the passages as they are touched in by the brush during the process of painting.

At Hospental, where the ancient tower of the Langobard barons still frowns down on the valley that was their domain, the Gotthard turns south across the mountains, and is seen swinging its rebuilt way up the left-hand valley-wall overhead, where the orderly border stones of its hairpin terraces once made a bewildering pattern across the slope above (Chapter VIII). The Furka road goes straight on up the middle of the Urserental as if drawn with a ruler, ignoring alike the windings of the young Reuss on the right, hurrying down from the crest of the Furka Saddle ahead and the curves of the narrow-gauge Furka Railway, which has tunnelled its way through its base on the long journey from Brigue. (This is the only direct rail link between the Rhone valley and the Engadine, for beyond Andermatt it continues to parallel the road over the Oberalp into the Rhine valley all the way to Chur, where it connects with the Albula Railway. The daily luxury observation-car 'Rhone–Rhine' express completes the journey from Brigue to Chur in six hours, and the traveller enjoys some, though by no means all, of the scenic beauties of the Furka *en route*.)

The Urserental has already been described in the introductory chapter as the 'navel of Switzerland', that extraordinary depression in the great upheaval of surrounding mountains, from which the only downward outlet is the 100-ft. slit the pounding of the Reuss has carved through the rock of the Schoellenen Gorge.

Its floor is a small green plain about 5 miles long, with bare, forbidding ridges on either side and two high saddles enclosing it at either end, to the east the Oberalp close behind Andermatt, to the west the Furka behind Realp, the last village on the level at the other end. The mountains at the Andermatt end are heavily fortified, and the acute zigzags of military roads leading up to forts and installations can be seen scarring all the slopes: and during the summer months when the Swiss army manoeuvres are in full swing, military traffic in and around Hospental and up to the Gotthard is often very heavy and liable to cause delay to civilian traffic, including that to the Furka.

The road to the foot of the Furka runs fast and straight the length of the little plain from Hospental to Realp (5,060 ft.), where it is suddenly faced with a broad green shoulder of the hills, about 1,500 ft. high and not unlike a Welsh mountain-side, as the only means of progress; for the exit of the Reuss from a long, deep ravine ahead offers no foothold for road or railway, which here resorts to the mile-long Furka Tunnel, over on the other side of the valley.

At the last houses of Realp the Furka road sets resolutely to work and overcomes this first obstacle in more than twenty loosely woven curves, looping their way up the full width of the great green mound to the small Galenstock Hotel at the top (6,595 ft.). As it mounts, a fine view opens up looking back along the straight bottom of the green Urserental, now far below, to the Oberalp ridges and saddle at its far end and the taut thread of the road which has brought you from Andermatt and Hospental to the foot of the climb.

Beyond the little inn, the road immediately enters the high, bare Furka ravine and for 5 miles clings its way up the huge right-hand retaining wall without the need for a single hairpin, high above the young Reuss foaming its way down in the bottom, several hundred feet but not precipitously below. The backward prospect is soon lost, and the road is imprisoned all the way as it climbs steadily and sometimes steeply to the high saddle ahead between the bouldery walls of this bleak and viewless corridor.

Relief from the generally sombre tone of this long final approach is, however, afforded at several points by little widenings in the shelf, with grass-fringed lay-bys from which there are fine upward glimpses to the broken blue-grey rock-combs of the Dammastock–Galenstock ridges (11,900 ft.) and their hanging glaciers to the right overhead. And at the Tiefentobel there is a fine waterfall roaring down from one of them, often throwing a mist of spray over the bridge which carries the road across it, when the hot summer sun is at work on melting ice.

The square shape of the Hospice is in view on the saddle for a long time as the shoulders of the hills close in and you gradually attain the 7,000-ft. level. Just before reaching the narrow neck of the pass the road steepens and is forced to wriggle a little past a small cluster of buildings to overcome the last slope to the saddle. And then, as you swing left-handed into the car-park outside the hospice at 7,970 ft., framed by huge turf slopes which form a perfect V, the Furka summit view bursts on you with overwhelming suddenness, its vast effect, as so often, sharply accentuated by the long claustrophobic hour spent with your bonnet's nose to the mountain-side, shut in from all wider vision of earth and sometimes even sky.

This is one of the immortal views, and since there is nothing about it that can be subject to a mountain change, it is perhaps appropriate to quote the description written by the master hand of a masterly observer nearly a hundred years ago. This is what Mark Twain said about it in *A Tramp Abroad*:

'No one can fail to be completely recompensed for his fatigue when he sees, for the first time, the Monarch of the Oberland, the tremendous Finsteraarhorn.

'A moment before, all was dulness, but a step further on placed us on the summit of the Furka; and exactly in front of us, at a distance of only 15 miles, this magnificent mountain lifts its snow-wreathed precipices into the deep blue sky. The inferior mountains on either side of the pass form a sort of frame for the picture of their dread lord, and close in the view so completely that no other prominent feature of the Oberland is visible; nothing withdraws the attention from the solitary grandeur of the Finsteraarhorn and the dependent spurs which form the abutments to the central peak.'

Like most similar prospects from more or less enclosed saddles, it can be improved and better photographic compositions achieved by shorter or longer walks on the neighbouring slopes or to dominating view-points a little farther afield, from the ten-minute strolls to the Schönblick or the Signal, west and north-west of the hospice, to the hour and a half to and three hours of the Blauberg (9,110 ft.) and the Muttenhorn (10,180 ft.).

The next short straight section of the road, the descent of a mile to the Furka Belvedère Hotel and neighbouring buildings is along the edge of a

tremendous precipice falling almost to the head of the Gletsch basin in
the bottom of the bowl 2,000 ft. below. As you drive along it with only
the comforting row of soldierly demarcation stones lining the route between
you and that deep, stony rift, the view gradually opens out to take in the
additional distant prospect, far beyond the tiny buildings of Gletsch, of the
upper Rhone gorges, and, beyond, the great 14,000-ft. giants of the Valais,
the Mischabel, the Matterhorn—from here a small black and crooked
spike thrusting over an intervening ridge—and the lovely gleaming white
pyramid of the Weisshorn (14,804 ft.) leaning against the sky 30 miles
away.

At the Belvedère Hotel (7,545 ft.) if you arrive at any time between
twelve and two in the summer season you will probably find facing you a
dozen or more enormous coaches, a high proportion of them yellow Postal
'Motors', occupying half the narrow roadway, bonnet to tail, for this is the
lunch halt when the round is done—as it more frequently is—in the opposite direction, taking the Grimsel first, and coming up from Gletsch.
(Another reason perhaps for driving it my way, for it is less trying to edge
past a string of the huge brutes coming to meet you than to get tucked in
behind their slow progress ahead of you—courteous as the Postal drivers
generally are in giving you a chance to overtake.) The occupants of the
parked juggernauts will be scattered all over the neighbourhood, as far
afield as the blue ice-grotto carved in the glacier for their delight, and root-
ling for souvenirs at the little brick kiosk along the path on the way to the
glacier's edge. You, too, should get out and stroll to one of the nearby
view-points on the path overlooking the glacier.

At Belvedère begins the astonishing series of six hairpins which lower
the road down a sheer thousand-foot precipice of rock alongside the
cataclysm of the Rhone Glacier's tongue. The top turn, with its petrol
pumps, is literally within a few yards of the edge ice and frequently below
the level of the icefall's crazy séracs—ice towers and pinnacles anything up
to 50 ft. high; and until recently the alternate bends used to bring the
road back to the rim of the glacier's steep tongue and into the chill breath
blowing off its riven ice.

As a spectacle, the Rhone Glacier has, however, suffered severely even
in the thirty years since I first saw it. For then its tongue cascaded all the
way down the thousand feet to the stony wilderness at the bottom, in a
welter of blue-and-green-shadowed ice-terraces; and from the arched
cavern at its foot the infant Rhone rushed out among the boulders a grey
and headstrong river of foaming turbulence. Now, having suffered like
all the glaciers of the Alps from a period of swift and steady recession
during the intervening years, the rather dirty ice-tongue hangs somewhat
limply and crookedly over the top third of the escarpment, the rest of
which is now revealed as a wall of bare blue-grey rock, polished smooth
by the action of centuries of ice-movement. Down it half a dozen rivulets
spatter from ledge to ledge and find their tortuous way across the flats
below to unite in a recognizable main stream some way out towards
Gletsch, which stands a mile away from the foot of the wall. Some idea

of the rapidity of the glacier's recession in a century and a quarter can be obtained from old early-nineteenth-century prints—one hangs in the hall of the Belvedère Hotel, and there is an interesting sketch in Brockedon's *Alpine Passes* (1829)—which show the tongue of the ice, piled hundreds of feet thick across the whole level mile, reaching out almost to the buildings of Gletsch.

Turning its back on the glacier at the lowest of six magnificently daring hairpins, the road now runs straight on down across the base of the rocky face until, in a barren re-entrant, down which the Muttbach rushes from the Muttenhorn's hanging glacier high above, it doubles back over a small stone bridge, at about 6,500 ft., to find a lodgement on the steep, turfy slopes of the Längisgrat on the other side of the bowl. These it descends in a long reach, passing full across the front of the Rhone Icefall, now seen across the flat, stony plainlet, with fine views up to the Gerstenhörner (10,449 ft.), and the Galengrat (8,520 ft.) containing it, of the great Belvedère windings, down which you have just come, and the six great hairpins of the Grimsel rising opposite. This is a favourite picnic spot, and there is room to get the car off the road in several places. Down below, trapped in the narrow rift, lie the hotels and other sparse buildings of Gletsch, a grim and cheerless staging-post of the old coaching days, when the night was spent here after a crossing of either of the great passes which spring from its opposing ends, only a few hundred yards apart. The road continues to contour the slopes till it is almost on a level with the plain and only a couple of hundred feet above the roofs, then suddenly winds its way steeply down the last slope in three or four sharp tourniquets.

3. THE GRIMSEL PASS (7,100 ft.)

Entirely in Switzerland (Valais–Bernese Oberland).

From Gletsch (5,777 ft.) to Innertkirchen (2,067 ft.): 20 miles.

Detail. Gletsch to the Grimsel Summit (7,100 ft.): 4 miles, ascent 1,300 ft.

> Summit to the Hospice turning (6,200 ft.): 2 miles, descent 900 ft.
> Hospice turning to Handegg (4,510 ft.): 5 miles, descent 2,600 ft.
> Handegg to Innertkirchen (2,067 ft.): 9 miles, descent 2,500 ft.

Total descent summit to Innertkirchen: 16 miles, 5,000 ft.

Open: Mid-June to late October. Postal Motor Route.

From Gletsch to the summit, six long, dog-legged hairpins, finely built out, up the Maienwang, then contouring past the Totensee to the top (car-park). Surface often poor, owing to heavy traffic. Good modern section past the hospice (on by-pass) to the upper gorges of the Aar, where it narrows inescapably to force a way through to the lower levels at Handegg. Very narrow at the Handegg lay-by and tunnel, heavily frequented in summer. Good, straightforward, and easy descent from one valley-level to another from Handegg to Innertkirchen. Maximum gradient: 1 in 10.

Traffic very heavy in summer (innumerable coaches and postal motors). Moderate to drive otherwise. Exceedingly interesting scenically.

Barrenly sited and architecturally sterile as it is, there is something romantic about Gletsch, hemmed in an arid neck where three important

roads meet.   For the little outpost houses more than the two great mountain roads writhing out of it to the heights.   The narrow ravine, through
which the young Rhone plunges its swift downward way between rocky
cliffs to the west of the hamlet, brings the valley road-link (and in modern
times the narrow-gauge railway) from the broad lower sector of the Rhone
valley, 20 miles below at Brigue.   This connecting-road from the Valais
climbs steadily from terrace to terrace of the river's narrow upper-basin,
through Naters, Ried, and Fiesch, to meet the passes in the heart of
Gletsch.

And here the traveller from the lowlands or he who had come over
either of the two great passes was glad to put up his weary horses and
spend the night before committing himself to the serious business of
another long, tiring journey next day.   Nowadays, the place does a good
business in lunches and teas, and there are petrol pumps for the thirsty
motor; but to many motorists Gletsch will remain in the memory only
as a bridge over the brawling Rhone, a sharp left turn, a quarter of a mile
of level street between big square buildings, another sharp turn, and the
first narrow, steep rise of the Grimsel road, safety-walled on the valley side.

There is nothing compromising about this southern side of the Grimsel
as it flings itself at the great green 1,500-ft. slope of the Maienwang.
Broadening immediately after its narrow exit from the village, it snakes its
way across the huge breast of the hills in six long dog-legs, with broad,
built-out walled turns between each.   At each the roofs of Gletsch sink
another couple of hundred feet below into the pit, and the tongue of the
Rhone icefall climbs down from high overhead to meet you.   Beyond it,
across the receding abyss of the Gletsch basin and the baby rivulets twisting
their way between the boulders to knit into a foaming thread of torrent,
the windings on the Furka wall steadily lose height till you are just on a
level with the Belvedère buildings, then above them; and at the fifth and
last hairpin you find yourself high enough to look down upon the crevassed
surface of the Rhone Glacier, level before its sudden precipitous fall over
the edge of the escarpment.   It is not always easy to park hereabouts,
especially when traffic is heavy, for there are few widenings; but if it is at
all possible it is well worth while, in order to scramble a few minutes on
foot to a grassy shoulder above that last great bend, from which there is a
superb view back, especially in afternoon light, to the rocky Dammastock–
Galenstock teeth rising high above the imprisoned stream of ice, the
barren chasm into which its tongue plunges, and the whole length of the
Furka road slashing its angular way up to the dark saddle on which you
were standing an hour two earlier.

That view is soon lost on the last long reach to the crest of the Maienwang, curtained behind the huge spur falling from the Gerstenhörner
above your head; but to compensate you, the distant Valais giants, far
to the west, lift momentarily into view again as you surmount the last of
the slope and the road flattens out at last into the stark and lonely basin of
the Totensee (7,034 ft.).   This sombre lake, on whose dark surface ice is
often to be seen floating late into the summer, owes its name not to the

Stein Glacier and Lake, with the Gwächtenhorn, from the Heuberg-Rank windings of the Susten (Bernese Side)

Looking down the Uri side of the Susten, into the Maienreuss Valley, from near the summit

Looking up the Uri side of the Susten from Maiendörfli

The Furka Pass: Rhone Icefall and Gerstenhörner, from the windings below Belvedère

deathly grimness of its setting, but to the dead who perished in this remote, unlikely spot during a fierce engagement between the French and the Austrians in 1799.

Through this wild and awesome hollow under great stony spurs the road skirts the water's edge for a short way before mounting what proves to be the last short slope to the watershed between the Rhone and the Aar. In a brief half-hour it has annihilated nearly 2,000 ft. from Gletsch to the Grimsel summit at 7,100 ft.

If the little hollow in which the Totensee lies cradled is stern and savage, the crater-like bowl on the other side of the divide below the very rim of the Grimsel car-park merits the epithet titanic, and is terrifying in its grim severity. It requires some adjustment of the eye before you can appraise the scale of this immense cauldron carved out of the surrounding ridges. First you have to take the measure of the scene on which you are looking down—the Hospice perched on the summit of a sizeable hill in the centre, with a service road sweeping up to it from the main carriage-way of the pass, after it has swung in two wide curves down 500 ft. of mountain-side into the bottom of the crater; the two curved sectors of the huge Grimsel Dam, itself over 100 ft. high, barring the entrance to the narrow lateral valley, to pen up a mile and a half of artificial water stretching away to the feet of the Finsteraarhorn, in discreet seclusion far behind; the minute ribbon of the road beyond and below the Hospice, writhing into the crevice by which it finds a way down to the great unseen valley rift to the north, whose presence you can only sense in the gap between cloud-capped ridges, embroidered with hanging glaciers, high up under their spiny crests.

The whole scene is one of utter desolation, relieved only by the beauty of its colouring, for the whole bewildering pattern of the polished rock strata sweeping downward to the heart of the bowl and of the gigantic smooth-worn boulders which everywhere litter the weather-riven slopes is of a wonderful mauvish pigmentation, startling in its intensity when the sun is lighting the scene, black, daunting, grim beyond words with lowering cloud.

When I first looked down into the Grimsel bowl thirty years ago there was a softening touch of beauty now alas removed in the cause of progress. There was no vast hydro-electric dam then, no artificial reservoir drowning the valley along whose green floor the path used to lead to the foot of the Oberaar Glacier, its pent up waters a hideous dirty ochre. Instead there lay at the heart of the bowl a small deep-green jewel of a lake divided into two by the causeway which then carried the road; and by its side, in the shelter of those enormous mauve slabs, stood the old original white-washed Hospice. Then, for years, the long and lovely rift from Innertkirchen to the Grimsel bowl was hideous and noisy with the ceaseless movement of disfiguring wire ropeways, whose bucket-containers whirred restlessly from pylon to pylon, as the massive 100-ft. walls of the barrage rose to block the openings on either side of the central rock mound, and a new Hospice-Hotel appeared on its summit. Then one day in 1932 nature's

L

green lake, the ancient old Hospice, and the old road running by its door were submerged to create a regular-sided man-made storage tank a mile and a half long, capable of holding twenty billion gallons and supplying half the power for the railways of Northern Switzerland.

As so often when man meddles with the mountains, the Grimsel scene is on so colossal a scale that his puny scratchings are in the end visible only as minor changes in detail, contemptuously absorbed by the overpowering and changeless magnificence of the surroundings. Still, if you were ever lucky enough to see the placid green lake glimmering below you in that fearsome setting, it seems to me that what you look down on now is no change for the better.

It is only when you have driven down the two long elbows between the colossal boulders into the heart of the chaos and from its level floor seen the height of the hillock in the middle, with the service road running up over its shoulder to the Hospice, and the enormous retaining walls of the catchment frowning down on you, that you can realize the true immensity of this mighty devil's cauldron churned out of the stony hills.

Then as the road dips, again towards the northern lowlands, with a fine glimpse of the Bächli Glacier high above to the left, there begins one of the most fantastic sectors on any of the great pass roads of the Alps. For here at about 6,000 ft. the Aar, born in the glaciers away behind the reservoir and released now from its controlling gates, comes plunging down to freedom in a series of headlong leaps, foaming and boiling; and through the centuries it has worn a passage a few feet wide through the towering cliffs—now a fine light grey—barring its downward course. Through this it thunders steeply down, frustrated at every turn, swirling and eddying through pools whose rocky rims are miracles of water-polishing, lashing at the walls which imprison it, throwing spray high in the air, where it beats in fury against the craggy barriers, for some 1,500 feet.

There was no room for a road here, so the engineers who had to find a way for one just strung it from ledge to ledge, close above the seething grey glacier torrent, now blasting it out of the living rock which is still left overhanging it, now forced to tunnel through the vast flying-buttresses rising vertical to the narrow strip of sky overhead. So low above the river's course were they forced to go that at times a fine mist of spray is thrown up over the guardian walls or rails protecting the roadway on its exposed side and the carriage-way is wet with it. And so the Grimsel road writhes and wriggles its frantic way like a hunted fugitive down through this veritable slit in the huge base of the Bernese Oberland, to reach the first more open ground for miles beyond the jaws of the rift.

At Handegg (4,510 ft.), in the very exit from the gorge and just before the final tunnel, there is at last room for a slight widening of the road sufficient to produce a usually crowded lay-by. Here everybody gets out of coach or car to lean over the parapet and marvel at the stupendous leap of the Aar, 250 ft. sheer, into an inferno of spray in the gloomy pit below, while at the same time, closer at hand, the silvery cascading Aerlenbach

pours down from overhead and burrows under the road to join the foaming
tumult below.   When the sun is shining and the time of day allows it to
penetrate into the dark and dramatic 300-ft. ditch at your feet, magnificent
rainbows arch the fine curtain of spray in the chasm, to produce a setting
fit for the last scene of *Rheingold*.

Below Handegg, the valley opens out a little, and for a time the floor is
almost level, with the containing peaks and ridges towering higher and
higher above the first dark shields of the pine-woods, as you gradually lose
height and re-enter the world of trees, grass, flowers, and ancient wooden
châlets again.

And so, through Guttannen (3,480 ft.), winding occasionally more
sharply and steeply from one terrace level to another, you float down the
widening valley as if you were in some swift, wheeled boat being lowered
by a series of locks from one level of a green-walled canal to another.
Every yard of the way is lovely, and the great green bases of the hills shoot
up on either side to fantastic heights as the deep Innertkirchen bowl, which
you left many hours and three passes ago, opens up ahead once more.
Everywhere are torrents and waterfalls, one of which gushes in a cloud of
spray over a tunnel in the road.   Flat, flowery meadows now open up on
either hand beyond the pine-railed fences; the old brown-beamed and
balconied Oberland châlets cluster more thickly; a familiar signpost
points, to the right now, in large white lettering on a blue ground—
SUSTEN; this is where you came in, and in Innertkirchen's small square,
with its welcome hotels and verandahed tea-gardens, the round of the three
wild and windy passes comes to an end in a quiet shade.

XXII

THE OBERALP PASS (6,720 ft.)

Entirely in Switzerland (Uri–Grisons).

From Andermatt (Urserental) (4,738 ft.) to Disentis (Rhine Valley) (3,760 ft.), crossing the Reuss–Rhine subsidiary watershed: 20 miles.

Detail. Andermatt to Oberalp Pass (6,720 ft.): total ascent 7 miles, 2,000 ft.

Oberalp Pass to Disentis (3,760 ft.): total descent 13 miles, 3,000 ft.

Open: Early June to November. Maximum gradient: 1 in 10.

A straightforward mountain-road with good windings and no outstanding scenic attractions. Important as the direct link across Switzerland between the Rhone and Rhine basins; also between the Bernese Oberland and the Rhine basin, using the Susten or the Grimsel and Furka *en route*.

Traffic usually only moderate. No difficulties for the driver.

THIS UNEXCITING and not particularly interesting pass is taken next because it provides the direct link between the three great passes dealt with in the last chapter and the three Engadine passes covered by the next.

Its true importance is that it provides the last stage in the long road linking the Rhone and Rhine valleys, thus affording the only direct road (and rail) highway between the extreme south-western and south-eastern corners of Switzerland. The route taken is, of course, by the upper Rhone valley some 20 miles to Gletsch, and thence over the Furka Pass and along the Urserental to Andermatt, where the Oberalp begins (see previous chapter and Chapter VIII, the St. Gotthard).

Directly behind Andermatt to the east, the lofty northerly spurs of the Rheinwald Alps form the watershed between the Reuss, which here turns northwards to burrow through the Schoellenen Gorge to the Lake of Lucerne, and the Rhine rising on its other side to flow at first eastwards. The Oberalp Pass, leaving the main street of Andermatt (4,738 ft.) unobtrusively, immediately winds its way up the grassy mountain slope behind the town in a series of nine wide turns, yielding splendid views back over the diminished roofs and the long, straight floor of the Urseren valley to the Furka at its farther end.

The road, accompanied by the diligent rack-and-pinion narrow-gauge railway, which connects Brigue and Chur (see Chapter XXI, p. 156) and has followed the road the whole way, now climbs into the Oberalp (6,300 ft.), a rather dreary corridor between bare rocky ridges, and keeps on along it for 3 miles to reach the village and station of Oberalp (6,670 ft.). It then skirts the long, narrow Oberalpsee, which occupies the defile beyond the village for nearly a mile, where the watershed lies at the actual Oberalp

Pass (6,720 ft.) with a view of the rugged peaks fringing the head of the Rhine valley ahead.

This is the frontier between Uri and Grisons as well as the Reuss–Rhone divide and, as the road descends the eastern side, the long view down the upper Rhine valley gradually opens up towards Disentis, the considerable town at the foot of the pass. A lengthy slope is traversed in the traditional manner, the road requiring 2 miles and twelve moderate-length dog-legged hairpins to fall to the first village, Tschamut (5,405 ft.), just before which it crosses one of the newly born Rhine torrents. It then continues to fall more directly for 5 miles, crossing several more torrents and passing a ruined castle, to Sedrun (4,737 ft.). Five miles farther on, the green valley levels are reached at Disentis (3,760 ft.), a thriving road junction and resort, with its huge medieval monastery founded by St. Sigisbert and its white-painted houses huddling round a slender campanile among the pleasant meadow-slopes. During its descent the road clings to the left-hand side of the re-entrant, while from high up on the right, in the mountains above the Oberalp, the Vorder–Rhein torrent, the most westerly of several arms eventually uniting to form the mighty Rhine, comes leaping down in a series of cascades to carve a deep ravine through the meadows below the town.

From Disentis the long valley-road runs straight on eastwards to Ilanz and Chur, 30 miles away at the first great northward bend in the Rhine, beyond the gorges of Versam and Conn, deeply scored in the valley-bed and overlooked by the much-frequented holiday resort of Flims-Waldhaus (3,618 ft.) on a high, sunny plateau to the north. A good road leads up from Ilanz to Flims, which, besides providing the usual opportunities for climbs (in the Segnes Group, 10,175 ft.) and high mountain-walks over the Flimserstein behind the village, with wonderful wide views, is famous for its natural bathing lake—the Caumasee, warmed by a hot-spring—and includes first-class tennis and a golf-course among its amenities.

If you are bound for Zürich, Liechtenstein, Germany, the Lake of Constance, or Austria via the Arlberg, you keep straight on along the valley to Chur. But, should you be seeking an alternative to the Gotthard in order to reach Northern Italy by way of Lugano, you turn right at Disentis and take the Lukmanier Pass between the high peaks of the Rheinwald Alps across the valley to the south (Chapter XIV).

XXIII

THREE LINKS WITH THE ENGADINE

1. THE JULIER PASS (7,493 ft.)

Entirely in Switzerland (Grisons). Rhine Valley–Engadine.

From Tiefencastel (2,821 ft.) to Silvaplana (5,958 ft.): crossing the main chain of the Rhaetian Alps: 27 miles.

Detail. Tiefencastel to Savognin (3,900 ft.): 6 miles, ascent 1,100 ft.
Savognin to Bivio (5,827 ft.): 11 miles, ascent 1,900 ft.
Bivio to Julier Summit (7,493 ft.): 5 miles, ascent 1,650 ft.
Total ascent Tiefencastel to summit: 22 miles, ascent 4,650 ft.

Total descent Julier Summit to Silvaplana (5,958 ft.): 5 miles, 1,500 ft.

Open: All the year round, chains often necessary in winter.

From Tiefencastel the road, of average width, climbs, curving from level to level of the valley in lovely scenery until the true foot of the pass is reached at Bivio. Splendidly engineered banks of hairpin-bends take the road on up the boulder-strewn slope to the Julier Saddle (car-park). Famous view of the Bernina peaks lifting above the southern wall of the Engadine far ahead. Magnificent, wide, and finely graded descent curving down to Silvaplana, with three final hairpins on the last slope above the woods, the village, and the green lakes of the Engadine.

Traffic not normally very heavy. An extremely interesting drive, easy to moderate. Postal Motor Route. Maximum gradient: 1 in 10.

THE JULIER is one of the passes for which I have no hesitation in expressing a directional preference. I am sure it should be driven, certainly on the first visit, from the Rhine valley upwards to the Engadine. For it is an example of that type of pass where a long, varied, and attractive approach from the lower levels suddenly reveals a glorious 'surprise' view of great snow peaks from the summit. And even if the Julier summit view were not one of those breath-taking visions, which are all the better for the slow whetting of the appetite before the abrupt moment of revelation, there is still a moment of sheer beauty of quite a different type, as the road drops down the short re-entrant falling from beyond the pass to the Engadine levels only 1,500 ft. below it. It is the first glimpse of the twin lakes cradled in that green valley as seen from the last bends in the road above Silvaplana; and it should be enjoyed facing it from the descent, not behind a reluctant shoulder as it is left regretfully behind.

Tiefencastel (2,821 ft.), where the northern side of the Julier properly begins, is a busy road-junction which can be approached from the Rhine valley by either of two parallel routes. It is also the starting-point of two roads besides the Julier leading to the Engadine—one branching leftwards to Davos and the Flüela Pass, the Albula Pass climbing straight ahead almost parallel with the Julier, to reach the Engadine at Punt, as far to the east of St. Moritz as the Julier does to the west (see below, this chapter).

Of the two approaches from the Rhine valley to Tiefencastel, that through Churwalden and the pleasant resort of Lenzerheide is the prettier, tamer, and more direct. If I have a preference for the *détour* through Reichenau up to Thusis (2,369 ft.), in its broad, smiling valley of the Hinter Rhein, it is because I always enjoy an overnight stop at a comfortable, old-fashioned hotel in that beautifully situated old village, with its straight and

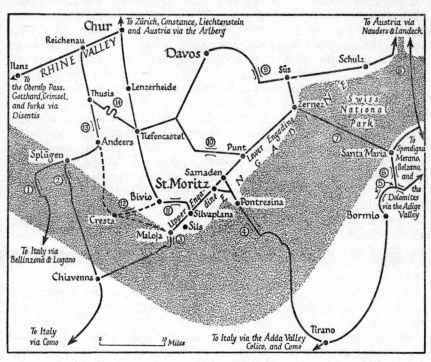

MAP No. 4. THE RHINE VALLEY–ENGADINE PASSES

Passes

1. San Bernardino	6. Umbrail	11. Julier
2. Splügen	7. Ofen	12. Septimer
3. Maloja	8. Resia (Reschen-Scheideck)	13. Via Mala
4. Bernina	9. Fluela	14. Schyn Gorge
5. Stelvio	10. Albula	

narrow hotel-lined street, from which a clutch of postal coaches set out in the morning on their journeys through the magnificently sombre gorge of the Via Mala and over the lofty Splügen Pass to Chiavenna (see Chapter XV).

The minor road from Thusis to Tiefencastel is narrow, steep, and exciting, snaking a precarious way for some miles through the rock of a fairly wild ravine, the Schyn Gorge of the Albula torrent, with the stream brawling down below in the depths. For this reason the less-confident driver on his first Alpine journey may perhaps prefer the approach by the easier Lenzerheide route; but the experienced will find it much more fun.

Tiefencastel (2,821 ft.) is in itself a remarkable spot. Here, where a stone arch spans the roaring torrent penned between precipitous rock walls 60 ft. below, the junction of four major roads and two rivers, the Albula and the Julia, is crammed on to a narrow shelf. Two white-walled hotels face each other across the first lift of the Julier road, the gaily painted balconies at the back of one overhanging the ravine. Crowning a hillock on the other side of the stream stands the slender-towered church, and that is all there is of the place. But if you look up the steep mountainside beyond the church towards the rocky comb of Piz Curver (9,764 ft.) against the sky, you will see a similar church tower, white in the sunshine, doing a perfect imitation act on a jutting terrace hundreds of feet up the green slope, marking the village of Mons. In the morning sunshine there are some lovely pictures to be taken here before you drive on your way up the first windings of the pass.

The road climbs pleasantly but busily, looping its way upwards through the hay meadows with fine glimpses of snow-streaked rock peaks on either side and presently, in 6 miles, reaches the first little plateau housing the tiny but very attractive resort of Savognin (3,900 ft.) with the rock walls of Piz Michel, the Tinzenhorn, and Piz d'Aela (10,958 ft.) rising grandly behind it. Then it climbs and twists again for 6 more miles to another terrace where once stood the hamlet of Marmorera (4,793 ft.), now submerged under the dirty-coloured water of the new reservoir built in 1954 to provide distant Zürich with additional electric power. The road follows the shore of this artificial lake in a wild, rock-strewn setting and then winds up again for 5 miles to reach the highest balcony in the valley, where stands the village of Bivio (5,827 ft.).

At Bivio the Septimer, a pass as famous since Roman days as the Julier itself, starts up a deep ravine in the mountain wall to the right—the Val Cavreccia—and takes a short-cut over the range, crossing a 7,600-ft. saddle, to the Val Bregaglia at Casaccia, thus by-passing the Julier–Maloja combination and saving many long miles for travellers on foot and other heavily laden mules. The track has two branches on either side near the summit, one arm leading down to Maloja, the other across the 8,000-ft. Stallerberg Pass to Cresta Avers and on to the Splügen road at Andeer (see Chapter XV, p. 126). Though regularly used since time immemorial, the Septimer has always remained a mule-track, and is not for motorists. Pass-walkers will find near its summit some magnificent views of the Bregaglia peaks across the deep rift of the valley and of the more distant Bernina giants, in a grand day's walking.*

The Julier road, however, finding all onward progress barred, swings violently to the left and climbs in earnest backwards and forwards across a huge boulder-strewn slope, high above the last level of the stunted pines,

---

* Correction: In the map (no. 4, p. 167) the main Septimer track from Bivio to Casaccia, just west of Maloja on the Chiavenna road, is missing and the numeral (12) has, wrongly, been attributed to the Stallerberg branch.

towards the bleak, narrow saddle slung between Piz Albana (10,184 ft.) and Piz Polaschin (9,900 ft.) still a thousand feet above. This is a wild, bare, and savage sector, and only the backward glimpses, from each successive hairpin-lift, far down the valley by which you have come contain a hint of kindliness and beauty.

The turns are at much closer intervals up the steep, final slope to the saddle and then by a little swampy tarn the road flattens out across a smooth greensward, and on the right of the road is the summit car-park, at 7,493 ft.

To enjoy the Julier summit view to the full it is advisable to leave your car, hot after its long grind of nearly an hour from the foot of the pass, to cool off in the park, and walk a little way down the forward slope of the saddle. There you can choose your own vantage point, and if you are a photographer choose the best foreground of boulder or descending road for your composition.

Whatever choice of foreground may result, you will be looking out through a V-shaped window between the grim and stony slopes of Piz Julier (11,105 ft.) and Piz Polaschin sweeping down from overhead to the Engadine's unseen rift before you. Beyond it again rise the long, snow-dappled ridges of Piz Rosatch and Piz Mortel (11,300 ft.), joined by the low, dark sweep of the 9,000-ft. Fuorcla Surlej saddle. And close behind that snowless, sombre-hued barrier, overtopping it by 3,000 ft. of rock, ice, and snow, there rise into the sky the gleaming heads of Tschierva (11,713 ft.), Morteratsch (12,315 ft.), and the Bernina (13,295 ft.) herself, the polished blade of the Biancograt slashing like a knife from the deep notch between the great peaks to her proud 13,000-ft. crest.

From the Julier Saddle, on the northern side, the downward road is a broad, splendidly surfaced, easily graded modern road, neat and tidy between its spaced-out boundary stones, with hardly a curve of note to it as it follows the Ova de Vallun torrent, till the last slope down into the Engadine above Silvaplana's roofs causes it to take a trio of wide sweeps to meet the pine-woods.

And here is the second surprise of the Julier road. As you descend from the pass, the great white peaks have long since retired behind the intervening screen, though Corvatsch (11,320 ft.) and its neighbours are in themselves fine enough mountains. Now there suddenly opens at your feet a contrasting picture of the most exquisite gentleness and colourful beauty. A few minutes ago you were among bleak and cheerless boulder-littered slopes of grey rock-rubble. Suddenly you are looking down across the heads of dark pine lances, at a distance of less than a mile and perhaps 300 ft. below you, on the gently curving shores of two unruffled lakes whose colour in the midday sun defies description, set in lush meadow green only less beautiful than their own more turquoise depth, and backed again by the deeper colour of the pine forest steeply banked at the foot of the opposing wall of the valley. Perhaps it is the violence of the contrast, but this seems to me to be one of the warmest, loveliest, most peaceful downward glances among all the mountains I have seen. I cannot think that anyone who sees it for the first time under a blue summer sky, with perhaps a few white clumps of cotton-wool cloud riding high above or among the summits, will ever forget it.

A few minutes later the Julier drops through a typically narrow space between Silvaplana's houses (5,958 ft.) into the bustle and traffic of the none-too-wide main street. If you are bound for St. Moritz you turn left; for Maloja right. Either way you will be bowling along by the edge of one or other of those enchanting lakes in one of the loveliest valleys in the world.

The Julier is, incidentally, one of the few really high passes which the shovel and the snow-plough proudly keep open from one year's end to the other. In winter the Engadine is, of course, one long, crowded, luxurious winter-sports-centre, and communications with it and between its scattered components are of the first importance. So the visitor to St. Moritz and Pontresina, to Sils, Silvaplana, Maloja, and the rest puts on his chains and sails merrily over the 7,000-ft. road to the snow and the sunshine, the ski-lift, and the Samba.

Let us hope that as he passes between the banks of snow piled 15 ft. on either side of his narrow strip of magic carpet, he gives a thought to the relays of hands that operate the cold shovels in all kinds of bitter mountain weather and to the snow-plough teams who spend the cracking winter nights up there on the wind-swept heights.

2. THE ALBULA PASS (7,595 ft.)

Entirely in Switzerland (Grisons). Rhine Valley–Engadine.

From Tiefencastel (2,821 ft.) to Punt (5,546 ft.) crossing the main chain of the Rhaetian Alps: 30 miles.

Detail. Tiefencastel to the Albula Summit (7,595 ft.): 25 miles. Ascent 4,750 ft.

Albula Summit to Punt (5,546 ft.): 5 miles, descent 1,950 ft.

Open: Early June to November. Maximum gradient: 1 in 10.

The Albula provides an alternative route between the Rhine Valley and the upper Engadine, but is less interesting than the Julier. The road ascends the steep slopes of the Albula Valley, the chief feature of which is the remarkable sustained engineering feat by which the Albula Railway (opened in 1903) twists its way up the successive steps in the valley floor through a series of spiral tunnels in the mountain-side and across wonderful airy bridges and viaducts. In the upper section road and railway eventually part company, the former crossing the Albula saddle into the Engadine, the latter tunnelling beneath it.

Traffic normally light. Sharp windings, moderate to drive. Postal Motor Route.

From Tiefencastel (see this chapter, above) road and railway, never very far from one another all the way to Preda, the last village below the mountain-barrier at the head of the valley, ascend the steep Albula re-entrant to Bad Alvaneu (4 miles, 3,285 ft.) near the Schaftobel Fall. Between Bad Alvaneu and Filisur (4 miles, 3,550 ft.) the railway is seen crossing the Schmittentobel viaduct and, just before Filisur, the beautiful, curved Landwasser Viaduct (200 ft. high) leaps over the wild gorge through which the branch-line ascends to Davos. Six more miles of steady ascent lead to another charming resort, Bergün (4,510 ft.), with Piz d'Aela (10,958 ft.) towering finely overhead. The next 6 miles to the small resort of Preda (5,880 ft.) are the most interesting, with the railway performing bewildering acrobatic feats in wide loops and spiral tunnels high above to surmount the steep slopes, while fine views of Piz Uertsch (10,738 ft.) and other rocky, snow-streaked peaks open up at the head of the valley in front.

At Preda the railway enters the 4-mile-long Albula tunnel under the dividing range to come down upon the Engadine at Bevers. The road ascends in wide hairpins past the Weissenstein Inn (2½ miles) to the saddle of the high, bare Albula Pass (7,595 ft.) between the rocky-toothed Crasta Mora ridge (9,635 ft.) and Piz Uertsch, skirting a lakelet on the way. The upper levels of the pass are incidentally a favourite hunting-ground for botanists and entomologists, who find there extremely rare specimens of plant and insect life.

From the summit the road falls along the bed of a stony, sombre valley, with fine views over the Engadine gradually opening up ahead, for 5 miles, to enter the green levels of the famous main valley of the Upper Inn at Punt (Ponte) 5,546 ft., a mile or two east of Samaden, through which St. Moritz is reached in another 4 miles, following the Engadine westwards, and where the Bernina Pass road through Pontresina (4 miles) branches off to the south.

3. The Flüela Pass (7,815 ft.)

Entirely in Switzerland (Grisons). Rhine Valley–Lower Engadine.

From Davos Dorf (5,174 ft.) to Süs (4,659 ft.), crossing the main chain of the Rhaetian Alps: 18 miles.

Detail. From Davos Dorf to the Flüela Pass (Hospice) (7,815 ft.): 10 miles, ascent 2,650 ft.

From the Pass to Süs (4,659 ft.): 8 miles, descent 3,250 ft.

Open: Late May to November. Maximum gradient: 1 in 10.

A long, winding road, well surfaced and average in width, penetrating a series of rocky ravines to the viewless pass. Good descent with one bank of long hairpins to the Engadine level.

Traffic normally light. An easy drive in spite of its height, through somewhat forbidding scenery. Postal Motor Route.

From Tiefencastel, as has already been seen, the Julier and Albula roads start out on parallel courses to cross into the Upper Engadine, which they reach at points roughly equidistant from St. Moritz, on either side of that great metropolis of the area. From the picturesque cross-roads by the bridge over the ravine, a third road pushes up into the mountains to the north-west, passing through Alvaneu (high on the slope above Bad Alvaneu on the Albula road) and Schmitten, then following the narrow valley of the Landwasser for 12 miles to reach the world-renowned convalescent-centre and pleasure resort—more famous perhaps in winter than in summer—of Davos (5,115 ft.).

The Flüela Pass starts at Davos Dorf (5,175 ft.), and is of comparatively modern construction, the carriage-road being built in 1866-7 to provid a short cut into the Lower Engadine, which it reaches at Süs (4,659 ft.). This achieves a saving of some hours over the old route, which dictated a return to and crossing of the Albula and, from its northern end at Ponte, the long descent of the Engadine's straight corridor.

Apart from the time-saving factor, there is, in spite of its considerable height, nothing of outstanding interest about the road either as a mountain pass or for the beauty of the scenery along its route, though near Carlimatte whole colonies of marmots are often to be seen at play. Indeed, its chief peculiarity as a high mountain-road is that on its western side, at least along the 10 miles from Davos to the summit at 7,800 ft., not a single hairpin was necessary to achieve an ascent of nearly 3,000 ft. Scenically, it is for the most part hemmed in by gaunt and uninspiring mountains, precluding any wide or distant view; at the summit the road runs straight and level as a causeway between two sombre lakelets which occupy a narrow, excessively stony funnel between the screes of débris chutes descending from the immense rocky slopes of the Flüela Schwarzhorn (10,335 ft.) and Weisshorn (10,131 ft.) on either side. Here in this chaos stands the lonely looking Flüela Hospice (7,815 ft.). (Flüela, by the way, stems from the old German 'fluoh', a rock or rocky outcrop, and the pass fully lives up to its name.)

From the summit the road descends the bouldery Val Flüela with a glimpse, far below ahead, of Ardez and the Lower Engadine and on the right up the grim Val Grialetsch to the jagged Piz Vadret (10,568 ft.) and its considerable glacier. Passing several winter-avalanche galleries and crossing a torrent, the road passes the Jägerhaus Inn (5,889 ft.) and presently climbs down in several long hairpin curves to gain the right-hand side of the valley, where eventually Süs, with its ruined castle and backed by the three rocky summits of Piz Mezdi (9,598 ft.), comes into sight in the trough of the green Engadine ahead.

If I were already staying at Davos and in a desperate hurry either on my way over the Resia to the Dolomites or intending to cross into Austria by way of Nauders at the bottom end of the Engadine and Landeck, I should use the Flüela as a useful time-saver; in any other circumstances if I wished to reach the Engadine from Davos (or below it)—and especially if I had not crossed the Julier for some time—I should deliberately retreat to Tiefencastel, for the sheer pleasure of driving over that long, high, and wholly delightful pass.

XXIV

THE KLAUSEN PASS (6,390 ft.)

Entirely in Switzerland (Uri–Glarus).

From Altdorf (1,512 ft.) to Linthal (2,135 ft.); 32 miles.

Detail. Altdorf to Urigen (4,200 ft.): 9 miles, ascent 2,700 ft.
Urigen to Klausen Summit (6,390 ft.): 6 miles, ascent 2,200 ft.
Total ascent Altdorf to summit: 15 miles, 4,900 ft.

Summit to Urnerboden (4,535 ft.): 6 miles, descent 1,850 ft.
Urnerboden to Scheidbächli (4,307 ft.): 6 miles, descent 250 ft.

Scheidbächli to Linthal (2,135 ft.): 6 miles, descent 2,150 ft.
Total descent summit to Altdorf: 17 miles, 4,150 ft.

Open: Early June to early November. Maximum gradient: 1 in 12.

A good modern road with a great many fairly sharp hairpins in banks at a number of places, but finely engineered and mostly broad. Gravel surface over the summit, bitumen approaches. Magnificent scenery along the whole road.

Traffic not normally very heavy, but like all the scenic passes much frequented in the high season and especially at week-ends. Postal Motor Route.

THE KLAUSEN, which leaves the main Lucerne–St. Gotthard highway at Altdorf (see Chapter VIII, p. 89) is a fine high pass in its own right, but affords a relatively minor link between the head of Lake Lucerne and the eastern end of the Lake of Zürich, by way of the lovely Linthal valley, Glarus, and Näfels, at the western tip of the beautiful Walensee. It can, however, be used as a through-route to St. Gallen and Lake Constance to the north; or, by way of Walenstadt, to Sargans in the Rhine valley; and so on, northwards to Feldkirch and the Arlberg; or southwards to Chur and the Engadine passes; as well as to the upper Rhine valley road through Disentis and the Oberalp Pass (Chapter XXI), leading back into the heart of Central Switzerland. Its main trouble is that it need not be used at all, for it is possible to reach any of those places by lower and more direct routes; but it is a fine mountain-road, set amid splendid mountain scenery, and is well worth a visit for its own sake.

From Altdorf (1,512 ft.) it swings away to the left into the heart of the great Clariden–Glärnisch group to the east, with its wild 10,000-ft. peaks, and climbs through Bürglen and a number of other villages to Spirigen (7 miles, 3,035 ft.), high above the tumbling Schächenbach, and thence to the finely situated resort of Unterschächen (9 miles, 3,260 ft.), at the mouth of the Brunni Tal, dominated by the 10,290-ft. Grosse Ruchen and its glaciers. In another 2 miles a wide curve winds up a thousand feet to picturesque Urigen (4,200 ft.).

The road now passes through a tunnel and climbs high up on the flank of the Schächental for 6 miles to the Klausen Pass Saddle (6,390 ft.), with splendid views of the surrounding mountains, their glaciers and torrents—the Claridenstock (10,730 ft.), Gries Glacier, Scheerhörner (10,815 ft.), Kammlistock, Grosse Ruchen, and the Windgällen. At the Hotel Klausenpasshöhe (6,050 ft.) the Uri-Rotstock also comes into view.

Beyond the summit the road descends rapidly through the wild, rock-girt cauldron of the Klus and its falls for 6 miles, by a staircase of magnificent hairpins—the scene of numerous motor trials and races—to Urnerboden (4,555 ft.).

Here the long, grassy valley of the Urnerboden, some 5 miles long, begins, and the road continues along it, almost on the level, past the high châlets used in summer when the cattle are brought up to pasture, and with the Clariden glaciers and snow-fields high above to the south. This is Switzerland's largest Alpine pasturage, housing seventy families and more than 1,000 cattle in the season.

At the northern end of the Urnerboden, beyond the obelisk marking the frontier between Uri and Glarus (1,307 ft.), near the Scheidbächli stream, the road falls steeply again by a long series of hairpin curves, with the fine Fätschbach Falls to the right, into the depths of the lovely, green-carpeted Linthal valley, finally passing through a couple of galleries to reach that pleasant summer resort (2,135 ft.) in another 6 miles.

XXV

THE COL DE LA FORCLAZ (4,997 ft.) AND COL DES MONTETS (4,793 ft.)

Switzerland–France (Rhone Valley–Arve Valley, Savoy).

From Martigny (Valais) (1,562 ft.) to Chamonix (3,412 ft.) crossing a subsidiary watershed, both sides of which empty into the Mediterranean: 22 miles.

Detail. Martigny to the Col de la Forclaz (4,997 ft.): 8 miles, ascent 3,400 ft.

Forclaz Summit to Trient (4,278 ft.): 2 miles, descent 700 ft.

Trient to Le Châtelard (3,704 ft.) (Swiss and French customs): 4 miles, descent 600 ft.

Le Châtelard to Col des Montets (4,793 ft.): 5 miles, ascent 1,100 ft.

Col des Montets to Chamonix (3,412 ft.): 8 miles, descent 1,200 ft.

Open: Late May to November. In exceptional winters mid-May–mid-October. Maximum gradient: 1 in 12.

This combined route of two minor passes affords an important direct link between the Rhone Valley, Central and Eastern Switzerland, and Austria over the Arlberg, on the eastern side, and the valleys of Savoy and Dauphiné on the western. This is in fact a splendid 'high-level' route from Innsbruck to Grenoble and the South of France.* Completely modernized in 1956–57, the Forclaz has lost its one-time terrors and the Col des Montets is also a good modern motor-road, presenting no difficulties. The scenery to which they lead, around Chamonix, is superb.

Traffic moderately heavy in the season, but the road is now adequate for the volume.

T HESE TWO passes are given a chapter to themselves on account of their importance as a link between Switzerland and France as well as for the wonderful scenery they traverse.

From Martigny (1,562 ft.) (see Chapters VI and VII) the road follows the Great St. Bernard route for a mile or more to Martigny Combe, where the fine new road branches to the right and, avoiding the sharp, narrow wriggling of the old ascent to the Col, whose savage gradient and extreme difficulty in passing made it such a trying road to drive, swings easily up to rejoin the discredited route in 4 miles and six fine, wide bends, and then climbs on to the Col de la Forclaz (4,997 ft.) without difficulty. The Col itself has no view, but only two minutes to the right is a point affording a fine prospect over the Trient valley.

The reconstructed descent falls in a little over a mile to the resort of Trient (4,280 ft.), with the Glacier du Trient falling from the Aiguille du Tour (11,620 ft.), the most easterly summit of the Mont Blanc chain, high on the left. Passing through a larch wood, high above the foaming torrent for the next mile, the road forces the passage of the wild Tête Noire ravine to the hotel of that name (3,966 ft.), a knoll above which has a good view over the ravine, with the Dent de Morcles and Grand Muveran rising to the north-east. Passing through a tunnel, the road then reaches the

* Innsbruck–Landeck–Feldkirch–Chur–Oberalp Pass–Andermatt–Furka Pass–Glersch–Brigue–Martigny–Chamonix–Albertville.

bottom of the pass and the Swiss–French frontier at Le Châtelard (3,704 ft.), in about 2 miles.

From the French customs, the road immediately rises again into the defile of the Eau Noire de Bérard and in another 2 miles comes to Vallorcine (4,137 ft.), the first French village and the frontier railway station on the narrow-gauge railway from Martigny via Salvan and Finhaut. An easy ascent leads in 3 miles to the Col des Montets (4,793 ft.), the true watershed between the Rhone and the Arve.

Here the wonderful and world-renowned view of the Mont Blanc chain opens up ahead, and all the way down to the valley-level, by long, easy windings through scattered larch-woods, changing aspects of the world of great peaks from the 12,800-ft. Aiguille du Chardonnet on the left, through the glorious Aiguille Verte (13,520 ft.) and the famous rocky comb of the dark Chamonix Aiguilles to Mont Blanc, soaring in its white majesty to nearly 16,000 ft., are an endless source of beauty and delight, along 2 lovely miles of road.

Half-way down the slope at the beautifully situated village of Trélé-champ stands the Col des Montets Hotel (4,650 ft.), which, of recent years, has become widely familiar through its use as the location for numerous films with a mountaineering background, notably *The White Tower* and *The Mountain*; thus ensuring that some ludicrously comic goings-on among the studio breeze-blocks and sugar-slopes were, in both cases, relieved from time to time by glorious shots of the real God-produced mountain scene.

Argentière (4,110 ft.), with its glacier snaking down between the Chardonnet and the Verte, is the highest and, in my opinion, the best holiday centre in the Chamonix valley. There is nothing in the way of ex-peditions on foot, by rail, or by *teleférique* in this wonderful region of peaks, glaciers, forests, and streams which cannot be done as well from it—though it may take a little longer—as from Chamonix, 5 miles down the beautiful valley road, especially if you have the mobility of a car at your disposal.

Chamonix-Plage (3,400 ft.), as its modern appellation suggests, has everything—Lido, Casino, Cinemas, 'le dancing', 'le bar', and milling crowds of worshippers of Mont Blanc (which is not seen particularly well from the enormous township which was once a climbing-village, because it is far too foreshortened from so deep and close beneath it). If you like peace and quiet on a mountain holiday you will not like the most famous, perhaps, of all Alpine centres. Moreover, if you occasionally crave for the bright lights and, when it rains—as, alas, it so often must among mountains—ache for a cinema and a chromium café, you can be at Chamonix in twenty minutes by car from Argentières or any of the delightful smaller resorts in the Arve valley—Les Tines, Les Praz, or Les Houches, below the town.

From Chamonix the road descends westwards to pleasant St. Gervais les Bains (2,680 ft.), and thence over the Col de Megève (3,700 ft.) (Megève itself is another pullulating summer-resort at 3,690 ft.) to Albert-ville, Chambéry, or Grenoble. Also by Cluses and Bonneville, a fine valley-road, to Geneva (for all these roads, see Chapter XXXI).

Gletsch, the infant Rhone, the Grimsel windings and the Oberland peaks, with the Furka road in the foreground

The Furka hairpins with Belvedère and the Rhone Icefall from the Grimsel windings

Tiefencastel, the junction of the Julier, Albula and Flüela Passes

MINOR LINKS

The Saanen-Moeser (4,193 ft.) and Col du Pillon (5,070 ft.)
The Jaun Pass (4,948 ft.) and the Col des Mosses (4,740 ft.)

For the motorist who wishes to proceed from the Oberland, anywhere in the neighbourhood of Thun or Interlaken to the Rhone valley and the Lake of Geneva, without exploiting any of the major Swiss passes *en route*, there is a pleasant and easy direct route by one of two minor inter-connecting passes, the Saanen-Moeser and the Col du Pillon.

The former, so gentle and low as hardly to qualify for the name of ' pass ', leaves the Lake of Thun at Spiez, with an immediate lovely view of the 12,000-ft. Blümlisalp, as the road runs almost level at first across a small plain. It then enters the gentle valley of the Simme, which it ascends steadily, through Erlenbach and Boltigen, to Zweisimmen (3,087 ft.), where the upper Simmental road branches off to the left to Lenk (3,510-ft.), the well-known resort at the foot of the 10,665-ft. Wildstrubel.

Here, too, the rather higher Jaun Pass road (4,948 ft.), narrow in places but scenically attractive, goes off to the right on its 60-mile journey to Vevey on the Lake of Geneva.

The Saanen-Moeser now rises gently through the charming meadows ahead, reaching its 'summit' almost imperceptibly in 5 miles at 4,193ft. It then curves equally gently down to Saanen (3,326 ft.) at its southern end —a similar distance. Here the road divides again, the left-hand end running through pretty country by way of the well-known summer resort of Gstaad (3,450 ft.) to Gsteig (3,911 ft.) 7 miles farther on, where the delightful and easy road over the Col du Pillon (5,070 ft.) begins. The other branch leads to Chateau d'Oex and over the modern but slightly lower Col des Mosses (4,740 ft.) back into the south side of the Pillon road on its descent to Aigle (1,358 ft.) in the main Rhone valley.

The Pillon winds easily for 5 miles up to its 5,000-ft. summit under the great crags of the Diablerets (10,650 ft.) and then descends through the summer resorts of Les Diablerets (3,822 ft.) (4 miles) and Le Sepey (3,208 ft.) (9 miles) and onward by the fine wide gorge of the Grande Eau for another 9 miles to Aigle. On this long descent, which affords fine views ahead over the Rhone basin and the 10,000-ft. Dents du Midi beyond, there are frequent exhortations not to loiter for fear of falling stones from the cliffs overhead.

At Aigle you are only a few miles from the western head of Lake Geneva if you turn right, and less than twenty from Martigny, on the way to the Simplon, if you turn left. The old town, a little off the main highway, is also a pleasant place for a break in the journey, with hotels and *confiseries* to suit the most exacting taste.

The Saanen-Moeser, by the way, is always open, the Col des Mosses usually so, with chains necessary at times in winter; the Jaun Pass is open from mid-April to late November, and the Pillon from mid-May to late November.   There are no gradients exceeding 1 in 10 on any of these roads.

PART V

TWO GREAT SUBSIDIARY LINKS

XXVII

THE ARLBERG PASS (5,912 ft.)

Entirely in Austria (Illtal–Valley of the Inn).

From Bludenz (1905 ft.) to Landeck (2,677 ft.), crossing a subsidiary watershed (Silvretta–Allgaü Alps) between the North Sea and the Black Sea: 42 miles.

Detail. Bludenz to Langen (3,990 ft.): 23 miles, ascent 2,100 ft.
   Langen to Arlberg Pass (5,912 ft.): 5 miles, ascent 1,900 ft.
Total ascent Bludenz to the Pass: 28 miles, 4,000 ft.

   Arlberg Pass to St. Anton (4,275 ft.): 5 miles, descent 1,600 ft.
   St. Anton to Landeck (2,677 ft.): 19 miles, descent 1,600 ft.
Total descent Arlberg Pass to Landeck: 24 miles, 3,200 ft.

Open: Usually open, chains sometimes necessary in winter.

The Arlberg is a long, easy pass, rapidly being modernized into a wide, modern motor-road, with a few steep, narrow, winding sections, near the top of its western side, still remaining. It is the historic through-route from Eastern Switzerland into Austria, and passes through interesting but undramatic mountain scenery. Facilities are available for rail transport through the tunnel (Langen–St. Anton) when the pass is (rarely) blocked by snow.

Traffic moderate to heavy in summer, but not normally uncomfortably so. The road presents no difficulties for the driver, though the usual care is necessary at some sharp bends at upper levels. Maximum gradient: 1 in 7.

CONSIDERING ITS importance as an artery and the distance between its two end points, the Arlberg, like other passes on which a main railway line accompanies the motor-road for the greater part of the way, is somewhat unexciting. Its long corridor, in which the road never really gets above the tree line, is too consistently and too steeply dominated by the great green, forest-covered slopes on either side; its saddle when reached is self-effacing and relatively viewless; and its engineering problems are not sufficiently exacting to have evoked any particularly imaginative treatment.

This long and vital international link is, however, equally pleasant whichever way it is taken; and the logical approach would seem to be from the plains of Switzerland into Austria, as a first passage through the mountain gateway, beyond which lie the alps of Austria and of Italy with their great highways—the Dolomite passes beyond the Brenner and the Glocknerstrasse farther east.

Let us look at it, then, as the driver sees it who has come, perhaps, by way of Bâle and Zürich, or maybe from Constance and Rorschach, along the lovely shores of Swiss lakes and through the trim fields and villas of Switzerland's eastern border, where he has crossed—almost without noticing it—the small independent principality of Liechtenstein, lying between him and the high lift of the Vorarlberg mountains to the east.

Heading north for a moment along the upper Rhine valley, by-passing Vaduz, the tiny capital of the Principality, a place of only 3,000 inhabitants, he comes to the busy railway-junction of Feldkirch on the Austrian frontier, just short of which the customs formalities take place.

The road, leaving the town by a short but impressive gorge, swings due east towards the mountains and, with the main railway to Vienna and Eastern Europe as its constant though often unobtrusive companion, heads straight for the tall barrier ahead. Accompanying it too, and not so unobtrusively, for the first 15 miles to Bludenz, are several lines of huge pylons carrying high-tension power along the broad and level floor of the green valley of the Ill.

At Bludenz, an industrial town with an attractive old quarter, the road begins its long 18-mile ascent to the top of the pass, at first in gentle steps from terrace to terrace of meadow-land, with some fine, fast sections of modern road linking the steeper rises. A great deal of building and widening was going on here in the autumn of 1956, and the whole western side of the pass may well be modernized by now.

About a mile after leaving Bludenz, the new Montafon–Silvretta toll-road forks off into the mountains to the right. This fine but rather narrow high mountain-road, opened in 1954, is one of two recently constructed by-passes to the Arlberg route; the other and less interesting, the Hochtannberg (5,232 ft.), runs through the Allgaü ranges to the north, through Schröcken and Lech, and was completed in 1953. Neither has been treated in this book as a main Alpine pass, because the Arlberg still remains the most direct and speediest major highway link between Switzerland and Austria. For anyone with the time and inclination, however, the artificially created Montafon–Silvretta 'pass' affords a splendid mountain drive, whose numerous and finely engineered hairpins lift him to 6,666 ft. in the very heart of the snowy Silvretta Group, lying so close to the north of the Arlberg, but hardly seen from it. This longer route, forming two sides of a triangle, and running through magnificent scenery, rejoins the direct pass just short of Landeck, at its eastern foot. The Silvretta road is subject to a toll.

The old Arlberg road ascends pleasantly through the meadows and slopes of Braz, Dalaas, Danöfen, and Klösterle in the Klostertal, the valley of the Alfenz, to Langen (3,990 ft.). Here the railway, which has for the most part clung to the slopes high above the road to the left, is seen below on the right, with the western end of the double-track Arlberg Tunnel, 6 miles long, built in 1880–3 at a cost of £1,300,000, just beyond Langen station. An alternative route on a goods-truck is thus always available if the top of the pass is blocked by snow.

A steep section of about a mile at 1 in 10 brings the road to Stuben (4,600 ft.), which has grown in a generation from a small cluster of châlets to a popular resort with several large modern hotels. And here the modern mountain road to the more famous winter-sports centre of Zürs climbs away along the mountain-side to the north, continuing across the intervening range to Lech on the Hochtannberg road (see above).

Only a short, bare slope separates Stuben from the Arlberg Saddle (5,912 ft.), the watershed between the Alfenz and the Rosanna, flowing eastwards to join the Inn at Landeck. This is the only point on the route where the scenery grows for a moment even moderately wild, and a fleeting impression of a high mountain crossing is evoked. The road swings right from the last houses of the village and twists its way up the projecting mountain shoulder in half a dozen steep and somewhat sharp hairpins, which may not be susceptible to modernization; for they remain much as I remember them from my first crossing of the pass in 1913, when, on an icy road early one morning, our temperamental Minerva Landaulette jibbed at each of them in turn, and I was kept warm by the duty which had been allotted to me as the youngest and most active member of the party, dodging round behind like a scrum-half in reverse and dumping a large and heavy block of wood against one of the rear wheels, in the hope of arresting the car's tendency to roll backwards even with the brakes on.

After the hairpin-bank there are several curves and sharp windings along the rather bleak left-hand slope to the summit (5,912 ft.), a small level saddle, occupied by the usual cluster of buildings. Here and for the 2 miles of descent to St. Christoph (5,740 ft.), the first village on the other side, the road has been modernized and the windings are broad and finely surfaced.

From St. Christoph to the famous winter-sports resort of St. Anton (4,275 ft.), 6 miles below, the road falls steeply, but its windings along the abrupt contours of the left-hand side of the narrow valley are excellently engineered and the surface is very good.

From the summit down to St. Anton's very narrow main street, below which the Arlberg Tunnel at last emerges from its long, dark passage under the saddle, the views from the road are very restricted, for the sombre, forest-covered slopes on the other side of the valley are close at hand beyond the stream in its deep ravine, and immensely steep and high. As at other points on the ascent to the pass, occasional and tantalizing glimpses of the tops of the Silvretta peaks materialize and are whisked away as the narrow entrances of deep lateral valleys to the south are passed all too swiftly.

Below St. Anton, however, the valley opens out somewhat, and the road shares its pleasant green bed with the river, which it crosses near Pettneu (3,950 ft.), and the railway on the far side. The road has been progressively rebuilt on this side of the pass and, except for a few sections of the original carriage road, rapidly being eliminated, is now a wider modern highway, well surfaced and well walled where protection is necessary. So far as is possible with a road which continually contours a steep mountain slope, the number of sharp bends has been brought down to a minimum, but a few still exist.

After a short section along this small green plain between the towering pine slopes, the road falls more steeply again, weaving its way along the left-hand wall, high above the river, through the hamlets of Schnamm,

Flirsch, and the larger village of Strengen (3,355 ft.) (extensive road building for some distance in 1956–7).

The valley at last begins to open out, revealing wider views ahead of the broad floor of the Inn valley still far below, and the chain of heavily wooded mountains containing it on the north.   The road steepens again and winds its way down the mountain-side towards the level of the main valley in numerous curves, but without the need to resort to a single hairpin turn.

Near Pians (2,990 ft.), the last village before Landeck, the other leg of the Montafon–Silvretta toll-road comes tumbling into the main Arlberg route from Galtur in a fine staircase of hairpins to the right.   Shortly afterwards, the road enters charming old Landeck itself, with its castle dominating the ravine from its rocky bluff, its lofty bridges, and its ancient coaching hotels, straddling the jaws of the Rosanna valley at its confluence with that of the Inn, which here comes racing through a narrow gateway to the south on its way down from the Engadine, then swings eastwards on its way to the Danube, along the deep, wide trench which houses it all the way through Innsbruck to the Kufstein gap.

From Landeck the main Austrian highway runs straight, level, and fast along that broad valley-floor, passing the Oetztal turning a mile or two short of Imst, to Innsbruck, 48 miles away.

If, however, you are bound for Merano, Bolzano, and the Dolomites by the shortest route, or plan to cross the Stelvio from north to south, or intend to visit the Lower Engadine, your road swings away to the right at Landeck, climbing away south-eastwards over the Reschen-Scheideck (Resia) Pass (Chapter XIX), past the delightful gorges of the Inn at Hochfinstermünz and then down gently into the upper reaches of the infant Adige; this is a beautiful valley-road to Merano, with the great wall of the Oetztal peaks to the north of you in its later stages and the magnificent Ortler Group to the south.   The road to the Engadine goes off to the right at Nauders (p. 145), the Stelvio Pass at Spondinig (Spondigna) (pp. 146, 191).

Julier Pass. Summit
windings on the Northern
side, above Bivio

The Flüela summit. The
Hospice and Lake, with the
Schwarzhorn

St. Anton, on the Arlberg road

Looking down the Trafoi windings from the Stelvio summit

The Meije from the Lautaret road at La Grave

Val d'Isère and the Mont Pourri from the top of the Iseran windings

The ascent from the Lautaret to the Galibier, with the Écrins in the background

XXVIII

THE STELVIO PASS (9,042 ft.)

Entirely in Italy (Adda Valley and Lake Como–Upper Adige Valley).

From Bormio (4,019 ft.) to Spondigna (Spondinig) (2,903 ft.), across the main ridge
    of the Ortler Group; both sides of which empty into the Adriatic:
    30 miles.

Detail. Bormio to 4th Cantoniera (Junction with Umbrail Pass) (8,160 ft.): 12
        miles, ascent 4,100 ft.
        4th Cantoniera to Stelvio Summit (9,042 ft.): 1 mile, ascent 900 ft.
Total ascent Bormio to Stelvio Summit: 13 miles, 5,000 ft.

        Summit to Trafoi (5,055 ft.): 8 miles, descent 4,000 ft.
        Trafoi to Spondigna (2,903 ft.): 9 miles, descent 2,150 ft.
Total descent Summit to Spondigna: 17 miles, descent 6,150 ft.

Open: Late June to mid-October. Maximum gradient: 1 in 9.

The Stelvio is not in itself an essential through-route, but is one of the most
magnificent mountain passes to be driven by experienced drivers for its own sake.
Till 1936, when the Iseran (Chapter XXX) was opened, the highest motorable pass
in Europe, it has only surrendered that honour by a matter of 46 ft., and is incomparably finer from the scenic angle: indeed, many consider it scenically the
finest of all the Alpine passes. The road itself is also a marvel of engineering
skill, the huge rises on both sides being overcome by some fifty hairpin bends
on either approach, the forty-eight on the north side between the summit and
Trafoi being probably the finest continuous hairpin sector in the Alps.

On the southern side the road worms its way up the immensely deep Braulio
Ravine, clinging from side to side and tunnelling frequently, between towering
rock walls, to the more open basin at the 4th Cantoniera, where the Umbrail
Pass (Chapter XVIII) comes in from the left. From the junction to the summit
is little more than a mile, the road winding more gently up 900 ft. of shaly slope,
but still relatively viewless.

From the summit, where the famous Ortler view is suddenly revealed, the
Trafoi windings lead down in face of superb views of peaks and glaciers to
Trafoi, just below the tree line. The rest of the road, falling along the Trafoibach
to the Adige levels in the main valley, is a pleasant descent with fine views ahead
of the Zillertal (Austrian) Peaks in the main Alpine chain.

Traffic can be heavy in the season and especially at week-ends (coach-trips
daily and Italian Postal Motors). No difficulty for experienced pass-drivers, but
might worry a novice or one not accustomed to looking down considerable slopes
while driving. Wonderfully engineered and surfaced corners: moderate
width throughout and gravel-surfaced in some sections.

W HEN I FIRST made acquaintance with the Stelvio, in the days of a
diligence drawn by three white horses, whose progress was heralded by
blasts physically blown on a post-horn by the gentleman in charge, it was
undeniably the King of the Alpine passes not only by virtue of superior
height and the magnificence of its approach to the snowy shoulders of a
high and splendid mountain, the Ortler* (12,800 ft.); it also possessed
that added sense of international dignity and importance which customs

* See footnote p. 24.

185

houses and frontiers somehow lend to high roads linking adjoining countries.

Not many years later, the first of two world wars resulted in a tragic re-adjustment of boundary lines, and a great slice of typically Austrian country, with typically Austrian inhabitants, language and habits—the South Tyrol—was surcharged 'Italy' on the map of Europe. In the process, the frontier which had separated Austria from Italy at the Stelvio saddle—the Stilfserjoch—where, too, the eastern corner of Switzerland came so close that the little view-point peak above the Hospice was charmingly and aptly called the Dreisprachenspitze, or Peak of the Three Languages—moved some miles northwards to the crest of the Oetztal–Zillertal–Tauern chain of the Central Austrian Alps. From that day the whole of the Stelvio road, from Bormio in the Val Tellina at its Italian foot to Spondinig, transmogrified into Spondigna, at its northern, in the Etschtal, now the upper valley of the Adige, lay in Italian territory.

In spite of the disservice done to it by that now long-distant and arbitrary demotion from international to purely intra-national status, I venture to suggest that this truly glorious road, imaginative in its concep-tion as it is superb in its engineering, still retains pride of place among the mountain-roads of Europe. Some indefinable quality of sentimental thrill may perhaps have been filched from it, but its essential dominance remains unimpaired as it vaults uncompromisingly from north to south across the highest saddle any major road had yet dared to tackle in the days when it was first conceived and constructed.

And though its carriage-way and impudently daring corners may now be a trifle wider, equipped with concrete surfaces and retaining-walls where once there were dusty ruts and white-washed guardian stones, its actual course up to those tremendous heights is the same as it always was in the days of horses and jingling bells. For a very good reason, too, which applies generally to all the major passes; if there was going to be a road up there over the divide, there was only one way it could be got there —the way it took then and the way it goes today. The great passes of the Alps do not change greatly over the years. Minor improvements and adjustments continue to be made as the demands of the traffic alter in kind and grow annually heavier; the passes remain essentially the same. That is, and has been for me over forty years, their greatest charm and attraction. Each of them has remained the same great experience renewed every time I have passed that way, on foot, by carriage, or driving a modern car which reduced the length of time taken by six; each of them is an old friend whose face has changed only by a few surface wrinkles in all that time; each has kept its individuality—and how different each of them is in character and lineaments from the other!—distinguishing it from its cousins, its sisters, its aunts, and its neighbours just as sharply as face and form and speech distinguish our lifelong friends.

The Stelvio is one of the few great passes which leaves me without a distinct preference for the end from which it should first be driven. The doctrine of the surprise summit-view delayed till the last moment dictates the southern approach; that of the logical ascent towards the dominant snow peaks instead of the continual regretful over-the-shoulder glance as they are left behind on the withdrawal from the heights, the northern. The happy fact is that whichever way you take it, the Stelvio is magnificent.

On balance, I think I should still recommend the southern approach for the driver coming to it on his first visit. After all, if he finds the route as wonderful as I think he will, he can always arrange to come back the opposite way on his homeward journey, or drive it in the opposite direction another time. I think he will want to come back to it; for the Stelvio is not the kind of pass one wants to see only once.

Coming from the south, then, with the narrow, twisting road along Lake Como behind you and the long, sun-drenched high road up the Adda valley allowing of more speedy progress between the fruit orchards and the famous Valtellina wine slopes, reaching up to the huge green mountains on either side, you pass through Sondrio and Tirano (where the Bernina road dives leftwards into the jaws of its narrow side valley— Chapter XVII). Here also, just before Tirano, a right-hand turning crosses the Adda and leads up the mountain slope on the other side of the valley to the easy and beautiful Aprica and Tonale passes, respectively 3,875 and 6,181 ft., providing a direct link with the Dolomites by way of the Adige's lower valley, which is reached at Mezzolombardo, 8 miles above Trento and 25 miles below Bolzano. This is a delightful journey of about 75 miles of lovely mountain motoring.

Sondrio (1,140 ft.) and Tirano (1,475 ft.) are typical white-walled Italian towns, with picturesque church towers and interesting church interiors. From Tirano the pleasant Valtellina continues straight and hardly less wide for 25 miles, rising gently to Bormio (4,020 ft.). A few glimpses of obviously lofty peaks, snow-streaked except in the hottest of summers, off to the right, overtopping the containing wall, are the first hint that you are approaching one of the great mountain-groups of the Alpine chain. Then suddenly Bormio lies before you, snugly set in the last level of the valley, and close behind it the great barrier rises unbroken to east and west, effectively blocking all apparent means of further progress.

Bormio is a pleasant little town, boasting at least one famous inn whose tradition survives from the coaching days, when you put up your tired horses overnight at the foot of the next day's tremendous undertaking— the crossing, by the following evening, of the 20 miles to Trafoi on the other side of the Alps. It can now be done comfortably, but without due attention to all there is to be seen along the road, in two hours.

The road immediately sweeps up in wide curves through the meadows to the Baths of Bormio (4,380 ft.), tucked in on the first step at the very feet of the great mountain wall, and then devotes itself in earnest to over-coming the rise of 5,000 ft. in 12 miles which brings you to the summit of the pass, without unduly pushing the car, in an hour.

To do so it forces its way up the narrow ravine of the Braulio, with magnificent rock walls towering on either side to the little strip of sky between their opposing crests. For some time it clings to the left-hand side, then crosses the torrent to a ledge on the other, where it is forced to resort not only to short banks of built-out hairpins with their familiar black-and-white striped safety barriers, but also to three fairly lengthy tunnels in the course of a mile or so. Climbing steadily by numerous hairpins—there are nearly fifty on either side of the pass—it lifts you rapidly into the rarer atmosphere of 6,000, 7,000, and 8,000 ft., while the rocky screens on either side diminish swiftly in stature. Then at the eleventh mile the road emerges at last from the imprisoning gorge to enter a high, relatively open basin at a level of about 8,000 ft., where the Umbrail road, rising from Swiss territory at Santa Maria, joins in on the left.

(The Umbrail (Chapter XVIII) is not a true pass in its own right, forming as it does a spur from below the Stelvio saddle to the valley-level in Switzerland, and climbing or descending all the way, according to the direction in which it is used. Its main purpose is to link the Stelvio road with the Engadine without having to follow the whole length to Spondigna and then take a tedious *détour* up the Adige valley to Schluderns (Sluderno) (Chapter XVIII, p. 142), where it would again be necessary to turn left-handed to reach Santa Maria (Chapter XIX, p. 145)—a circuit of many unnecessary miles.)

From the junction with the Umbrail, at the Fourth Cantoniera of Santa Maria (8,160 ft.), to the saddle, on which the Hospice is now visible ahead, is only a few minutes' drive; but you are still almost entirely shut in by ridges lifting overhead. It is not till you swing out on to the tiny plateau at the crest of the pass, 9,042 ft., that the overwhelming view to the northward is revealed with breath-taking suddenness.

The impact of the Ortler's great snowy dome (12,800 ft.) crowning 6,000 ft. of precipitous rock, with the great riven tongue of the Unter-Ortler Glacier cascading below you into the depths between it and the snowy summits of the Gran Zebru (Königsspitze, 12,655 ft.) and the Cristallo—all so close before you that it almost seems possible to touch them—is such that at first it is difficult to take in any other details of the scene. The great 12,800-ft. peak still lifting the height of Snowdon above you seems to fill the whole earth and sky with its magnificence and bulk.

Then, gradually, drawn downwards by the plunging line of rock-face and icefall circling the right-hand sector of the view, the eye swings across to the broad, slanting precipice of rock, out and away towards the valley-levels beyond the deep rift to the north, framing at its far end the distant wall of the Zillertal Alps with their snow-crowned battlements from the Weisskugl (12,290 ft.) to the Similaun (11,835 ft.).

Even more compelling than that distant line of mountains beyond the hazy green of the Adige valley, however, is the man-made wonder of the Stelvio road as it defeats the great slabby curtain of rock between the saddle on which you are standing and the green, pine-clad oasis of Trafoi, 3,000 ft. below at your feet.

Wriggling and writhing, darting and dodging, now this way now that, by a continuous bank of walled hairpins, now built out one above the other

like the landings of a gigantic spiral staircase, now spaced out at the end
of long, straight sectors where it clings to exiguous ledges, the narrow
white ribbon of this incredible road literally slashes its way over a height
differential of over 3,000 ft. of precipitous mountain-side in fifty looping,
swirling bends which leave the beholder almost dizzy as he tries to sort
out the interweaving pattern of its bewildering course.

There are many sets of marvellous windings up steep mountain flanks
in the course of a complete voyage over all the main mountain roads of
Europe—notably the forty-eight noble hairpins in an almost directly
vertical line up the Val Tremola face on the Ticino side of the Gotthard
(Chapter VIII), the long staircase of acute back and forth on the southern
face of the Splügen (Chapter XV), the broad, swinging progress in twelve
great loops up the north side of the Iseran (Chapter XXX), the amazingly
imaginative assault on the east buttress of the Susten, the short, steep
ladder up the Maienwang of the Grimsel and the sheer rise from the foot
of the Rhone Glacier to the Belvedère on the Furka (all three in Chapter
XXI). Nowhere in all these varied victories over verticality is there anything as sensational, from the engineering point of view alone, as the
desperate defeat of the Stelvio north face by road. Set, as it is, within
a stone's throw, across the chasm, of the tremendous upsurge of mountain
and glacier scenery which faces and dominates its heroic traceries, the
effect is overwhelming. Most of the great passes have their individual
and varied glories, of engineering skill and scenic beauty. For me the
Stelvio has everything any of them has, and more than all of them put
together.

There is a little terrace in front of the Hospice, at whose small round
tables coffee in the sun with the great snow dome as a background is a
most pleasant relaxation after the grim, grey climb through the shadow
of the southern ravine. The whole thing is, as usual, vastly improved if
time is taken to walk up one of the neighbouring bumps that flank the
narrow balcony of the pass and so broaden the prospect, which is slightly
constricted by the containing slopes. Certainly, the path towards the one-
time trilingual peak, the Dreisprachenspitze (9,325 ft.), should be taken
till you look steeply down on the roofs of the Hospice buildings and widely
out over icefall and rock-curtain and the piled-up maze of the windings
staggering up the left-hand wall of the (ex-)Austrian side's narrow rift to
meet you. All too soon you will be losing height down them with incredible rapidity and looking steeply up at the tops again instead of out at
them, for once on equal terms. It is one of the places not to be left with
undue haste.

Once on the downward way, however, there is plenty to provide a
different kind of wonderment. Immediately, the concrete-surfaced turns,
built wide out from the mountain face and separated by only a few yards of
straight from one another, lower you so swiftly that at each you look
vertically down on the roof of any car on the next turn below you. And
as you sink, locking-full-over at each walled balcony of a tight hairpin
turn, bend after bend, only some 50 yards apart, so the great helmet of the

Ortler and its ice draperies acquire fantastic stature and go shooting up higher and higher to the sky overhead.

Presently it is time to leave this close companionship with the rock buttresses and the steep ice-tongue opposite, as the road reaches out in longer dog-legs across the face of the precipice whose annihilation is its main business.   Long, straight reaches linked by short pairs of walled-up turns carry the exciting business on, always at the sheer edge of the deep ravine, past the Franzenshöhe (7,180 ft.) and the Cantoniere del Bosco, opposite the magnificent Madatsch Glacier, till at last, just above Trafoi, the last of the forty-eight hairpins wriggles off the great slabby wall on to normal ground, and a level terrace, fringed by spearheads of the first high pines, receives you on its kindly green cushion.   The finest view-point along this sector is at the platform of the Weiss Knott (6,110 ft.), with its marble obelisk to Joseph Pichler, who in 1804 was the first to climb the Ortler.   The panorama of rock, snow, and ice lifting above the pines in the deep rift below, sheltering the little Chapel of the Three Holy Springs, to a height of 6,000 ft. overhead, is truly magnificent.

This is altogether a supreme half-hour of mountain motoring, and I would not like it, for many reasons, to be less; though it is a horrid fact that in the days of the motor-races from Trafoi to the summit Mario Tadini in an Alfa Romeo lowered the record for the upward course to 13 min. 53·8 secs., an average speed of just under 40 miles an hour.   Well, if he absorbed any benefit from some great Alpine scenery it must have been on some other occasion, when off duty.

The pine-woods of Trafoi (5,055 ft.) are a gentle relief after so much stark grandeur.   Here there stood in the coaching days a huge white, black-beamed hotel where passengers in either direction used to spend the night, with the great climb before them next morning or safely behind them in a long day from distant Bormio.   It was entirely burnt down in 1913, and perhaps it was the smoke of things to come in which it was consumed; for these frontier peaks, for all their icy heights, were bitterly fought over between 1914 and 1918.   The charming little hill-station has its modest caravanserai again, but who, nowadays, wants to stay the night at Trafoi, once so busy a terminus for the traffic over the road, when you can easily drive from Bolzano to Milan, or Como to Zürich in a long summer's day?   And yet I have an idea that one day it would be very pleasant to come down over the Stelvio from Bormio on Trafoi and spend all the long afternoon—perhaps the next day too?—idling afoot among the pines with the Ortler peaks lifting their gleaming heads above, withdrawn now and in middle distance; then, the following morning, to turn the car's nose up the hill again for a repeat of those fantastic windings to the saddle, before finally coming down again through Trafoi and Gomagoi (4,175 ft.) (3 miles) on the continuation of the northward journey.

From Gomagoi a narrow spur road (Postal Motor Route) climbs 5 miles eastwards into the heart of the mountains to reach the delightful little climbing centre of Solda (Sulden) at 6,050 ft. and the Sulden Hotel above it (6,235 ft.), set in tremendous mountain surroundings.   It is from here that most of the mountaineering routes in the Ortler Group are under-taken, by way of the Payer and other famous Club Huts.   This side-valley is, by the way, a *cul de sac*.

From Gomagoi the Stelvio road runs prettily down, below the village of Stelvio high up on the left, to the flat valley-levels at Prato, with the snow-capped peaks of the Austrian Alps rising ever nearer and higher ahead. At Spondigna (2,903 ft.), which is more important as a road junction than as a place, it crosses the Adige by a famous bridge, beyond which it strikes at right-angles into the great highway running through the wide, level, and pleasant valley of the Upper Adige.   This road links the foot of the Arl-berg, 30 miles to the west, at Landeck, by way of Hochfinstermünz, Nauders, and the Resia (Reschen-Scheideck) Pass (Chapter XIX) with Merano, Bolzano, and the Dolomites 30 miles to the east; it is perhaps superfluous to add that you turn left if bound for the former, right for the latter destination, for you will probably have a map, a sense of direction, or both, with you.

PART VI

THE PASSES OF THE FRENCH ALPS

XXIX

THE ROUTE DES ALPES

I. THE COL DU LAUTARET (6,751 ft.) AND THE GALIBIER (8,399 ft.)

1. The Col du Lautaret

Entirely in France (Dauphiné Alps; Isère Valley to Durance Valley).
From Bourg d'Oisans (2,359 ft.) to Briançon (4,396 ft.): 41 miles.
Detail. Bourg to La Grave (5,000 ft.): 16 miles, ascent 2,650 ft.
La Grave to Lautaret Saddle (6,751 ft.): 7 miles, ascent 2,750 ft.
Total ascent Bourg to Summit: 23 miles, 4,400 ft.
Lautaret Saddle to Le Monêtier les Bains (4,890 ft.): 8 miles, descent 1,850 ft.
Le Monêtier to Briançon (4,396 ft.): 9 miles, descent 500 ft.
Total descent Summit to Briançon: 17 miles, 2,350 ft.
Open: April to December. Maximum gradient: 1 in 14.

A long and at times fairly narrow road, whose surface varies from excellent to indifferent, especially at the many tunnels, which are usually very wet and rough. Narrow, twisting sectors in the lower gorges and some steeply banked hairpins below La Grave make for slow progress in heavy summer traffic conditions, overtaking being impossible for long sections. From La Grave to the summit and again below it on the Briançon side the road proceeds in wider, easier curves without the same difficulties.

Traffic at week-ends in summer is very heavy indeed, and the growing volume calls for modernization. Moderate, and in heavy traffic, tedious to drive, but scenically magnificent.

GRENOBLE (700 ft.), a splendid city set in a splendid plain at the foot of magnificent mountain walls, is the gateway to the chain of mountain passes driven through the heart of the Dauphiné Alps and on southwards through the Lower Alps of Eastern Provence (Basses Alpes) to the Mediterranean.

This linked garland of passes, loosely known as the *Route des Alpes*,* provides a wonderful mountain highway linking the Isère valley and Rhone basin, into which the Isère flows over 30 miles to the west of Grenoble, with the Côte d'Azur by a high-level route of supreme beauty and magnificence.   Divorced from those continuations—the Cols d'Izoard, de Vars, d'Allos, and de la Cayolle, together forming the *Route des Alpes*— the Lautaret and Galibier respectively also afford direct routes to Italy, if the Mont Genèvre is linked with the former and the Mont Cenis with the latter.

The less adventurous motorist, for whom this book is not written, will be content to reach the southern sea by one of two more direct and less mountainous routes skirting the wild massif of savage peaks which rises

* Often more widely applied to the whole of N.202, from Evian on the Lake of Geneva to the Riviera, and all the mountain-roads and passes joining it from Chamonix, Grenoble, etc.

to the east and north of them. The most direct and least mountainous of these runs due south by the Grasse valley, at the head of which it crosses the modest Col de la Croix Haute (3,850 ft.) to Aspres, Serres, and Sisteron. Thence, by only moderately hilly roads, it reaches Cannes or Nice by way of Digne, Castellane, and Grasse. The other follows the valley of the Drac, crossing the low Col Bayard (4,117 ft.) to Gap, whence there are several mountain and valley routes connecting with the lower end of the *Route des Alpes*, to reach Nice via the Col d'Allos or the Col de la Cayolle (see below, this chapter), or convenient branches leading back into the valley-route described above, either at Sisteron or at Digne, the latter involving a minor road over a pass 4,000 ft. high, the Col de Maure.

Both routes command fine sub-mountainous scenery and involve sectors of quasi-mountain road and the crossing of minor passes; both by-pass some of the finest and most rugged high-mountain scenery to be viewed from the safety and comfort of a major mountain highway anywhere in the Alps.

My advice to the motorist who has not driven the *Route des Alpes* or any of its components before and wishes to enjoy it to the utmost the first time is to take it on his southward journey, returning if he prefers by one of the valley routes described. At least, so far as concerns the Lautaret and Galibier, it is the logical approach, leaving the level of the plains, and soaring, at first by gradual degrees then more steeply, to the heart of the Dauphiné Alps in a climb of nearly 7,000 ft. over a distance of 45 miles. All the way you are driving deeper and deeper into the tangled mass of the mountains and draw near to the feet of the great snow peaks in your approach, instead of leaving them regretfully behind your shoulder on the long descent.

In this way you see them first as remote fragmented summits overtopping the lower ranges and cliffs which contain your approach route, whetting your appetite for the delayed revelation of their loveliness and magnificence, from the first breath-taking beauty of the Meije at La Grave to the unfolding of the neighbouring peaks *en route* to the Lautaret Saddle and the unveiling of the Barre des Écrins at the Galibier summit.

From Grenoble an astonishing speedway lined with poplars cuts straight across the plain, without a bend for some miles, to the ancient and historic town of Vizille with its fine, dark gateway. An alternative narrower and slower route is provided by the true *Route Napoléon*, whose milestones bear the Imperial Eagle, through Uriage les Bains, a slightly faded watering-place 7 miles from Grenoble.

At Vizille (10 miles) the road begins to rise, entering the towering jaws of the valley of the Romanche and climbing gently but sinuously past immense electrical and engineering works, which harness the power of the swift-flowing river, through the impressive gorges of the Livet past Allemont until it emerges at right-angles into the level green valley floor of the Oisans (2,300 ft.). Unfortunately the passage of these fine gorges is not infrequently marred by a heavy sulphurous cloud from the chimneys of the great local industrial enterprises which hangs trapped between the

MAP No. 5. THE FRENCH PASSES

1. Lautaret		
2. Galibier		
3. Col d'Izoard		Route des Alpes
4. Col de Vars		Main
5. Col d'Allos		
6. Col de la Cayolle		
7. Tenda		
8. Larche		
9. Sestrière		Trans-Alpine
10. Mont Genèvre		(International)
11. Mont Cenis		
12. Petit St. Bernard		

13. Iseran		
14. Col du Chat		
15. Col de Grimone		
16. Col Bayard		
17. Col de la Croix Haute		
18. Col d'Ornan		Minor Passes
19. Col de Glandon		
20. Col de la Croix de Fer		
21. Col des Aravis		
22. Col de Megève		
23. Col de Maure		

lofty mountain walls and blots out the light of the sun even on a fine summer's day.

At Rochetaillée, where the road swings right-handed into the pleasant green level of the enclosed Oisans plainlet, with its maize-fields on either side of the river, its tall poplar-trees, and the little grey town of Bourg d'Oisans (2,390 ft.) nestling in the middle 3 miles ahead, comes the first intimation that you are on the threshold of a great mountain complex. For the valley is bordered on either side by huge vertical cliffs of ochreous limestone, strangely striated, and every now and then, lifting over them or between them, you are granted a glimpse of snow-streaked rock ridges and peaks shyly revealing themselves at some distance beyond and above— the shoulders of the Grandes Rousses (11,400 ft.) red as their name suggests, the Belledonne Range (9,780 ft.), or an occasional glimpse of the great ridges towards the 11,000-ft. Muselle in the main Dauphiné Massif to the south.

Bourg d'Oisans (2,390 ft.) is a compact little holiday resort with narrow streets and grey-stoned buildings, not unlike its counterparts among the Welsh hills.   There are two or three hotels, a number of pensions, and a profusion of rooms 'to let', crowded to overflowing by French families during the holiday season.

The main road to the Lautaret crosses the Romanche half a mile after leaving the town.   Just before the bridge, a modest-looking road branches off to the left, and very soon acquiring a very adequate width, begins almost immediately to climb into the limestone cliff bordering the valley on the north.   This beautifully graded modern road swings its way up the almost vertical wall in a dozen wide, well-protected hairpins to reach first the village of Huez, nestling on a ledge 1,500-ft. above the valley around its ancient church-spire, and later, by a few more wide sweeps across the bare breast of the higher slopes, the lofty Alpine resort of Alpe d'Huez at 6,500 ft., 7 miles from Bourg d'Oisans.

Magnificently situated far above the tree line, with a fine view over the Muselle and Ornan peaks across the deep intervening rift of the Oisans, and a more distant one from its immediate environs of the great Dauphiné snows some 15 miles away, Alpe d'Huez, of post-war origins, boasts numerous fine hotels of every category, and though perhaps more famous as a winter-sports centre, can offer a wide variety of summer recreations from tennis to boating and swimming, magnificent mountain-walking, and fine opportunities in the chain of the Grandes Rousses (11,350 ft.) which stand close behind it, for the mountaineer, whether novice or expert. The only asset of a hill station lacking here is shade, and this can be acquired by taking the many attractive walks down towards the valley-level.

Crossing the Romanche, the Lautaret road continues on the level between the poplars for 4 straight and pleasant miles to Pont St. Guillerme (2,435 ft.), where a sudden transformation takes place.   Almost without warning the mountains range themselves in a towering barrier of solid rock ahead, and for a moment it is difficult to see any breach in them.   There are in fact two narrow chinks in their defences.

The more important is that through which the Romanche has bored a narrow way in a series of immense precipitous-sided gorges—the Gorges de l'Infernet—through which the Lautaret road now rises sharply, clinging to ledges in the right-hand (true left) wall, twisting, turning, and frequently tunnelling its way, for about 3 miles to reach the next, more open, step in the valley-level at Le Freney (3,090 ft.). This is a truly magnificent sector of the road, with the torrent foaming in the depths hundreds of feet below and the cliffs fully a thousand feet high sweeping vertically to the sky overhead.

The other gap in the mountain wall at the bridge of St. Guillerme is well worth a diversion. A minor road swings off to the right from the main Lautaret highway just before it leaps into the Romanche gorges and finds, at first, a quiet, unsensational way into the deep valley of the Romanche's main tributary, the Vénéon, which has its springs in the glaciers of the great horseshoe-shaped mass of the Dauphiné peaks some 15 miles ahead to the east and south-east.

Then at Bourg d'Arud it crosses the Vénéon and for 12 miles to its end— for it is a *cul de sac*—at the tiny climbing centre of La Berarde, it piles sensation on sensation as it climbs through a series of wild and precipitous gorges from valley-level to valley-level, past St. Christophe (4,820 ft.) and Les Étages (5,230 ft.), through some of the most awesomely rugged scenery in the whole Alpine chain. At several points the road is perforce so narrow, as it clings to its ledges in the living rock, that progress has to be made from one lay-by broad enough to take two passing cars, to the next (picturesquely named '*garages*'), while traffic in the opposite direction waits its turn to proceed. For the non-mountaineer La Bérarde has nothing to offer but the overwhelming grandeur of the 6,000-ft. piled-up rock-faces of the Écrins (13,462 ft.) and its satellite giants, as seen either from the valley-level or, if an energetic scramble up a rough, steep, and sometimes exposed path is acceptable, from the glorious belvedere of the Tête de la Maye (8,500 ft.). If the ascent to this—one of the classic middle-altitude view-points in the Alps—is undertaken, not less than four hours should be allowed for the round trip from the little car-park by the Vénéon bridge at La Bérarde and back to the comfort of a seat in the car. The view from the top is best in afternoon light; but the average driver will probably prefer not to drive those sensational 12 miles down from La Bérarde in the dark. He may, indeed, find them testing in daylight.

At Le Freney (see above) the main Lautaret highway emerges into a broader section of the Romanche valley and is immediately confronted with the great 300-ft. concrete dam of the Barrage du Chambon (built in 1927–35), which harnesses the Romanche's power for the benefit of the industrial works down below, already mentioned. Here, too, is the first sense of approach to the great snow peaks, with a glimpse of the Meije's dark summit belfry peeping shyly over the intervening ridges. A side road climbs up into a lateral valley to the small mountain resort of Mont de Lans (4,200 ft.), where there is unassuming hotel accommodation and walking and mountaineering in pleasant scenery.

The barrage has formed a deep green artificial lake nearly a mile long, and the road, crossing the top of the dam, climbs steadily along the farther bank, passing through a couple of longish tunnels, whose roofs have never altogether solved the question of keeping out adjoining streams in the rock, and where the heavy plashing of water has usually resulted in heavy deterioration of the road surface.

Emerging on yet another relatively open terrace in the floor of the valley, you drive on for another 3 miles, at the foot of enormous grey cliffs, down which falls at least one superb cataract with a very ugly name common in these parts, leaping 500 ft. sheer in emulation of Lauterbrunnen's famous Staubbach. Along this sector, in summer, the air is likely to be heavy with the scent of lavender, which grows here in profusion and provides a flourishing local industry.

Suddenly the valley contracts, the road is forced into a short, steep bank of hairpins—the only half-dozen on the whole pass—and a minute or two later, after passing another fine waterfall, the Saut de la Pucelle— to the left—you are driving into the narrow main street of La Grave (5,000 ft.), a grey cluster of stone houses clinging to the hill-side above the willows of the Romanche, which tumbles in a deep gorge between you and the sudden stupendous revelation of the lovely, snowy 13,000-ft. Meije, towering—if the epithet was ever rightly applied—on the other side.

The little mountain- and climbing-resort boasts two good hotels on the left of the main road and, opposite them under the shade of the trees, is a car-park and terrace whose invitation it would be criminal to neglect. For the Meije from La Grave—and better still from the paths and minor roads winding up to the Plateau du Paradis behind its church tower and huddled roofs—is one of the glories of the Alps.

Quite apart from the shock of surprise with which she unfolds her creaming glaciers and savage rock-ridges when approached from this direction, and from the inherent beauty of her structure and the lovely sculpture of her draperies, dazzling white and sombre black in turn, there is the overpowering effect of her proximity and height. For from the roadway and car-park at La Grave the 13,034-ft. summit is distant only $4\frac{1}{2}$ miles and lifts overhead at an angle of 30°, as compared with the 16° of the Matterhorn when seen from the main street of Zermatt. Indeed, the real mountain lover and enthusiastic Alpine photographer may well be tempted to break his journey here overnight and continue only after a fuller exploration of the glorious views obtained by pleasant walking on the heights behind La Grave towards the picturesque Chapel of Le Chazelet and other famous view-points commanding even finer aspects of the Meije and her snowy neighbours, the Râteau (12,317 ft.), the Pic Gaspard (12,730 ft.), and many other rugged and splendid peaks.

Beyond La Grave the characteristics of the pass alter completely. As it makes its long, steady approach to the Lautaret Saddle the road swings gently upwards through a broad, smiling valley, curving widely among meadows and corn-fields as it rises. And close at hand, on the right as it ascends, one by one the great peaks of the Dauphiné Group tower grandly

up in a huge wall, broken into first by the lovely green re-entrant of the
Upper Romanche valley, at whose distant head the shapely Agneaux
summits (12,008 ft.) lift their snow-powdered rocks, and later by the steep
Glacier Blanc cascading from between the fierce dark ridges of the Pic
Gaspard and Pic de Neige Cordier (11,830 ft.) almost to the level of the
meadows.   Then, almost before you realize that the considerable ascent
to over 6,000 ft. has been accomplished, you are at the little Inn on the
broad green saddle of the Lautaret (6,750 ft.).

The Romans used this route extensively.   Close by the road is the
hillock—Collis de Altareto—where they laid votive offerings on an altar in
gratitude to the gods who had granted them safe passage, whence the name
of the pass to this day.

The Lautaret summit is not one of those which commands a wide or
striking view except the fine backward glimpse of the Glacier du Bon-
homme plunging from between the Roche Faurio peaks, and the long vista
back towards the lowland levels and the now distant Grandes Rousses.
It is ringed in by minor rocky ridges of no great beauty, dominating it on
all sides.   The true glory of this road is enshrined in the 24 miles of the
ascent from Bourg, and especially in the wonderful section from La Grave
to the summit.

2. *The Col du Galibier* (8,399 ft.)

**Entirely in France (Dauphiné Alps).   Dauphiné to Savoy.   (Valley of the Guisane
to Valley of the Arc Maurienne.)**

**From the Lautaret Saddle (6,751 ft.) to St. Michel de Maurienne (2,366 ft.): 26
miles.**

**Detail.   Lautaret Saddle to Galibier Summit (Tunnel under Col) (8,399 ft.): 4
miles, ascent 1,650 ft.**

> **Galibier Summit to Valloire (4,690 ft.): 12 miles, descent 3,700 ft.**
> **Valloire to St. Michel (2,366 ft.): 10 miles, descent 2,300 ft.**
Total descent Summit to St. Michel: 22 miles, 6,000 ft.

Open: Late June to mid-October.   Maximum gradient: 1 in 8½

From the Lautaret to the Galibier the road ascends steeply in wide bends,
recently modernized, and is easy to drive.   The surface at the north (Savoy)
end of the tunnel is subject to the ravages of winter, and is often in a bad state for
half a mile; recent rebuilding may, however, have removed this defect.   Onwards to Valloire is a fine sector of modern mountain-road, wide, well graded,
and beautifully cornered and surfaced.   From Valloire to St. Michel is a long,
old-fashioned road, gravel-surfaced and somewhat narrow.   Undulating at first,
it descends the last 4 miles in interminable sharp hairpins, high on the slope of
the Maurienne Valley: this exposed section could worry an inexperienced
driver.

Traffic heavy at week-ends in summer, otherwise average; coach trips.
Easy, except for the old section of bends above St. Michel.

Paradoxically, the true summit view of the Lautaret road is from the
top of the adjoining Col du Galibier (8,399 ft.), which here leaves the
Briançon route to cross the northern range into the Maurienne and
Savoy.   In clear weather it would be criminal not to diverge by the
necessary half-hour to that magnificent view-point, even if the direct line

of your journey lies straight on down the Lautaret's eastern flank to Briançon and the continuation of the *Route des Alpes* beyond.

I therefore propose to include the southern side of the Galibier as an integral part of any description of the Briançon route, by virtue of its obvious extension and enlargement of the Lautaret's attractions.

The modern road from the Lautaret summit to the Col du Galibier is wide and well surfaced, mastering the ascent of 1,650 ft. by a series of well-graded bends, easily driven in twenty minutes to half an hour. Just before the 200-yd. tunnel which pierces the last vertical 200 ft. of the true saddle, there is a spacious car-park and a small inn which dispenses refreshments, postcards, and local literature.

There is a magnificent view from here eastwards down the long trench of the upper Guisane valley towards the mountains behind Briançon and far beyond to the distant Cottian Alps and Monte Viso (12,615 ft.); to the south, close at hand, the great Dauphiné peaks stand saw-edged to the sky from the Écrins to the Meije. The latter sector, however, is masked to a great extent by the huge intervening spur of rock, up whose base the road has wound its way from the Lautaret bowl; and in order to enjoy the prospect to the full and to add to it the whole vast northern vista across the tumbled rock ranges of Savoy to Mont Blanc—on a clear afternoon—lifting incredibly over them at a distance of 80 miles, the half-hour's walk up the old mule-path to the true (8,720 ft.) pass and back is extremely well worth while.

From this exceptional vantage point the nearby Dauphiné massif is seen in all its savage crenellated wildness, and for the first time the magnificent ice-armoured north face of the Barre des Écrins, the 13,680-ft. monarch of the group, is seen lifting untrammelled above the screen of the lower Agneaux–Faurio comb, which effectively masks it from all points lower down. Northwards and eastwards, the panorama sweeps away into the haze of immense distances, beyond the piled-up brown and grey ranges of Savoy, the Tarentaise, and the Cottians on the borders of Italy.

In this way the Galibier can be enjoyed as providing nothing more than a 'summit' to the Lautaret. Of recent years there is even a loop road to save your having to revisit the Lautaret saddle down there below; it winds down to join the Lautaret road about 2 miles along the descent on the Briançon side.

Lest this be considered somewhat cavalier treatment, it should at once be said that the Galibier is a fine pass in its own right and affords an important link with the valley of the Maurienne to the north and thence through Modane over the moderately low and direct main route of the Mont Cenis to Turin and Italy (Chapter IV).

The ravages of winter on a north slope at so great an altitude often play havoc with the first half-mile beyond the Galibier tunnel—the last time I went that way there was a complete absence of surface, and a traffic jam caused by the resulting single-line crawl cost an hour's tedious and uncomfortable frustration. This apart, a magnificently graded road with fine views over the stark grey ridges of the Grand Paré now swings down the broad valley of the Valloirette to the pleasant holiday resort of Valloire (4,690 ft.). Beyond, the road is much narrower, and after skirting the side of a green and wooded dale it winds endlessly down the huge steep flank of the Maurienne valley, blue and remote in the depths, dropping 3,000 ft. to St. Michel de Maurienne in a series of somewhat constricted turns, yielding at times a considerable sense of exposure. Not, I think, a beginner's drive, but otherwise a fine road.

3. Continuation of the Lautaret Road to Briançon

From the Lautaret saddle the road dips steadily down the less-interesting side of the pass, following the newly born Guisane down its long, straight valley, lined on either side by rocky ranges from which, as you gradually lose height, dense tongues of pine-forest sweep down into the green and temperate valley-levels. There are pleasant villages here along the road and, just before the valley bends southwards around the eastern wall of the Dauphiné Massif, there is the little resort of Monêtier les Bains (4,890 ft.) with the high rocky chain of the Rochebrune (11,000 ft.) behind it. Lateral vales bite westwards into the main mountain group opposite, whose outstanding feature on this side is the triple-headed massif of the Pelvoux (12,970 ft.), and a *teleférique* now affords easy access from here to a splendid view-point over the great peaks at Serre Chevalier (8,760 ft.).

The descent continues pleasantly rather than excitingly till, 17 miles from the Lautaret summit and 3,900 ft. below it, you reach the fine old fortified town of Briançon (4,330 ft.), whose walls, towers, jumbled roofs, and plentiful hotels are crowded on a rocky hillock which straddles the valley at a point where it is joined from the east by that of the Durance. The provision of historical detail about Briançon is left to the guide-books: suffice it to say that it was the *Brigantium* of the Romans.

The continuation of the Route des Alpes beyond Briançon is over the Cols d'Izoard and Vars, described immediately below. Motorists bound for Italy, however, take the easy Col du Mont Genèvre across the frontier range due east of Briançon, to descend on Turin either by Susa and the Dora Riparia valley or over the Colle di Sestrière down to Pinerolo (Chapter XIII). To the south, the main valley highway follows the Durance, swinging south-westwards through Embrun back towards Gap and Sisteron on the direct high road from Grenoble to the Riviera (see beginning of this chapter).

II. THE CONTINUING PASSES OF THE ROUTE DES ALPES

1. The Col d'Izoard (7,743 ft.) *

France (Dauphiné). Continuation of the Route des Alpes.
From Briançon (4,396 ft.) to Guillestre (3,248 ft.): 33 miles.

* Extensively damaged by floods in July 1957. Temporary repairs effected by October, but surface then still very poor. Although it is intended to have the road in order by summer 1958, enquiries are advisable before driving over this pass.

Detail. Briançon to the Col d'Izoard (7,743 ft.) between the Pic de Côte Belle and the Clot de la Cime: 13 miles, ascent 3,350 ft.

Col d'Izoard to Guillestre: 20 miles, descent 4,500 ft.

Open: Early July to late October. Maximum gradient: 1 in 6.

Steep and narrow, with sharp hairpin bends and narrow bridges. Not too well protected on the precipice side. Great care required. Impressive scenery. Moderate to difficult. S.A.G.A. coach route.

On leaving Briançon, the road immediately rises in hairpins to gain the valley of the Cerveyrette. It then follows a ledge high above the river through a narrow gorge, whose cliffs are crowned by forts, to Cervières, in an open basin formed by the junction of the valley and that of the Bleton, descending from the Izoard. Here there is a fine view back on to the great peaks of the Pelvoux and the 13,000-ft. Barre des Écrins, the highest summit in the Dauphiné Massif.

By-passing the narrow and immensely steep main street of Cervières, the road ascends the valley of the Bleton for 5 miles to the Izoard Refuge (5,905 ft.) just short of the Col, with several hairpins on the way. The neighbouring rock formations, above fine pasture slopes and woods of larch and fir, are impressive, particuarly the turreted south ridge of the Pic de Rochebrune (10,905 ft.) high overhead.

Half a mile beyond the Refuge lies the wide saddle of the Col d'Izoard (7,743 ft.) commanding a fine view of the upper Durance mountains to the north, dominated by Mont Thabor (10,440 ft.) and the Chaberton (10,295 ft.) above the Col du Mont Genèvre. A column erected in 1934 commemorates the *Chasseurs Alpins*, who, in the last years of the nineteenth century, built the strategic roads which were the forerunners of the present Route des Alpes. There is a limited view southwards over the Queyras valley, towards which the road now descends for about 10 miles.

Several hairpin windings lead down to the extraordinary barren amphitheatre of the Casse Deserte, whose yellow-and-white sandy slopes support the strange shapes of orange-coloured pinnacles. The descent to Arvieux (8 miles from the Col) continues through more cultivated scenery of rich green alps and slopes. The little hamlet boasts a sixteenth-century church with a Roman tower.

The road continues down the valley of the Rivière torrent till, passing through a narrow gateway between steep rocks, it emerges into the main Queyras valley—the valley of the Guil—at the cross-roads of Esteyère. Little more than a mile away to the left the picturesque fortified rock of Château Queyras (4,400 ft.) appears to block the valley. In that direction lies the narrow and difficult road which penetrates the upper Guil valley to Abriès and l'Échalp, from which an even narrower mule-track offers the energetic walker a way over the Col de la Traversette into Italy.

It is over that inaccessible, almost impassable nick, just on 10,000 ft. high, in the most savage and inhospitable rock barrier of the whole frontier range that the most recent theory contends Hannibal led his men and his elephants. Well, there's nothing like doing things the hard way!

The main road now turns right-handed to descend the valley of the Guil, westwards, for the remaining 10 miles to Guillestre (3,116 ft.).

This is a truly magnificent sector of the route, forcing its way through the awe-inspiring gorges of the Guil, which the road is compelled to cross five times by very narrow bridges, frequently clinging to narrow ledges 200 or 300 ft. above the brawling stream in its savage trench, and tunnelling three times through the mauvish rock, simply because there is nowhere else for it to go. (Unless the ground has changed out of all knowledge, Hannibal and his elephants must have had quite a jolly time along here in the pre-tunnel and pre-bridge era.)

Then suddenly the view broadens out over the Durance valley, with the Pelvoux and the Écrins rising magnificently to the right, and a gentle descent brings the road down to picturesque Guillestre, with its silvery-grey roofs, backed by the bulk of the rocky-headed Pelvoux (12,970 ft.) and the Glacier Blanc falling from its peaks.

2. *The Col de Vars* (6,939 ft.) *

France (Dauphiné). Continuation of the Route des Alpes.

From Guillestre (3,116 ft.) to Barcelonnette (3,740 ft.): 32 miles.

Detail. Guillestre to the Col de Vars (6,939 ft.): 11 miles, ascent 3,800 ft.

  Col de Vars to St. Paul sur Ubaye (4,820 ft.): 8 miles, descent 2,100 ft.
  St. Paul to Barcelonnette (3,740 ft.): 13 miles, descent 1,100 ft.
Total descent from the Col to Barcelonnette: 21 miles, 3,200 ft.

Open: Late April to late November. Maximum gradient: 1 in 10.

Many hairpins, road average to narrow in width, many steep sections. Careful driving necessary; not always too well protected on precipice side. Moderate to difficult.

After crossing the river on leaving Guillestre (3,116 ft.), the road attacks the limestone escarpment to the east of the valley by a number of steep, sharp hairpin bends. The view back towards the great Dauphiné peaks to the west broadens and improves at every turn, the finest view-point being reached at the lay-by and indicator between the third and fourth hairpins.

At Vars (6 miles, 5,445 ft.) the road enters the valley of the Chagne and then mounts in hairpins for 3 miles through pleasant pine-woods to the Refuge du Col de Vars, 2 miles above which it reaches the Col de Vars (6,939 ft.). The saddle consists of grassy pastures and is completely hemmed in; on it stands a pyramid commemorating the opening up of the route in 1891 by the 5th *Chasseurs Alpins*.

The steep descent of the valley of Riou-Monal beyond the Col provides fine views of the rocky frontier ridge, from the Aiguille de Chambeyron (11,160 ft.) to the Cuguret (9,970 ft.) above the Col de Larche (see Chapter XII, p. 117). Three miles down the slope stands the pretty hamlet of Le Serre, set in meadows, shaded by poplars and beeches on the banks of the stream. As the road descends, cut into black rocks, past Le Mélézen, the Ubayette valley opens up gradually to the right, and to the left the lovely basin of the Ubaye comes into sight below. Two miles farther on, the pass proper comes to its end at Saint Paul sur Ubaye (4,820 ft.) in its

* Also extensively damaged by floods in 1957. Enquiries should be made before driving over this route, as in the case of the Col d'Izoard (see footnote p. 203).

pleasant green plainlet at the foot of the Tête de Paneyron. (The valley of the Ubaye was the scene of much wanton destruction by the Germans at the end of the Second World War.)

The continuation of the road to Barcelonnette takes a wide curve to St. Paul, and many of the villages on the road down the lower valley were seriously damaged and in some cases totally destroyed. It crosses the Riou Monal, reaching the Pont de la Fortune after a mile or so, and then enters the fine gorge of the Pas de la Reyssole, through which it cuts steeply in cliffs of curious stratified rock, the Ubaye below being confined in a narrow chasm at times only 10 ft. broad.

Continuing the descent of the Ubaye valley for 3 miles, the next landmark we meet is the road-junction near Gleiznullas, at which the Col de Larche road goes off to the left up the Ubayette valley on its way across the frontier range to Italy (see p. 117).

The remaining 10 miles to Barcelonnette fall into two distinct sections. The first immediately enters a wild amphitheatre entirely enclosed by rocks, dominated by the extraordinary fort of Tournoux or Grouchy, a visit to which is quite an experience.

A mile farther on stood Condamine-Châtelard, astride the broad Parpaillon torrent, with Châtelard high on its rocky perch. (Condamine suffered total destruction at the hands of the Germans in 1945.) Here, to the right, an amazing strategic road climbs up by a series of exceedingly steep and narrow hairpins over the 8,500-ft. Col de Parpaillon, or rather through a perilous 500-yd. tunnel under it, to Embrun. This is *not* an excursion for the ordinary motorist, but the very intrepid, with a short wheelbase-car or a Jeep, will find plenty of excitement and a very fine view indeed, over the Dauphiné and Frontier Alps and away to distant Mont Blanc, in the neighbourhood of the summit (closed November to April).

After Condamine the main valley-road enters a 3-mile section of wild and narrow gorges, the Pas de Gregoire, where there is frequently only just room for the road and the river to force a passage. Emerging at ancient Jausiers (4,262 ft.), the road traverses a series of immense and bleak débris-cones for the last 5 miles to reach Barcelonnette, in its broad and pleasant valley fringed with willows and poplars.

Barcelonnette is an interesting old town, part of whose ancient fortifications still stand to bear witness to its medieval fame as a frontier fortress, and the *Place Berwick* commemorates the prowess of the illegitimate son of James II who became a Marshal of France and by a great strategic defence won the town and district for the country of his adoption. Here too some surprisingly fine near-châteaux testify to the successful princes of the silk trade which flourished here till in the nineteenth century, it transferred itself to Mexico, but whose well-endowed descendants have since returned to the place which founded their fortunes.

The valley road continues westwards to join the main road along the Durance from Embrun to Sisteron (see p. 196 above).

3. *The Col d'Allos* (7,382 ft.) *and the Col de la Cayolle* (7,630 ft.)
(*Continuation of the Route des Alpes*)

From Barcelonnette there are two routes, both involving high and somewhat difficult passes, constituting alternative final sectors of the *Route des
Alpes* to Nice.   These are the Col d'Allos (7,382 ft.), whose southern exit
is at Annot on the main valley route from Digne to Puget Théniers; and
the Col de la Cayolle (7,630 ft.) leading down to Guillaumes and Puget
Théniers itself.   Both are narrow and extremely tortuous roads and in-
dulge in sections of unfenced progress on the precipice side, which might
make them something of an ordeal for the less-experienced mountain
driver.   Both are also used by the S.N.C.F.* and other coaches, which
daily traverse the *Route des Alpes* in summer, so that progress may be
very much hampered by the difficulties of overtaking and passing.   The
mountain scenery through which they pass is fine and rugged, but on the
whole barren and without any features of outstanding beauty or importance.

The Col de la Cayolle is taken first as being slightly the more direct and
perhaps the more generally used alternative.   Both roads pass through
remarkable scenery, though the wide views near the top of the Col d'Allos
are not matched anywhere on the Cayolle.

4. *Col de la Cayolle* (7,630 ft.)

Entirely in France (Basses Alpes; Provence).
From Barcelonnette (3,740 ft.) to Guillaumes (2,687 ft.): 40 miles.
Detail.   Total ascent Barcelonnette to the Col (7,630 ft.): 20 miles, 4,000 ft.
Total descent Col to Guillaumes (2,687 ft.): 20 miles, 4,050 ft.
Open: Mid-June to early November.

**Narrow and winding, gravel surface, with special care necessary on the
southern side.   Many unfenced sectors with considerable drops below.   A long,
high, and moderately difficult pass.   Motor-coach traffic (S.A.G.A., etc.).**

From Barcelonnette (3,740 ft.) the road climbs into the valley of the
Bachelard, where the route by the Col d'Allos soon diverges to the right
(see below); it then continues along the right bank for 3 miles to Uvernet,
a picturesque village, where the stream is confined by strong embankments.   Crossing and recrossing the river, it then ascends with a view of
the graceful Viaduc du Faut, carrying the Col d'Allos road, on the right.
After another 5 miles, near Villard d'Abas (4,888 ft.) at the foot of a limestone cliff the valley widens, and on the next part of the ascent (past Fours
St. Laurent (5,446 ft.) and Bayasse) the fine cliffs of Mont Pelet (10,017 ft.)
to the right and the Cime de l'Eschillon (8,890 ft.) with its Refuge are
gradually seen to advantage.   It is 10 interesting miles from Villard to the
Col de la Cayolle (7,630 ft.), where the Refuge at the Pass stands on the
north side of an opening between slopes littered with limestone slabs.

The descent winds continually through savagely wild scenery, passing
some foresters' huts at Le Garet (6,550 ft.), near which the Var rises in a
limestone hollow to the left.   Continuing down the course of the Var, we

* See p. 252.

come to Esteng (5,512 ft.), the highest hamlet in the valley, at the foot of Fort Carré, some 7 miles from the Col.

Four miles farther down in less rugged surroundings, lies picturesque Entraunes (4,134 ft.), a small mountaineering centre, below which fine views open up to the Aiguilles de Pélens on the right and the Cime de Chamoussillon on the left.   At St. Martin d'Entraunes (4 miles, 3,460 ft.) there is an interesting Gothic church with an A.D. 1555 reredos and some good Renaissance wood-carving.   Crossing to the left bank of the Var, the road reaches Villeneuve d'Entraunes in another 3 miles: here, too, there is an interesting old church.   The bleak ravine of the Barlatte now opens up on the left, overlooked by Châteauneuf d'Entraunes, while the main valley is flanked by fine limestone escarpments, with a good view back to the Aiguilles de Pélens.

Twenty-one miles from the Col the true pass comes to an end at Guillaumes (2,687 ft.), the chief village of the upper Var valley, charac-teristically southern in aspect, with the remains of ancient fortifications and a ruined castle dominating the little square of the town below.

Below Guillaumes the road crosses to the right bank of the Var by the Pont Roberts and enters the Gorges de Daluis, one of the most remarkable ravines in the Maritime Alps.   For nearly 2 miles the road clings hazardously above the torrent, far below in its narrow chasm, crossing tributary streams by dizzy bridges and threading a succession of tunnels. The vivid red-and-yellow rocks, seen against the green of trees and the blue Provençal sky, provide a beautiful and colourful contrast all the way to Daluis (7 miles).   Four miles farther on, at Pont de Gueydan, the 'Porte du Var' suddenly leads out into the open main valley, down which the road and railway run from Digne through Puget Théniers (6 miles) to Nice, 47 miles beyond.

Puget Théniers (1,320 ft.) is a small town in a wild situation on the banks of the Roudoule, set between the gorge of that torrent and its junction with the Var.   It contains the ruins of an old feudal castle, an ancient church ascribed to the Knights of Malta, some quaint Renaissance houses and the remains of its medieval ramparts.

From here to Nice is 47 miles by the pleasant valley highway, with its occasional gorges and tunnels.

5. *The Col d'Allos* (7,382 ft.)

Entirely in France (Basses Alpes; Provence).

From Barcelonnette (3,740 ft.) to Colmars les Alpes (4,085 ft.): 27 miles.

Detail.   Total ascent Barcelonnette to the Col (7,382 ft.): 13 miles, ascent 3,650 ft. Total descent Col to Colmars (4,085 ft.): 14 miles, 3,400 ft.

Open: Late May to early November.   Maximum gradient: 1 in 10.

Narrow, tortuous, gravel-surfaced, requiring care and attention: generally lacking in protective fencing.   S.A.G.A. and other coaches in summer.   Never-theless a fine pass for the experienced driver to drive, through varied scenery and with a striking summit panorama.   Moderately difficult to drive.

The start from Barcelonnette (3,740 ft.) is the same as for the Col de la

The summit of the Sella Pass, with the Langkofel Group

The Sella precipices from the lower Pordoi road

THE DOLOMITE ROAD

Canazei and the Marmolata

The Pordoi summit with the
Marmolata

Pieve and the Civetta

Cayolle, which is very soon left to take its more easterly course.   The Col
d'Allos road goes off to the right and embarks on a picturesque ascent with
numerous windings.   Rounding a side valley, it overlooks the deep gorge
of the Bachelard and later on skirts the ravine of the Malune to Les
Aqueliers-Bas (7 miles) beneath the Grande Séolane (9,535 ft.).   Continuing to climb through the Bois de Gâche and leaving the hamlet of
Morjuan below, the road ascends an exciting sector, hewn out of the rock
and at places overlooking sheer precipices, to near the summit.   At the
Refuge National just before the Col there is a fine, wide panorama, with a
mountain indicator.   The Col d'Allos itself (7,382 ft.), 13 miles from
Barcelonnette, a saddle between the Sestrière to the right (8,261 ft.) and
the Grand Cheval de Bois (9,321 ft.) on the left (both easily accessible in
little over an hour from the pass), also has a striking view, especially eastwards.

The descent begins by passing the Cirque de Sestrière, passing La Foux,
with its inn on the left bank of the Verdon, after 4 miles and, falling continually for 5 more miles past several hamlets sheltering under sheer crags,
reaches the more open Allos (4,675 ft.) at the foot of the bare, rocky
pyramid of the Roche Grande, an excellent centre for excursions in the
surrounding mountains, and also latterly developing as a skiing resort in
winter.   The most attractive simple expedition is the three-hour ascent
by a winding path of the Mont Pelat (10,017 ft.), the highest summit in the
Provençal Alps, passing the Châlet Restaurant at the Lac d'Allos, famous
for the seigning of salmon-trout.

Beyond Allos on the left rises the curious Roche-Cline (8,373 ft.),
consisting of a pyramid between two almost perpendicular peaks.   Before
reaching Colmars (5 miles) the old Fort de Savoie is prominent, perched
on a rocky hillock, with the Verdon curving round its base.   Colmars-les-
Alpes (4,130 ft.) is a tiny walled town and ancient fortress, attractively
situated in the Upper Verdon valley, and is much favoured by the inhabitants of Nice and Marseilles as a summer resort.   Here the true pass ends.

The narrow main street of Colmars, bordered by tall houses, boasts a
sixteenth-century church and an interesting southern gateway.   The
neighbourhood provides fine easy mountain-walking facilities.

The road now descends the valley, crossing the Verdon below the old
Fort de France, with the handsome pyramid of the Gardette, one of whose
peaks is crowned by a natural arch, rising on the right.   It descends just
past Villars-Colmars (3 miles) on the slope of the wooded Montagne du
Puy and, 2 miles farther on, Beauvezer (3,940 ft.), a quiet little summer
resort.   Presently an arch carries a mountain torrent across the road and
the Crête de Pasquier becomes prominent on the left; while, to the right,
a little above the road, rises the copious spring of the Rieu du Trou.

After 4 miles the descent ends at Thorame Haute (3,775 ft.), a small
summer resort on a green plateau, with a sixteenth-century church containing some good stained-glass.   Here the road to Castellane goes off on
the right.

The road now rises again for some miles, keeping above the left bank of the Verdon to reach the intervening watershed at La Colle–St. Michel (4,941 ft.), whence the 6-mile descent of the valley of the Vaire is accomplished by a lengthy zig-zag. At Le Fugeret the road crosses the river and joins the high road and railway from Digne, to reach Annot (2,313 ft.) in another 3 miles.

Annot is a considerable village set among rugged mountains, full of interesting old buildings, and presenting a picturesque pile of irregular streets on the mountain-side. From here to Puget-Théniers (see above, Col de la Cayolle) along the main valley road from Digne and Castellane to Nice is 12 miles.

XXX

THE COL D'ISERAN (9,088 ft.) *

Entirely in France (Savoy). Graian Alps–Tarentaise.

Valley of the Arc–Upper Isère Valley.

From Bonneval sur Arc (6,030 ft.) to Val d'Isère (6,065 ft.): 22 miles.

Detail. Bonneval to the Pont des Neiges (8,432 ft.): 8 miles, ascent 2,300 ft.
  Pont des Neiges to Summit (9,088 ft.): 3 miles, ascent 750 ft.
Total ascent Bonneval to Summit: 11 miles, 3,050 ft.

Total descent Summit to Val d'Isère: 11 miles, 3,000 ft.

Open: late June to mid-October. Maximum gradient: 1 in 10.

A fine modern road (1936) of fair width and good surface (gravel on south side) ascending the steep mountain-side above Bonneval in an immensely long dog-leg, moderately exposed on the valley side. From the Pont des Neiges more steeply and by some well-engineered windings up the combe of the Lente, finally contouring the huge bouldery slope to the summit in a wide curve. On the northern side, after a gentle descent of the summit corridor for a mile and a half, the road swings down the broad mountain face in half a dozen splendidly graded dog-legs of great length, with finely built-out hairpin turns, to the level of the infant Isère. Thence straightforward to Val d'Isère.

Traffic not unduly heavy normally. Coaches in summer season. Moderate to easy: not walled on the valley side and mildly exposed in places, but the road is broad and there is plenty of passing room.

TILL 1932 THE Col d'Iseran was a humble and somewhat obscure mule-track 10 miles long, providing a highly convenient short cut between the upper Isère valley and the head-waters of the Arc, a journey which if executed at valley-level required a fantastic *détour*. By carriage road this added up to some 130 miles, for there was no alternative but to start off in precisely the opposite direction, descend to Bourg St. Maurice, turn west there the length of the Isère valley through Moutiers to Albertville, then sharply back into the valley of the Arc at Aiguebelle and so to climb eastwards to your objective by the endless Maurienne road through St. Jean, St. Michel, Termignon, and Lanslebourg (see Chapter IV, the Mont Cenis.)

In 1932, for prestige and strategic reasons, the French Government decided to convert the track over the dark and sinister Iseran hump into a great military motor-road which, besides providing a long-required strategic link over a vital sector just inside the Franco-Italian border, would at the same time wrest the distinction of being the highest motorable pass in Europe from the unfortunate Stelvio, which had already been shorn of international status by a peace treaty of some twenty years before. With all the advantages of modern engineering skill, methods, and

* The most seriously damaged of all in the 1957 floods, bridges being washed away, villages badly damaged, and long sections of the road destroyed. It seems improbable that it will be in good order in 1958. Enquiries are advisable.

material at the disposal of the engineers, it was also planned as a super-
lative example of an ample, gently graded carriage-road, in spite of having
to climb over a narrow 9,000-ft. neck at the top of a grim and stony
mountain mass, both sides of which are extremely steep.

All these things it achieved brilliantly in due season.* Yet there is something about the Iseran, quite apart from the exceptional bleakness of its
summit sectors, which leaves one with a feeling of artificial contrivance
and of having, in a way, been 'sold the pass'. For this manifestly major
triumph of engineering enterprise goes up—very far up—and it goes down
again, rather like the noble Duke of York, without a shred of that sense of
essential purpose which is the hallmark of the great mountain passes.
The fact is that if it were not there as a show-piece the civilian motorist
would hardly have missed it, for it leads not across a frontier, nor across
the main chain of the Alps, nor even from one main city centre to another,
but from one remote and neglected mountain valley to another a little less
remote and containing nothing more than a popular but small holiday
centre easily reached from elsewhere.

True, it provides a link which can be used for a rather strange combination of passes, in that a mountain-pass enthusiast, based on Turin, willing
to start early enough in the dawn and driving a sufficiently fast car, could
in the space of a very long day indeed, traverse a round of glorious mountain scenery by just crossing the Mont Cenis, turning right handed at
Lanslebourg to Bonneval, climbing over the Iseran, and continuing northwards from its foot to Bourg St. Maurice, there again turning right over
the Little St. Bernard down to Aosta and back by the long valley road to
Turin. But he would probably arrive home very late, very tired, and
suffering from a surfeit of good things.

As an excursion pure and simple, the Iseran is, however, a fine experience, if only for the boldness of its conception and the splendour of its
execution.

The approach from the south side as far as Lanslebourg has been
described in the Mont Cenis chapter (Chapter IV), and it is proposed to
continue the description from that point, both for the sake of convenience
and because I think it is the more attractive way to drive it for the first
time. (The northern approach will be found in Chapter V, the Little
St. Bernard.) In this direction the best views are more continually ahead,
though the road across the pass itself is everywhere so wide that there is no
difficulty about pulling in and looking back wherever you want to, if you
take it from the opposite end.

From Lanslebourg the upper valley of the Arc runs straight for 15 miles
to the wall of the Graians, closing it behind Bonneval sur Arc (6,020 ft.).
It is a wide, gently terraced corridor with high ranges rising on either side—
the wall of unglaciated peaks from the Grand Roc Noir (11,605 ft.) to the
Aiguille de Méan Martin (10,790 ft.) rising to the left and, opposite to the
south, the more lofty and glacier-covered frontier range between France
and Italy, with narrow lateral valleys carved deeply into it. These are the

* The north side was completed in 1935, the southern in the following year.

western peaks of the Graian Alps, containing numerous summits of over 12,000 ft. extending from the Roche Melon, above the south side of the Mont Cenis, through the fine glaciers and snows of the Chalanson and Albaron ridges (12,000 ft.) to the neat teeth of the Levanna (11,875 ft.), forming an amphitheatre at the far end of the valley above their glitter of hanging glaciers. As you drive up the long valley road and pass the entrance of one lateral gorge after another the great peaks are seen shining above in fine momentary glimpses rather than continuously, for they are set back somewhat to the south behind the high shoulders which bound the valley.

The road climbs up the valley floor from terrace to terrace, amid sparse and spasmodic cultivation, sometimes steeply and by short lacets as at the shabby-looking village of Bessans (5,645 ft.) perched on a bluff. It is a narrow road hereabouts, running mostly between meadow levels, and last time I passed over it the whole long stretch was in indifferent surface condition, which I was told was not unusual. It is to be hoped that money may since have been found to remedy this defect, for the approach was quite unworthy of the contrasting perfection found on the pass itself.

As Bonneval (6,020 ft.) is approached, the Levanna, at the head of the valley in front, is seen to continually greater advantage. The situation of the small, rather seedy looking resort, rich in walking and climbing attractions, is very beautiful, the white buildings occupying the smooth green carpet of the last little plain in the Arc valley on either side of the stream, backed by the abrupt mountain wall barring all further progress, with the Levanna's dark, regular teeth sharp against the sky.

The Iseran road proper now begins. On leaving the town it immediately turns sharply backwards and starts to climb steadily along the huge slope below the Méan–Martin range, in the direction from which you have come. Very soon you are high above the Arc valley, with Bonneval falling away into the depths behind and the valley-road on which you were motoring a short time ago a white ribbon far below; and as you drive straight on and up, with nothing more than a gentle contouring curve, on a broad carriage-way with a good gravel surface, the frontier peaks across the valley to the south begin to appear finely above the masking ridges.

After about 2 miles the road takes a wide hairpin swing back on itself and continues its beautifully graded ascent back in the direction of Bonneval and the Levanna, with a safe but tremendous drop beyond the road's edge, now to your right. This reach across the mountain face is even longer than the first, and succeeds in gaining sufficient height to force an entry into a high hanging valley above, dominated by the dark, rocky peaks of the Aiguille Pers (11,320 ft.) and Ouille Noire (11,925 ft.).

A wide curve, clinging to the right-hand wall of the re-entrant, now follows, and grand views open up southwards to the fine glaciers of the 12,000-ft. Chalanson and Albaron, as the road gains height and surmounts a steeper slope on the other side. This it does by a couple of long windings, having crossed the Lente torrent, which comes leaping down from the pass—still out of sight behind great intervening spurs of rock.

At about 8,000 ft. the hanging valley contracts sharply and the road forces a narrow ravine, recrossing the stream directly afterwards at the Pont des Neiges (8,432 ft.) in the high basin below the grim, grey summit slopes, a wilderness of dark scree and boulders, shut in from all view of the outside world, desolate, lonely, and seamed all the year round with patches of unmelted snow, often corniced by the sun to fantastic shapes. As the road climbs gradually by a long, wide curve, clinging to the great slabs of the right-hand slope, below small hanging glaciers, the crest of the Col is still hidden by a screen of rock. A sense of immense height is experienced here in spite of the completely enclosed and isolated nature of the vast and gloomy Cwm. You cannot help being conscious of the length of the climb since leaving Bonneval, and the actual height differential is in fact 3,000 ft. Suddenly the road takes a couple of sharp turns to surmount a steep final step, and the signpost on the broad Iseran saddle looms up before you, at 9,088 ft.

The saddle, on which stands a T.C.F. refuge hotel and a couple of dark, small stone buildings, one of which proves to be a chapel, is a wide and roomy level between the unprepossessing rocky combs of the Lessières and Aiguille Pers rising on either side, overtopping the pass by little more than 2,000 ft.; but there is a savage austerity about it, partly due to the fact that all the surrounding rock is almost black, which can, especially under low cloud on a windy day, invest it with a sombre air of gloom and depression. Nor should it be forgotten that at 9,000 ft., after so sharp a rise from valley-levels, your halt to admire the rather restricted view to the north and south will be in a place where the temperature is likely to be very cold and the atmosphere, if even the mildest local excursions are undertaken, very thin and rarefied.

In both directions the view from the Iseran is rather like looking out through a narrow window high in the hills, and consists of a fairly close survey of vividly contrasting tops of the mountain ranges, each seen beyond an intervening rift—to the south the three truncated cones of the Albaron rising from the shining glacier-field at their feet, to the north the twisted ridges of the snowless Tsanteleina (11,830 ft.) and the black, rubbly pyramid of the Grande Sassière (12,325 ft.). So high is the point at which the observer is standing that their extra 2,000–3,000 ft. of stature seems of little account; one appears to be hob-nobbing with them on very familiar terms. It is certainly impressive, but not one of the great summit views; and the Stelvio, beaten by 46 ft. for height, need not lose any sleepless nights about it.

A far more attractive, though still limited, prospect opens up about a mile down the northern side of the pass, after the road has gently descended another bare and scree-scarred re-entrant between parallel ridges of fluted rock. Here we reach the front rim of the Iseran Massif, which suddenly falls away more than 3,000 ft. into a narrow abyss cradling the ribbon of the infant Isère. Immediately beyond and almost vertical in its upward sweep, the immense wall of the Tsanteleina–Grande Sassière plinth goes surging up high overhead—a fantastic screen of beige and grey rock, stratified and twisted by titanic pressures. To the left in the deep bottom of the broadening valley, scattered over a smooth green plain, lie the Lilliputian houses and roads of Val d'Isère, backed by the peaks of the Vanoise Massif; and, looking straight down the corridor which leads to Bourg St. Maurice, the twisted skein of the Isère and its accompanying thread of road are lost in the blue distance at the foot of the grim dark cliffs of Mont Pourri (12,430 ft.).

There is a lay-by here and an observation point with an indicator, reached in less than two minutes by a short path. A halt here is well worth while, for it provides, I think, the finest view on the whole Iseran route.

The road now begins its amazing plunge down 3,000 ft. of bare mountain-side, which it achieves by half a dozen zig-zag sweeps across the face, each about half a mile long, as well as a few minor curves and banked hairpin turns. This is the show piece of the Iseran road. The gradient is moderate, the road broad and well surfaced, and the great hairpin turns are of wide radius and beautifully built out. One has the sensation of floating swiftly down to the blue depths of the ravine in a long, gentle, spiral glide, as if on wings. The Tsanteleina's fearsome precipice, close opposite, towers higher and higher into the sky; and in an astonishingly short time you find yourself crossing the foaming torrent of the infant Isère at a stone bridge in the uppermost eastern recess of the Cwm, where the feet of the great hills make an acute angle. The road swings leftwards hard back on itself, and descends straight along the river's bank to Val d'Isère (6,065 ft.), 3 miles away.

The beautiful approach sector up the upper Isère valley from Bourg St. Maurice to the resort and mountaineering centre of Val d'Isère has been described in the Little St. Bernard chapter (Chapter V, p. 63).

XXXI

THE MINOR PASSES OF SAVOY AND DAUPHINÉ

1. Savoy

From Geneva a main valley route runs due south to Annecy, Aix-les-Bains, Chambéry, and Grenoble, thus connecting Southern Switzerland by a direct and speedy link with the lowland feet of the Petit St. Bernard, Mont Cenis, and Lautaret-Galibier–Mont Genèvre routes into Italy.

For those who prefer a more leisurely and scenically more exciting drive through the Alps of Savoy there are several very attractive routes available which, without constituting major mountain passes, deserve a brief mention.

The first is a valley route, with occasional views of the great peaks of the Mont Blanc Massif almost all along it, through the beautiful basin of the Arve, which has its source in those distant glaciers. The road leads through Annemasse, Bonneville, and Cluses to Sallanches (1,788 ft.), just before which there are continuous views of the whole snowy chain. Four miles farther on (and about forty from Geneva) is Le Fayet–St. Gervais les Bains (2,075 ft.) a charming resort within easy reach of Chamonix, 10 miles higher up the road into the upper Arve valley (Chapter XXV).

From Le Fayet and St. Gervais an attractive road runs south-west to the highly popular and populated summer resort of Megève (forty hotels) (3,690 ft.) and over the low Col de Megève beyond it, down the vale of the Arly, with one or two grand glimpses of Mont Blanc's western faces, to Flumet (3,000 ft.) and so onwards to the main Isère valley at Albertville, 15 miles beyond (Chapter V, p. 62).

At Flumet the very picturesque Col des Aravis road comes in on the right from Annecy and Chambéry by way of the Nom valley and La Clusaz, and the pass (25 miles). This 4,915-ft. pass, much frequented in summer by coaches, has a wonderful view of the Mont Blanc range beyond the nearer and lower Aravis peaks, and provides the most attractive drive of all the routes into the heart of Savoy. From the Col it descends the valley of the Arondine to Flumet, a distance of 8 miles.

For those driving along the Savoy (south) shore of Lake Geneva from Geneva, intending to enter Switzerland at the eastern end of the lake, and who have had their fill of water-side roads by the time they reach Thonon, there is a fine mountainous alternative at that point. Instead of keeping along the lake to Evian, it branches off to the right and ascends the Drance valley through Abondance (19 miles, 2,982 ft.) and Châtel, reaching the Swiss frontier at the Col de Morgins (4,725 ft.) and so on down on the other side to Morgins and Monthey in the Rhone valley, near Aigle

(Chapter XXVI, p. 177).   This road traverses the fine if lowly mountains of the Grammont and Dent d'Oche chain (7,000 ft.), so well seen from all the resorts of the Swiss shore across the lake.

2. DAUPHINÉ

Besides the great passes described in Chapter XXIX, the Dauphiné has a number of very attractive minor mountain roads, some of them of considerable elevation and interest.

Two of the finest of these diverge from the lower approach to the Lautaret at Rochetaillée (Chapter XXIX, p. 198) just short of Bourg d'Oisans.   Leaving the Route des Alpes highway and striking due north to the little resort of Allemont, it penetrates between the Grandes Rousses (11,350 ft.) and the slightly lower Belledonne range by way of the Col de Glandon (6,260 ft.) to St. Avre-Lachambre in the Maurienne valley or by combining a more easterly arm, breaking away at the Col itself, over the second fine pass, the Col de la Croix at Fer (6,947 ft.), to St. Jean de Maurienne.   Both routes abound in fine mountain scenery, with wild ravines and fine waterfalls; but the finest view is probably that of the huge Aiguilles d'Arves, between La Grave and the Galibier, towering up, apparently vertical, to 11,500 ft. to the south-east of Saint Sorlin d'Arves on the early part of the descent from the Col de la Croix de Fer to Entraigues and St. Jean.

Another fine minor road in this area, if somewhat constricted by the neighbouring mountain walls, leads from Bourg d'Oisans over the Col d'Ornon (4,460 ft.) to La Mure, in the broad valley of the Drac, on the route from Grenoble to Corps, the Col Bayard and Gap, mentioned at the beginning of Chapter XXIX.

Leaving this main route at Corps is a useful cross-country link with the Grenoble–Sisteron highway to the Riviera (ibid.) climbing modestly over the Col du Festre (or de la Cluse) (4,820 ft.) to Veynes on the valley road from Gap to Serres and joining the main route at that charming town, which boasts a hotel with the engaging name of *Fifi-Moulin*.   This road penetrates the wild and barren Devolouy country and leads through some magnificent ravines, particularly the savage gorge of the Souloise.

Farther west, affording an entry route from the main Rhone valley at Livran to the Dauphiné and its southern roads, is another interesting valley and gorge route through Saillans and Die, from which the low Col de Grimone leads through a bare and rocky defile to a surprise view of gentle greenery and woods in the Lus valley, with the Devolouy crests beyond to the east, and then descends on Lus La Croix Haute on the same main Grenoble–Sisteron route referred to just above.   The Col de Grimone, by the way, has recently attracted attention as the route which Hannibal may have taken from the Rhone valley to the foot of his ascent to the final Alpine crossing, if, as the latest expert argument confidently asserts, he conjured men, horses and elephants over the 10,000-ft. Col de la Traversette—a pass so difficult that to this day no reasonable road has ever been built across it.

PART VII

THE DOLOMITE PASSES (ITALY)

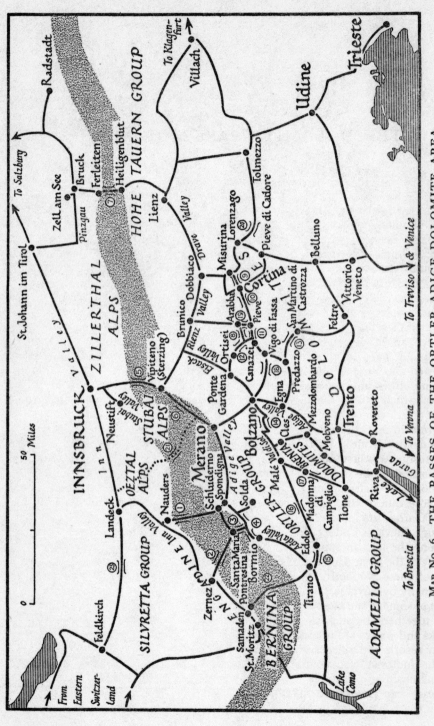

MAP No. 6.   THE PASSES OF THE ORTLER–ADIGE–DOLOMITE AREA

Passes

1. Resia (Reschen-Scheideck)
2. Ofen
5. Brenner
6. San Giovo
9. Tre Croci
10. Falzarego
13. Rolle
14. Mendola
17. Campiglio
18. Costalunga (Karer)
21. (Projected) Timml Joch
22. Bernina

XXXII

THE DOLOMITE ROAD
(PORDOI, FALZAREGO, AND TRE CROCI PASSES)

GENERAL

THE AREA approximately 40 miles wide by 50 deep from north to south, occupied by the fantastic rock towers, spires, fingers, and walls of the Dolomites, is a rough oblong, whose shorter northern and southern sides run east and west, situated many miles to the south of the main Oetztal–Stubai–Zillertal–Hohe Tauern Alpine backbone, and separated from it by the deep and often broad trench of the Pustertal valleys, housing the east-to-west course of the Rienz and the west-to-east channel of the upper Drave.

The whole of this unique mountain complex (the former Austrian province of South Tyrol), broken up by deep valleys into a number of distinct ranges and groups remarkable for their variety of contour, texture, and colour, has lain, since the arbitrary dictates of the peace treaty which followed the First World War, in Italian territory. There is therefore nothing either international or trans-Alpine about the fine series of lofty passes which thread their way between the isolated explosions of rock, from one lovely valley to another. Nor are any of them essential to progress in any direction once the main Alpine chain has been crossed from north to south; for the whole area occupied by the higher and more picturesque massifs dotted about it can be by-passed by fine highways in the bottom of the deep valleys which bound their outer confines. Thus the northern Italian plain can be reached by following the Adige valley far more quickly and easily through Bolzano and Trento to the head of Lake Garda; its more easterly regions and Venice by the low-level route through Pieve di Cadore and Vittorio Veneto.

None the less, in spite of their purely local and internal character, no survey of the great Alpine passes would be complete without some description of these wonderful roads, designed primarily to take the traveller (originally by carriage, more recently by motor car and coach) through the heart of some of the most astonishing mountain scenery in the world and to link together—passing close to the very feet of these unique, bizarre blocks and wafers of up-ended rock—some of the most beautifully situated valley resorts and villages imaginable.

The motorist who comes from the north, having crossed the main Alpine chain either by the Brenner to the west or the Glocknerstrasse to the east, can choose whether he will enter the Dolomite country from its northern perimeter at Dobbiaco (Toblach) or continue by valley roads to breach its western flank either from Ponte Gardena half-way between the foot of the Brenner and Bolzano, by the Val Gardena (Grödnertal) and its two alternative passes—the Gardena and the Sella—or from the fine centre of Bolzano itself—the normal gateway to the Dolomites. If the approach has been over the Arlberg and Reschen-Scheideck (Resia) down the upper valley of the Adige through Spondinig and Merano (Chapter XIX)—it is completed by the shorter and milder Costalunga (Karer) Pass, somewhat farther to the south.

If, however, the final objective is to see as much as possible of the Dolomites and emerge finally at their southern fringe, on the way to the Italian plains or *en route*, perhaps, to Venice, there is little choice but to enter by the northern gateway at Dobbiaco, half-way along the broad Val Pusteria (Pustertal) and follow the length of the three linked passes, together constituting what was once the Dolomitenstrasse and is now the Strada dei Dolomiti—the great Dolomite through-road—which carves its splendid way right through the centre of the area from the north, with a strong south-westerly bias all along its course. The three passes are, in this order, the Tre Croci (5,932 ft.), starting at Carborin and ending at Cortina, 12 miles away; the 6,913-ft. Falzarego, linking Cortina and the foot of the Pordoi, 16 miles away, through Arabba and Pieve; and the Passo di Pordoi (Pordoijoch), at 7,346 ft. the biggest and steepest of the trio, covering the wonderful 12 miles from Arabba to Canazei in the lovely Avisio valley.

Here the long sector of high mountain passes ends, and the road— which, by the way, is broad, magnificently surfaced throughout its length, and energetically maintained in first-class condition for the heavy traffic it understandably attracts—continues along this truly beautiful valley, always falling away gently southwards. As it passes through a string of charming villages all with melodious names—Campitello, Vigo di Fassa, Moena—with the Avisio bubbling merrily alongside through the meadows, there are glimpses on either hand of nearly all the more famous groups and summits. In 10 delightful miles of fast motoring Predazzo is reached; and here Trento, on the Valley Highway from Bolzano to Brescia is only another 45 miles ahead down the gently tilted floor of the Val Fiemme (Fleimstal) and the main Adige valley below it. From Trento it is only 20 miles more to the level of the Italian plains at the head of Lake Garda.

This, then, is the *sine qua non* of a visit by road to the Dolomites from north to south—the absolute minimum required to give some idea of the fantastic and varied beauties the region has to offer. I suggest that, if time allows, there are three digressions along the route which will add considerably to both knowledge and pleasure. The first two are relatively short—an hour or at most an hour and a half would be ample for each— the third is really an additional half-day's motoring, and so lovely is its objective that a day or two's stay at the end of it might well result before returning to the main north–south highway.

They are respectively, from north to south, the ascent of the eastern side of the Sella Pass (7,264 ft.) from the junction just short of Canazei;

the ascent of the Costalunga Pass (5,752 ft.) from Vigo di Fassa as far as
the famous Karersee (Lago di Carezza), which lies a few miles down the
western slope beyond the summit; and the splendid drive eastwards over
the Rolle Pass (6,463 ft.) from Predazzo, descending on the far side to San
Martino—in my view the loveliest of the Dolomite resorts. These are all
dealt with in detail under the separate sections below devoted to the passes
named.

Incidentally, if it is desired to make these deviations and give oneself
sufficient time to enjoy them, there are plenty of good hotels along the road
at which to break the journey. Canazei, about half-way, is an excellent
stopping-place if two days are to be devoted to the route; and there is a
particularly attractive-looking newly built hotel about a mile south of the
village. Karersee and San Martino are, of course, famous resorts with
ample hotel accommodation. Plainer hotels are to be found at Vigo and
Predazzo and at the summits of the passes.

From Cortina to Predazzo, taking in the suggested Sella and Costalunga
deviations, is about 100 miles and can be done in a long day's motoring—
depending, naturally, on the length of stops at the various beauty spots and
for roadside picnics—but I should not like to attempt more, lest fatigue
should blunt the pleasure, which would be a pity.

In the detailed sections which follow, the Dolomite road has however
been described from south to north for reasons given in Chap. XXXIII;
the Sella and Rolle from west to east because they seem to me to lose their
whole point if a first complete crossing of these two roads is made in the
other direction. The long mountain road from Bolzano to the head of
Lake Garda by the Mendola and Campiglio passes has been taken from
north to south because, although all its finest views seem to me to lie ahead
if it is driven in the opposite direction, it has been delineated from north to
south in the combined route suggested on p. 233. The Costalunga,
although it affords the most convenient approach to the southern end of
the Dolomite road and to the western foot of the Rolle Pass from Bolzano
itself, has been taken from east to west for the same reason.

The Dolomite Road

1. *The Pordoi* (7,346 ft.)

Italy (Dolomite Road).

From Canazei (4,806 ft.) to Arabba (5,253 ft.): 14 miles.

Detail: Canazei to the Pordoi Pass (7,346 ft.) between the Sella Group and the
Marmolata: 8 miles, ascent 2,550 ft.

Pordoi Pass to Arabba (5,255 ft.): 6 miles, descent 2,100 ft.

Magnificent wide hairpin windings from Canazei to the summit, very steep
in the lower sections: fine bitumen surface. Narrower, sharper, and more
closely-banked groups of hairpins on the northern side, but everywhere ade-
quately broad and well surfaced. A first-class road.

Open: Early June to mid-October. Maximum gradient: 1 in 10.

Easy to moderate.

Although the actual Pordoi Pass proper begins at Canazei (4,806 ft.) and its northern end is at Arabba (5,253 ft.), a distance of 13 miles, the long valley approach from Predazzo, 17 miles to the south, is so attractive and such an integral sector of the Dolomite road as a whole that its inclusion in any description of the Pordoi seems obvious.

From Predazzo the road runs almost straight, with occasional curving

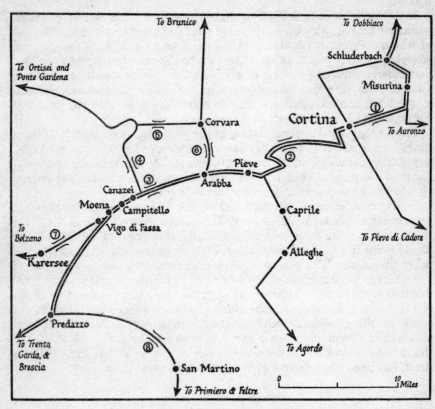

SKETCH MAP No. 4. THE DOLOMITE ROAD
(*Strada di Dolomiti*)
and adjacent passes

Passes
1. Tre Croci   3. Pordoi   5. Gardena   7. Costalunga
2. Falzarego   4. Sella   6. Campolungo   8. Rolle

sections, rising gently from level to level of the long and almost straight Avisio valley—a delicious corridor of meadows, pine-covered slopes, white-walled villages and their slender church towers, by the rippling stream, with occasional glimpses of the high, rocky combs of the Latemar

* It is difficult for anyone familiar with the long history of mountaineering to think of this by its neo-Italian name, Catinaccio. The same applies in the case of the Langkofel—Sasso Lungho—and the alteration of Marmola*t*a to Marmola*d*a.

The Cimone della Pala above the summit of the Rolle Pass

The Brenta Dolomites from the Campiglio road, below Madonna

The northern gateway to the Dolomites: Lago di Dobbiaco

(9,165 ft.) and Rosengarten (9,780 ft.) Groups on the left and the minor but lovely Punta Vallacia (8,665 ft.) on the right, rising above the dark heads of the pines. Passing through Moena, it continues for 10 miles to the turning for Vigo di Fassa—just to the left, off the main highway—and for the Costalunga Pass to Karersee and Bolzano. Here the distant Sella Group comes into sight ahead, apparently barring the end of the valley, which now narrows and steepens a little. As the road climbs, still quite gently, through Pozza, Fontanazza, and Campitello, closer now to the slopes and the forests, one enchanting prospect after another opens up ahead, and there are delightful picnic places on small green shelves fringing the Avisio, in the shade of tall pines. The white church towers of the villages are now charmingly silhouetted against the tremendous bulk of the Sella Massif, whose smooth, ochre-coloured precipices lift higher and higher as the road approaches the last level of the valley at Canazei. A little before reaching that resort, beautifully situated in a green plainlet at the foot of the great mountain barrier ahead, the road curves a little to the right and, at a point where a modern hotel has been most intelligently sited, a superb view of the shapely, dark, triple-headed Marmolata—the 'Queen of the Dolomites' (10,970 ft.)—is revealed behind the village and to the right of the Sella peaks, separated from them by the huge shoulder, entirely pine-covered, of the Pordoi wall.

The pass begins directly after leaving the main street of Canazei and gets to immediate grips with its 2,000-ft. problem, some of the lower hair-pins being extremely steep, as it swings in fairly abrupt turns up through the pine-forest.

The Marmolata is soon lost behind a great projecting spur of the forest, and for some time the dominating factor is the Sella Group (10,340 ft.), high overhead to the left, its fantastic yellowish blocks of sheer cliff gaining in stature and broadening in perfection of form at every turn in the steep, but splendidly engineered, road. About 3 miles up from Canazei, the gravel-surfaced Sella Pass road, rough and white in contrast with the velvety grey bitumen of the Pordoi, comes tumbling in on the left. Soon afterwards as the Sella, now close overhead, loses dignity and proportion by too much foreshortening, the three incredible wedges of the Langkofel Group (10,425 ft.)*—the Grohmannspitze, Funffingerspitze, and the Langkofel itself—shoot up into the sky farther round to the left, with the long green curve of the Sella saddle between them and the Sella cliffs, the windings of the pass and the summit buildings clearly visible high above.

The Pordoi windings now reach out more widely and less steeply across the upper slope—still between the pines—in a more easterly direction. Presently the trees are at last left behind and a narrow gateway between the foot of Sella precipices to the left and a small rocky subsidiary comb to the right is revealed above the breast of a final, broad, turfy slope. This is surmounted by a few steeper, shorter windings, and the Pordoi saddle (7,346 ft.) in the narrow jaws of the gateway, is reached after 7 miles of

* See footnote, previous page.

P

continuous climbing from Canazei, now 2,000 ft. below there in its green strip of plain, apparently a few inches broad.

Directly beyond the saddle the wide, northward view to the heads of the distant Dolomite groups towards and beyond Cortina opens up, and the road dips slightly to the considerable village of hotel and other buildings which occupy the brief green upland dell, about a mile long, between the feet of the Cima Boë (10,340 ft.), the easternmost of the Sella peaks, rising tremendously to the left with the Cima Pordoi beyond it, and the low comb of the Cima di Rossi (7,790 ft.), which borders the right-hand side of the view.

If time permits, the rather restricted view from the Pordoi corridor can be greatly improved by shorter or longer excursions on foot on either side of the road. By ascending the grassy slope on the left towards the screes at the foot of the Boë for only five or ten minutes, the Marmolata, with her beautiful snow cap and pale-blue glacier-shield streaming valleywards— the only sizeable sheet of ice in the Dolomites—lifts into view to the east through a convenient gap in the Cima Rossi–Sasso di Capello comb; the farther you go on towards the marked view-point about three-quarters of an hour above the pass, the more grandly she soars above the little upland valley at your feet and the diminishing roofs of the buildings clustered about the thread of the road. On the other side of the road behind the hotels, a relatively level path, which used to be known as the Bindelweg, strikes off around the foot of the rocky spurs away from the pass and the buildings, leading in half an hour to a point where the view of the whole mass of the Marmolata, streaming down in great buttresses of dark rock, relieved by the great sweep of the glacier's tongue, stands up even more magnificently, with nothing but the deep-green rift of the upper Avisio valley in between. (There is, incidentally, an attractive but narrow road along that valley, leaving the main route at Canazei and penetrating as far as Penia (5,060 ft.), from which the glacier-level can now be reached with the aid of the inevitable chair-lift.) The path, which eventually leads in two and a half hours to the Fedaja Pass (6,150 ft.) with its famous view, can also be used for the ascent of the Belvedère (8,695 ft.) and of the easy Cima di Rossi (7,790 ft.), each about an hour from the path.

From its summit-level the Pordoi road descends at first gently down the bare green alp, then with increasing steepness, by a bewildering pattern of long, looped windings, well built out at the corners, for 6 miles to the meadows and woods of Arabba (5,255 ft.), deep in its own lovely valley of the Cordevale. Here, on the left, the Campolungo Pass (6,125 ft.) road comes in through a narrow cleft from delightful Corvara, finely situated at the foot of the Gardena Pass and its junction with the direct valley road from the north, which ascends the Val Badia (Gadertal) to Corvara from Brunico in the Pustertal. Colfosco, at the foot of the immense Dolomite cliffs stretching behind Corvara, is one of the most picturesque villages in this whole region, and the drive across the Campolungo is very well worth-while.

From Arabba to Pieve di Livinallongo (4,815 ft.)—for once the

Italianization is an improvement, for this used to be plain Buchenstein—the road clings high up on the flank of the beautifully wooded winding valley, contouring for 4 miles hundreds of feet above the gorge of the river and the deep-green lake which it forms at one point, with backward glimpses to the Marmolata's snows, and the isolated Civetta (10,565 ft.) gradually lifting her broad and shapely outline ahead.

The classic view-point is perhaps just short of Pieve, which the road approaches on a narrow shelf; here the church tower and white houses piled up the steep left-hand slope of the valley are seen as a perfect foil to the immense screen of the Civetta, still nearly 10 miles away. This broad, crescent-shaped wall of fluted organ pipes, mauvish grey and delicate in hue, its supporting ridges beautifully balanced, marvellously crenellated, is surely the masterpiece of all the magnificent and varied Dolomite architecture. This is also the nearest point of view on the Dolomite road, which shortly after Pieve turns away northward into the Falzarego's southern flank.

There is, by the way, a celebrated close-up view—surpassing in splendour—of the Civetta, rising like Aphrodite in all her beauty from the blue depths of the tiny lake of Alleghe (3,170 ft.) at her very feet. And when the day is calm, those still waters reflect her loveliness for double measure.

Alleghe is reached by a steep and narrow road (it leads eventually to Agordo) which drops away at Andraz beyond Pieve into that deep valley to the right and winds monumentally down to Caprile (3,375 ft.) at its bottom, whence Alleghe and its lake are reached in another mile or two. A word of warning is, however, necessary for those who, tempted by paintings or photographs of that lovely picture, decide to make the digression required to enjoy its reality. Alleghe is twelve miles and 1,500 ft. off the road—12 miles which require not a leisurely three-quarters of an hour in each direction. Moreover, when you have reached your objective, it is necessary to leave the car and proceed on foot around the head of the lake, and then some way along and up the wooded slope away from the village—from which the Civetta is totally invisible behind intervening spurs—before the full glory of the view is revealed. This requires at least another hour, if it is to be enjoyed. So, if one is determined to see this almost uniquely beautiful view, it would be wise to add two and a half hours to the day's run, to cover the digression; and not to imagine, as the author did on his first, somewhat unsatisfactory attempt, that it is ' only just off the road, over there'.

2. *The Falzarego Pass* (6,913 ft.)

Italy (Dolomite Road).

From Pieve di Livinallongo (4,815 ft.) to Cortina d'Ampezzo (3,983 ft.): 16 miles.

Detail. Pieve to the Falzarego Pass (6,913 ft.), between the Tofana and Nuvolao groups: 6 miles, ascent 2,100 ft.

Falzarego Pass to Cortina (3,983 ft.): 10 miles, descent 3,000 ft.

Wonderfully engineered broad modern hairpin ascent, starting at Andraz, 2 miles from Pieve and a few feet lower, all the way to the Pass. Several tunnels, one spiral. Building and improvement still in progress 1957. Easy, broad descent, straight and level at first, then winding in fine curves down the northern slope into the Cortina basin.   Bitumen surface throughout.

Open: Subject to intermittent closure between November and June.

A first-class motor road, easy to moderate.   Maximum gradient: 1 in 12.

At Andraz (4,665 ft.) the ascent of the Falzarego begins in earnest.   It is a magnificent staircase, with hairpin piled on hairpin, up a wooded slope so steep that there are no wide views as you swing up for 5 miles from corner to corner.   Splendid and beautifully graded as the road is, widening work at the bends near Raggazzi, towards the top, were still in hand in 1957.   After this tiny hamlet, the road steepens and, in another mile, reaches the saddle (6,913 ft.)—much narrower than the Pordoi's—by a superb section consisting of built-out hairpins, some tunnels and even some hairpin tunnels.

The Falzarego Pass has much in common with the Pordoi.   Both have steep, wooded, winding climbs on their southern side; both penetrate a narrow gate-way to emerge into a lofty, bare corridor between greater and lesser rock-ridges; both suddenly offer an extended view forward to the north towards the heads of far-off surging ranges, seen as through a high window in the great hills.

The corridor stretching northward from the Falzarego saddle is, however, almost level for a considerable distance, and the great cliffs dominating it on the left are—unlike the Boë at the Pordoi—at their lowest level above the pass, rising to the climax of the Tofana's huge domed head of rock (10,565 ft.), which in certain lights shines as white as that of any snow peak, at the far end of a continually ascending curtain of pale-beige vertical cliffs.   The peaks on the right, the Nuvolao range (8,460 ft.), are set farther away from the pass and rise much higher than the Pordoi's corresponding containing ridge, which is insignificant.   Moreover, against the clustering Pordoi habitation there is, at the Falzarego summit, only a single hotel of most appropriate modern design, nestling under those stupendous crags, its single-span roof steeply tilted to shed the winter snows.

It is something of a surprise to find a magnificent side-road here, turning sharply back from the saddle and cutting upwards round the base of the cliffs into a steep sided re-entrant.   This is in fact Mussolini's famous military road, since thrown open to civilian traffic, which climbs some hundreds of feet higher than the Falzarego's level to drop down over a watershed into the Val Travenanzes and so to Ospitale and Carborin on the main valley road from Cortina to Dobbiaco.

The gentle descent, untortured by windings, of the long corridor to the north of the Falzarego Pass, until eventually the uppermost pines crowning the rim of the Cortina bowl are reached, is magnificent and beautifully withdrawn from the world.   On the left the unbelievable precipices of the Tofana mount and mount till they have completely obscured the rounded belfry above them and present the aspect of a vertical wall rising thousands of feet into the sky.   Away to the right, beyond the meadows and the wooded slopes of the ravine which carries the torrent downwards parallel with the road, the beautifully slender spires of the rose-coloured Croda di Lago (8,885 ft.) cluster high above the shallow vale and the incredible blocks of the much lower Cinque Torri stand jumbled like some fantastic outsize Stonehenge above the bare wilderness of scree at their base.

Then between the pines ahead, dove-grey and vast, the Cristallo (10,495 ft.) lifts his broad and riven front. One by one the neighbouring sharp outlines of the Sorapis (10,520 ft.) and Antelao (10,710 ft.) are added, as the road plunges through the pines in another fine cascade of hairpin curves and the wide, deep floor of the Ampezzo bowl is revealed outspread far, far below, with Cortina a tiny map straggling across its broad and gentle slopes.

Down and down the road bends and curves, past the two hotels of Campo, and reaches by half a dozen last hairpins across the wide, meadow-covered slopes down into Cortina (3,983 ft.). And as the roofs rise up to meet you, and the white, red-roofed buildings—including the bright pine boards of the beautiful Olympic stadium and the tall tower which is in summer the skeleton of the famous ski-jump—take shape, so the surrounding galaxy of wedges, peaks, and spires, Tofana, Cristallo, Sorapis, Antelao, and lace-like Croda di Lago go winging unimaginably high above into the wide reaches of rock-girt sky.

It is 10 miles from the Falzarego's cool and lonely summit to Cortina's hot and overcrowded streets. On a fine day, best of all in the rosy-fingered sunset hours of it, the 3,000-ft. descent from the fantastic feet of the Tofana cliffs is half an hour of continuous and colourful delight.

3. *The Tre Croci Pass* (5,932 ft.)

Italy (Dolomite Road).

From Cortina (3,983 ft.) to Misurina and Carborin (Schluderbach) (4,730 ft.): 13 miles.

Detail. Cortina to the Tre Croci Pass (5,932 ft.), between Monte Cristallo and the Cadini group: 6 miles, ascent 1,900 ft.

Tre Croci Pass to Misurina (5,760 ft.): 4 miles, descent 250 ft.
Misurina to Carborin (4,730 ft.): 3 miles, descent 1,000 ft.

Usually open, but chains sometimes necessary in winter.

Broad, very moderately graded windings from Cortina to the summit: bitumen surface. Gravel on the north side, fairly broad winding road with few hairpins.
One of the easiest of all passes. Maximum gradient: 1 in 11

Even if the discriminating may prefer the quiet beauties and modest seclusion of such smaller places as San Martino or Madonna, Cortina (4,000 ft.) is the undisputed queen of the Dolomite resorts.

Easily accessible by one of the two only narrow-gauge railways which penetrate the outer wall of the Dolomite fastnesses, beautifully poised for the better exploration, by road, of all the treasures stored in the region's innermost recesses, set on a broad green carpet in a landscape of surpassing beauty, it was destined from the first to become the touristic capital of the area, long before the winter Olympic Games of 1955–6 set their seal on its development and made it world-famous.

A secluded mountain village, grown in a relatively short space into a sophisticated town of considerable proportions, it has somehow, surprisingly, contrived to retain its native charm. Everything the pampered modern tourist can demand is to be found in Cortina now—luxury hotels, cafés, bars and dance-places, tennis courts, swimming-pools, a golf course, a wide choice of chair-lifts and cable railways to view-points and places of refreshment, at varying altitudes, to say nothing of the vast and, I think, beautiful Olympic open-air stadium, on whose rink ice-skating is practised and enjoyed by hundreds on the hottest summer day. Crowds mill around the narrow main street, strings of gigantic coaches block, bar, and nose their chromium way along it, sleek, expensive cars purr and park up and down its length; and yet Cortina, sitting firmly with her foot on the neck of the Dolomite road, remains a lovely place.

Having described the more important sections of the Dolomite road from its southern end into Cortina, it is logical to continue northwards over the Tre Croci, the third leg of the trio, as if you were bound for Dobbiaco (Toblach) and the northern exit from the region, on the way to the Brenner or Grossglockner crossings into Austria.

There is, however, no preference involved in this case, for I think it must be conceded that the Tre Croci Pass, charming as it is and delightful the scenery it traverses, is very much the 'little brother' of this family of passes, and it does not matter in which direction you take it. Nor is it an essential link in the road, for there is a shorter valley road to Dobbiaco, the two routes re-uniting at Carborin (Schluderbach). If, therefore, you had used up too much time over the more exciting things to the south of Cortina and were in a hurry to get out of the Dolomites, and so opted for the pleasant valley now, I would go so far as to say that it was a pity you had to miss your glimpse of pretty Misurina and of the astonishing Drei Zinnen, but that the loss is not irretrievable after all that you had already seen.

The Tre Croci road starts right among the shops and hotels at the northern end of the main street and heads purposefully up the long, sloping meadows towards the foot of the Cristallo. On reaching the belt of pines above the sunny fields it winds amiably enough upwards, without much to look at except the tall pine stems; and then, about twenty minutes after leaving Cortina, just when you think it is time for something exciting to happen, there—unexcitingly—you are (5,932 ft.).

There is a fine, if rather foreshortened, glimpse up at the Cristallo's towering cliffs (10,495 ft.) on the left. On the other side, behind the hotel —the Russians used it as their team headquarters during the winter Olympiad of 1955–6, thus elevating it from its obscurity as a mere mountain hospice, which humble status it has enjoyed since long before the Olympic Games were revived at the end of last century—rises the long, spiky screen of the Sorapis (10,520 ft.). The view ahead is a pleasant one, out over the heads of pines and more pines at nothing of any particular importance.

And yet here, where everything looks so peaceful, stands—in the form of a memorial—an incredible reminder that these vertical cliffs and apparently inaccessible pinnacles, thousands of feet overhead, were the scene of some of the bitterest fighting between Austrian and Italian Alpine divisions during the First World War. To this day the 10,000-ft. ridges of the Cristallo and Sorapis are honeycombed with machine-gun emplacements blown out of the living rock, trench systems, dug-outs, and a labyrinth of connecting tunnels in which an unbelievable mountain warfare of vertiginous attack and counter-attack, sap and counter-sap was carried on for months, with front line facing front line across abysses hundreds of feet deep, at a distance of only a few yards, 5,000 ft. above the nearest level ground. And up there, among the beige crags and gullies, the rusty coils of barbed wire still bear witness to a form of war the possibility of which even the toughest commando-trained plainsman of today might take leave to doubt.

Beyond the gentle pass, the road winds down through vast acres of pines much as it wound gently up on the Cortina side, till presently it emerges and divides, the right-hand branch—and, I suppose, the true northern continuation of the pass—falling away down the valley to Auronzo and Pieve di Cadore, past Lorenzago, where begins the road over the Mauria Pass (4,258 ft.) to Tolmezzo, Piani, and Udine if you are eastward bound to Trieste and Jugoslavia; or southwards to Vittorio Veneto and Venice. This is a well-engineered road with fine bends and tunnels and is in continual process of modernization. The other branch, more usually thought of as the northern leg, keeps on an almost level course for 5 miles with no particular features to make them memorable, to reach the pretty lake of Misurina. I think this favourite holiday spot over-rated, perhaps because I have read too many fulsome descriptions of its beauty, perhaps because I like my lakes deeper set between steeper-sided hills, and probably because its famous solitary hotel of days gone by has of recent years achieved too much barrack-like company, at both ends of the lake. And since this rather small almost oval sheet of water lies high and open, with somewhat prim and regularly shaped banks, the square and ugly blocks of buildings—a little modern white-walled hotel at the northern end is a nicely contrasting exception—tend to dominate the surrounding mountains, which stand well back from the saucer in which Misurina lies. The whole result is for me slightly artificial, as if the Round Pond had been greatly inflated and after being dropped in a spot near, but not near enough, to some mountains, had suffered the invasion at either end of two miniature Brighton hotels. I should, however, at once add that the twin summits of the Monte Cadini (9,320 ft.) stand up magnificently in the northern background and the long, grey serrated backbone of the Sorapis, rising rather closer behind the opposite end of the lake, affords a picturesque contrast. I have no doubt that Misurina would be an excellent centre for a delightful if slightly limited holiday combining the pleasures of walking, motoring, bathing, and boating in charming surroundings. And if it proved, owing to persistent bad weather or other mischance, too limited, a car-owner is within half an hour's comfortable reach of Cortina's flesh-pots, with cinemas, dance-floors, and other attractions at his disposal.

From the northern end of the Misurina bowl the main road dips immediately to descend a long and not very interesting defile till at Carborin (4,730 ft.) it meets the valley road from Cortina to Dobbiaco and so out of the Dolomites. But if time allows there is, directly after leaving Misurina, a good but fairly narrow mountain-road leading up into the hills on the right and penetrating them as far as Rimbianco, no great distance from the base of three of the most remarkable of all the Dolomite peaks—the famous 9,500-ft. Drei Zinnen or Tre Cime di Laveredo. These three massive vertical upheavals of smooth-faced stone, standing in a row almost touching one another, can boast some of the most appallingly difficult climbing routes in the world, and are certainly well worth seeing from the easily approached plinth on which they stand poised. The distant glimpses of them high up on the right, from the Misurina–Carborin road, show them off to immeasurably less advantage.

From Carborin the road continues its quiet descent of the deep Rienz valley for some 9 miles into the broad and sunny Pustertal and emerges through a narrow gateway, among whose level meadows lies Dobbiaco (Toblach), astride the high road and the railway line which link Bressanone and the Brenner to the west with Lienz and Austria to the east. You are out in the lowland world again, with hardly a hint that the great Dolomite ridges and wedges lie a few miles away behind the green wall to the south.

But only a mile or two before that final exit into the lowlands the Toblach road has reserved a small gem, which you might well miss if you did not know it was there. To the left of the road, hidden by a shallow screen of firs, lies the small sombre Lago di Dobbiaco, only a hundred yards walk from a parked car. To my mind this smooth sheet of dark-green water, trapped at the base of sheer, high crags, is far lovelier than its bigger, more celebrated sister of Misurina. You may disagree, but it will cost you only five minutes to go and look.

XXXIII

THE OTHER DOLOMITE PASSES—A COMBINED ROUTE

For the motorist who comes into the Dolomites from the Brenner intending to go out again by their northern exits and back into Austria, either retracing his route or through Lienz and over the Glocknerstrasse, I would suggest the following route.   If it looks at first sight slightly complicated, it has the merit of showing him almost all the best things the Dolomites have to offer.   And while a week, with interruptions at least at Madonna and San Martino, would not be by any means too long to spend over it, it could, with rather unceremonious haste, be traversed in three long days.

From Brixen at the foot of the Brenner, follow the main valley-road to Bolzano southwards as far as Ponte Gardena, turning left there over the Eisack bridge into the Val Gardena, from the head of which the Sella Pass climbs over its high saddle and drops down into the Dolomite road at Canazei.   From Canazei continue south as far as Vigo di Fassa, and there turn right over the Costalunga Pass, westwards, back to the Adige valley and Bolzano.   At Bolzano take the Mendola Pass road southwards, continuing along the Val di Sole to Malé, where the leftward road over the Campiglio Pass leads to Madonna just beyond the saddle.   (The right-hand road is the approach to the Tonale and Aprica Passes leading to Tirano in the Adda valley (Chapter XVII).)   From the southern foot of the Campiglio Pass at Tione a fascinating link road penetrates some wonderful gorges back into the Adige valley below Trento.   Heading northwards again through Trento, you turn right again at Ora* (Auer), and climb pleasantly past Fontane Fredde to the gentle San Lugano 'Pass'. The road then descends to Cavalese (15 miles) and onwards up the Val Fiemme, a lovely 8 miles, to Predazzo and the start of the Dolomite road. Before, however, retracing the short and pretty sector through Vigo to Canazei which you have already traversed, cross the Rolle Pass to San Martino, returning to Predazzo when (and if) you have exhausted the delights you find there.   Then drive the whole Dolomite road from Predazzo to Cortina, finally leaving the district, as planned, by Dobbiaco, there either turning left for the Brenner or right for the Glockner-strasse (see Sketch Map 5, p. 235).

A brief description of the other passes involved is given below, in the order in which they would be encountered if the above route is followed.

* The turning used to be at Egna, but a fine new road has been opened at Ora, a mile or two further on.

1. THE SELLA PASS (7,264 ft.)

Entirely in Italy (Dolomites).   Gardena Valley (Grödnertal) to Valley of the
      Avisio.

From Santa Cristina (Val Gardena) (4,685 ft.) to the junction with the Pordoi
      road 3 miles short of Canazei, at c. 5,000 ft.: 12 miles.

Detail.   Santa Cristina to the Sella Pass, between the Langkofel and Sella
      Groups, total ascent: 9 miles, 2,600 ft.

Total descent Sella Pass to Pordoi Junction (c. 5,000 ft.): 4 miles, 2,250 ft.

Open: Early June to mid-November.   Maximum gradient: 1 in 9.

A comparatively new, well-engineered road of comfortable width, but at
present only gravel surfaced.   Few hairpins on the Val Gardena side.   From
the pass (car-park) a long descent in wide loops to the Pordoi junction.   Construction and improvement still in progress.

Traffic moderate.   Steep in places, but in no way difficult to drive.

The attractive Isarco (Eisack) valley, with its picturesque towns and
perched castles, carries the main highway as well as the international railway link from the Brenner to Bolzano and on to Italy.   While the road is
excellent, considering the mountainous character of the country it traverses, it is of necessity only moderately broad, and the traffic in the high
season can be very heavy indeed.

In such conditions it can be a very comforting relief to turn off it and
cross the big single-span girder bridge over the river at Punta Gardena
(1,545 ft.) to find oneself immediately climbing steeply into the seclusion
of a lovely, wooded upland valley, out of all the noise and the bustle and
the lorry fumes.   The Val Gardena—once the Grödnertal—is long and
really charming; the road climbs on from green level to green level, now
gently, now more steeply, threading the meadows below the fringes of the
woods, while the second of the two narrow-gauge lines to penetrate the
Dolomite 'island' straggles unobtrusively alongside as far as Ortisei
(St. Ulrich).

Ortisei (8 miles, 4,055 ft.), the home of an ancient wood-carving industry,
and Santa Cristina (3 miles farther on, 4,685 ft.), in the highest step of the
valley, are both delightful holiday resorts set among their own particular
meadows.   And here, all of a sudden, there is a thrilling hint of things to
come, as the rounded fang of the Langkofel's* utmost tip (10,445 ft.) shoots
up above the woods unbelievably sheer and high.

At Santa Cristina where the enormous wall of the Sella's cliffs (10,340 ft.)
looms up ahead to bar all progress, the valley contracts and the Sella Pass
road begins its steep climb up the great turfy slopes at their feet to the
7,000-ft. saddle between the Sella and Langkofel groups.   The road, the
latest of the local mule-tracks to be converted to a motor highway, is at
present only gravel-surfaced, but its long, white reaches across the alp are
well graded and its infrequent hairpins easy.   As it climbs steadily to the
saddle there are fine views back across the Gardena valley and its containing ridges; and at every turn, close under the Sella's vertical cliffs, the

* See footnote p. 225.

three fantastic spikes composing the Langkofel Group shoot higher and
higher into the sky on the opposite side, to the right.

Not far below the summit the road divides and the few short windings
of the Gardena Pass (6,970 ft.) swing off to the left around the northern end
of the Sella Group to a low green col, over which it drops down steeply to

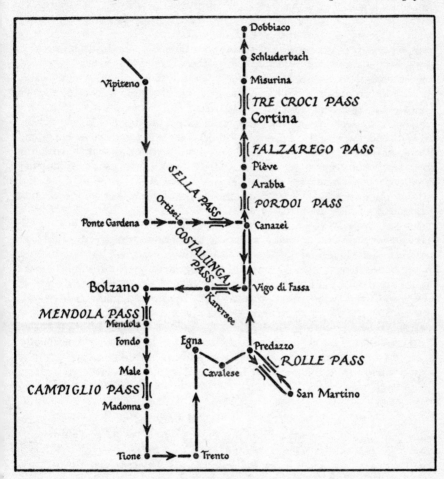

SKETCH MAP No. 5. COMBINED ROUTE OF THE DOLOMITE
PASSES
(As recommended in Chapter XXXIII.)

Corvara (see above, p. 226), another charming holiday centre, at the head
of a lovely valley-road running due north to the Brunico in the Pustertal.
The white thread of the Gardena, zig-zagging up the green slope, is a
picturesque feature in the view back from the higher reaches of the Sella
road, which overtops its subsidiary by only 300 ft.

At the saddle, where there is a modern hotel and an adequate car-park, the vast view eastwards is suddenly disclosed. As you stand perched between the solid ochre-coloured mass of the Sella's great unbroken blocks and the riven, fluted spires of the blue-grey Langkofel trio—the Langkofel itself, the Fünffingerspitze, and the Grohmannspitze—you look out from a high balcony across the depths of the Avisio valley, with Canazei's houses and thread of road minute in their green bowl 5,000 ft. below, to the rocky ridges heaped beyond away to the distant San Martino peaks. To the left, at the feet of the Sella's imminent and monstrous bulk, the road curves across on its way to Canazei, while through the dark, matted pine-woods on the opposing slope the upper windings of the Pordoi slash their half-concealed way up to the Pordoi Saddle, only a mile or two away as the crow flies and on just about the same level as one's own stance, but separated from one as the road winds by 10 miles and many thousands of feet—first down the Sella, then up the Pordoi's southern flank. And behind the Pordoi, in middle distance, its wings outspread like those of some huge grey bird, her breast glittering bluish with the great glacier pouring down from her blunt snowy head, the Marmolata's lovely mass lies dreaming against the sky. For the 'Queen of the Dolomites', alone in this vast area of barren rock peaks, boasts the shining raiment of a full-sized glacier robe.

As you drop down, hairpin after hairpin, into the woods below, the yellow Sella cliffs, topped by a broad, continuous terrace of rubble on which a few gigantic boulders lie miraculously poised, are an endless source of wonder, in colour, form, and changing outline. Not long before the junction with the Pordoi road, almost at the bottom, there is a point at which the whole stupendous screen, with hardly a wrinkle in it, stands unfolded above the pines—surely one of the most astonishing bastions of vertical, unbroken rock in the world. To point a contrast across the way, the dark Langkofel spikes stand ruined to the sky like splintered lanceheads.

A few more hairpins through the pines, and the Sella's white and gravelly serpent melts into the smooth, dark ribbon of the Pordoi's bitumen surface, a couple of miles short of Canazei. It is truly a lovely pass, the Sella.

2. The Costalunga (Karer) Pass (5,752 ft.)

Entirely in Italy (Dolomites). From the Val d'Avisio to the Adige Valley.

From Vigo di Fassa (4,565 ft.) to Bolzano (880 ft.): 28 miles.

Detail. Vigo to the Pass (5,752 ft.), between the Latemar and Rosengarten Groups, total ascent: 5 miles, 1,200 ft.

Pass to Karersee (Lago di Carezza) 5,030 ft.: 3 miles, descent 700 ft. Karersee to Bolzano (880 ft.): 20 miles, descent 4,250 ft.

Total descent Pass to Bolzano: 23 miles, 4,950 ft.

Open: Usually kept open, but chains sometimes necessary in winter.

A beautifully engineered, short ascent from Vigo to the Pass, contouring the somewhat exposed mountain flank without hairpin bends: excellent bitumen surface. Pleasant winding road, gravel surface, on west side of the pass down broad slopes and later through ravines: no definite hairpin bends or unduly exposed sections.

Traffic light to moderately heavy in summer (coaches). Mainly very easy, especially on the western Bolzano side. Maximum gradient: 1 in 10.

Ten miles to the south down the lovely Avisio valley from Canazei, just off the main highway running to Predazzo, lies picturesque Vigo di Fassa (4,565 ft.), which takes its name from this section of the vale, the Val di Fassa. (You have to turn right off the main road and hard back to reach Vigo, just off it.)

The Costalunga road, leading back through the hills to Bolzano and the Adige, branches off to the right, twists its way through the narrow village street, and immediately ascends the right-hand (western) slope of the valley by a long, straight climb across the flower-starred meadows. Having gained considerable height, it then burrows into a re-entrant to the right and contours its tortuous way on a narrow ledge at the base of the Rosengarten spurs till they almost meet the opposing spurs thrown out by the Latemar Group to the south. Here is the Costalunga neck and the summit of the pass. The whole thing from Vigo is only a matter of 5 miles and 1,200 ft., and its chief joy a series of lovely views back up the vale of the Avisio to the distant Sella, Pordoi and Marmolata rising far beyond the green, village-studded valley.

Beyond the crest of the pass the road winds gently downwards through a fine belt of pines, and soon reaches the few scattered hotels composing the tiny pleasure-resort of Karersee (Carezza al Lago) (5,400 ft.). These are dotted about the shady woods and broad, grassy slopes at the foot of the extended wall of the magnificent Rosengarten Group (9,780 ft.)*—so well seen from Bolzano as a distant backcloth. Here are charming walks in the forest, longer excursions into the Rosengarten on the one side, the Latemar (9,165 ft.) on the other, and the inevitable chair-lift and a golf course. Here also, close beside the road a few hundred yards beyond the original barrack-like luxury hotel which once constituted the whole resort, is the Karersee (Lago di Carezza) itself (5,030 ft.).

I would as soon hit a woman as disparage the character of a virtuous and respectable mountain lake, but it is only fair to warn you about the Karersee. Generations of cunning photographers, armed with wide-angled lenses and all the distorting and deceiving aids which have debased that proverbially truthful innocent, the camera, into one of the world's most facile prevaricators, have in this case of a world-famed sheet of water, pulled the wool over the world's eyes; to do so, some of them must, I think, have swum out into its middle with waterproofed gear and taken their pictures holding the apparatus over their heads as they trod water— or maybe you don't even have to swim, but merely to wade out the few yards involved. For the sad truth is that this widely publicized jewel of the mountains, beautifully set among the magnificent pines at the foot of the grey Latemar flutings and admittedly glorious in its colouring—an indescribable deep 'royal' green—is hardly more than a pond or a pool or a puddle, ringed by muddy shallows and fringed on its opposite side by a large and unpicturesque bank of shingle. Indeed, lying as it does in a hollow steeply below the left of the road, you might easily miss it altogether, were it not for the hideous ornamental fencing and the cluster

* See footnote p. 225.

of roadside snack-bars and ice-cream booths which advertise its presence. I, for one, shall never forget my disappointment, after years of hearing and reading about this aquatic marvel and of seeing it most invitingly portrayed in picture and photograph as a wide, horizontal expanse at the foot of the vertical mountain wall, at finding this famed emerald of the hills so small a chipping.

Far more attractive, to my mind, are the broad green alps stretching away on the other side of the road to the feet of the Rosengarten's fine and jagged wall, and the glorious open vistas westwards from among their meadows, flowers, and trees. For ahead, now, the land falls away gently down the wide slopes all the way to the great trench of the Adige valley, and down those slopes the Costalunga road winds unenclosed to follow the pleasant course of the Ega torrent through the Val d'Ega till, narrowing through a series of fine ravines, it in turn meets the Adige in the still wider, vineyard-furrowed plain of Bolzano.

From those pleasant meadows behind Karersee the eye roves out over the heads of the valley pines, far across the distant Adige rift, far beyond the green hills which range beyond the Mendola Pass down towards the Brenta, and then out and away across the grey-green distances to where suspended in the vast horizon sky, some 50 miles away, the great snow-capped summits of the Alps from the Ortler to the Oetztal float in ethereal detachment, minute links in a long-drawn chain of silver.

There is a minor but scenically fine gravel road leaving the Costalunga to the right just short of Karersee and skirting the base of the Rosengarten all its great length, to the Col Nigre (5,510 ft.) on the way to St. Cyprian (3,560 ft.) in the Val Tires. For a while it runs high and level through the woods above the meadows, with those great vistas of dark forest, misty vales, and distant shining snows intermittent between the pines on the left. A couple of miles along its gravel surface there is a point offering a quiet picnic spot in the shade of enormously tall pine-trees, with the creamy cliffs of the Rosengarten's western face sweeping prodigiously upwards, close above.

We lunched there one incomparable September day in 1956, with our backs to the Rosengarten and the great westward sweep outspread before us at far greater advantage than anywhere along the main Costalunga road, by then several hundred feet lower down the slope below us. There, against the sky, severed from all earthly contact by a blue noonday haze, dreamed the Cevedale, the Ortler, the Weisskugel, the Wildspitze, and a long intriguing fret of darker, less snowy crests. And I thought, as the smoke of my after-lunch pipe curled lazily on the windless air, of how, many years ago, I had sat on just such a day upon a hummock of green, wooded foothills and seen beyond the sundering gulfs, the mightier summits of the Himalaya—100 miles away—ringing the northern sky. Nor, I was surprised to find, was there anything odious about the comparison.

The Costalunga is not by any means a great mountain pass, but it takes you to places where there are, if you have time to look for them, many pleasant things to see.

3. THE MENDOLA (MENDEL) PASS (4,475 ft.)

Entirely in Italy (Dolomites).   Adige Valley to Val di Non and Val di Sole.

From Bolzano (880 ft.) to Fondo (Val di Non) 3,240 ft.: 21 miles.

Detail. Bolzano to Mendola Pass (4,475 ft.): 14 miles, ascent 3,600 ft.

Mendola Pass to Fondo (3,240 ft.): 7 miles, descent 1,200 ft.

Open: Usually open, chains sometimes necessary in winter.

A modest pass, winding up through woods by comfortable hairpins from a terrace in the broad Adige valley till about 2,000 ft. above the valley. It then climbs (splendidly protected on the valley side) straight across the Great Wall of the Mendelwand for some distance, finally ascending again by short but easy hairpin turns through a pine-forest to the summit. Surface excellent throughout. The descent on the southern side is by broad, gentle, and well-surfaced windings with no difficulties whatever. Maximum gradient: 1 in 10.

Traffic light to moderate. An easy drive with superb views over the valleys.

The Mendola Pass is one of those peculiar passes whose journey is not strictly necessary—for there is a valley route available of not much greater length from Bolzano to the places it leads to—but without which, mainly because of the lovely prospect from its comparatively humble summit, the motorist would be much the poorer.

From Bolzano's busy streets the road crosses the wide and sunny Adige plain to Appiano (1,365 ft.), where it surmounts a low step on to a slope covered, like the rest of the broad and lovely valley below it, with vineyards. After a mile or two of gentle ascent between the vines it reaches the foot of the immense, extremely steep flank of the mountains forming the western border of the Adige valley and known as the Mendelwand. Having found its way on to this wide mountain face by a few somewhat tight hairpins, it then proceeds to climb diagonally and steeply across it, contouring in and out of its buttresses and ravines for some miles, with the valley falling away into the depths to the left and the beautiful view eastwards broadening out at every yard of its magnificent progress. Along this airy stretch it provides several convenient lay-bys to enable you to enjoy the panorama of tumbled hills, miles of valley serrated with vine-yards, and the pink haze of Bolzano's roofs filling the plain, with the splendid wall of the distant Rosengarten* surging up behind it as a backcloth.

This enormous reach across the face of the hills brings the road in one bound to something like the 3,000-ft. level, where it encounters a broad, projecting spur covered in pine-woods. Through these it winds serenely by a number of hairpin turns, and very soon surmounts the remaining 500 ft. to Mendola, the little holiday resort of hotels and pensions which has grown up on the summit still deeply embedded in the pine-forest (4,475 ft.).

From the little open terrace at the northern end of the village there is a glorious view across the wide Adige rift, more that 3,000 ft. below, to the piled-up ranges of the south-western Dolomites and the valleys biting deep into them. Down in the green depths at your feet lie half a dozen

* See footnote p. 225.

towns white-walled and red-roofed, and a most lovely turquoise jewel of a lake.   It is a wide scene of calm and colourful beauty without a savage note in it, and the benches scattered in the shade of pines all around offer a most attractive site for a roadside meal.   If time allows, an even more extensive version of the Mendel view can be obtained by the ascent of the good path to the Penegal (5,700 ft.), a rocky crest overtopping the little resort by about 1,300 ft. and requiring about an hour and a half of uphill walking.

Southwards, the road wanders amiably through woods of pine and larch, winding down past two or three small hamlets and at least two attractive hotels on the way to Ronzone (3,555 ft.) and Fondo (3,240 ft.) in the Val di Non at the southern foot of the pass.

4. THE CAMPIGLIO PASS (5,580 ft.)

Entirely in Italy (Brenta Dolomites).   Val di Sole to Val Nambino.

From Dimaro (Val di Sole) (2,660 ft.) to Pinzolo (2,525 ft.): 20 miles.

**Detail.   Total ascent Dimaro to Campo Carlo Magno (Campiglio Pass) (5,580 ft.):
9 miles, 2, 950 ft.**

**Campiglio Pass to Madonna di Campiglio (4,970 ft.): 2 miles, descent
600 ft.**

Madonna to Pinzolo: 9 miles, descent 2,500 ft.

Total descent Pass to Pinzolo: 11 miles, 3,100 ft.

Open: Usually open, but chains sometimes necessary in winter.

The northern ascent from Dimaro is at present gravel surfaced, with a number of good hairpins on its lower reaches.   The descent from the pass to Madonna is the steepest section of the road, which on its southern side is well graded, excellently surfaced (bitumen), descending steadily with numerous easy windings.   Maximum gradient: 1 in 10.

Traffic light to moderate (coaches).   An easy pass, with much fine scenery and one superb view, of the Brenta Dolomites, just below Madonna.

The valleys linking the Mendola and Campiglio Passes, the Val di Non and Val di Sole, are long and broad and smiling, and the road keeps fairly high to their right-hand slope as you go south, finding the way from shelf to shelf through open meadows from one picturesque narrow-streeted, twisting village to another.   Near Cles (2,150 ft.) lying deep in the valley beneath, the river, often carving its course far below at the distant bottom of the slope, is artificially pent up in the interests of hydro-electric power into an obviously artificial lake of a deep-green colour.

And so after 10 pleasant, unexciting miles the floor of the valley flattens out, road and river run comfortably through it side by side on the same level, and at last you come to Malé (2,420 ft.) and 4 miles farther on to Dimaro (2,650 ft.), where at the foot of two passes the road divides.

The right-hand branch is the approach to the beautiful Tonale Pass, leading over between the Presanella peaks on its south and the Ortler's southern spurs on its northern side to Edolo and Tirano, in the Adda valley at the approaches to the Stelvio and Bernina Passes (see Chapter XVI, p. 140).

The left-hand road to the Campiglio Pass rises at once into magnificent pine-forests which cover the immense slope of a re-entrant some miles deep, biting into the mountains ahead and culminating in the narrow green saddle between the Brenta Dolomites to the east and the Presanella–Ademello snow groups to the west. This is the Campo Carlo Magno Saddle (5,580 ft.)—where Charlemagne is reputed to have encamped on one of his forays into Italy. The road, gravel-surfaced on this side, swings up by long reaches and occasional hairpins through the forest, with deep views back along the Sole valley and down into the gorge below over the heads of the massed pines; occasional glimpses of minor rocky outliers of the North Brenta Group are all it offers of the peaks lying close at hand but unseen, till the summit is reached and the view towards the Brenta opens out a little. But the classic road view of that magnificent group is still some miles down the southern side of the pass, beyond the charming resort of Madonna di Campiglio.

Madonna, with its cluster of hotels and small bathing lake in a very pretty clearing among the pines, lies only 2 miles down the windings from the summit of the pass, at a height of 4,970 ft. It nestles too deeply under the wooded ranges on either side to have much of a view of the great peaks hidden behind them, but offers splendid opportunities for even moderate walkers to view them with a minimum of effort. Chair-lifts go up on either side of the valley to crests of the containing ranges, 1,500 ft. higher up above the tree line; and from their upper stations gentle alps and pastures spread and slope to the very feet of those wonderful mountains, so shy and withdrawn from the valley below.

If I were limited to one such expedition only, I should unhesitatingly choose the twenty-minute chair-lift to Monte Spinale (6,900 ft.) on the eastern side of the valley, at the top of which there is, without any further journeying, a wide and splendid view across the valley westwards to the broad Adamello snowfields (11,640 ft.) and the long, serrated rock-ridge leaning away to the Presanella's keen, dark pyramid (11,690 ft.) fluted with ice; while, closer at hand behind the billowing green of the alps which stretch gently back from Spinale's steep edge, rise the fantastic blocks, wedges, whorls, and spikes of beige rock, flecked with small hanging glaciers, which are the Brenta Group (9,000–10,500 ft.).

Much more can be seen by extending the excursion up the gentle track across the alp, which in an easy hour and a half leads to the Graffler Hut (8,200 ft.) and if desired, in another hour, to the watershed above it, at the very base of those astounding cliffs. From the hut the view westwards is magnificently extended by the appearance above intervening spurs of the great 12,000-ft. chain of the Ortler* Peaks, 20 miles away, with the Cevedale (12,380 ft.), a broad and shining white throne, its masterpiece as seen from here; farther to the north the line of the main Alpine chain swings round more distantly towards the Oetztal Alps northwards with occasional far-off glimpses of the sharp white teeth of the Weisskugel (12,290 ft.) and other high peaks above the blue of lower snowless ranges. And as you come down again to the head of the lift at your leisure in the late afternoon,

* See footnote p. 24.

the terrific 4,000-ft. vertical face of the Crozzon di Brenta (10,245 ft.) will be with you all the last part of the way, lit to its best advantage by the westering sun.

Madonna is, of course, an ideal centre for longer and more arduous walks to and around the Club Huts below the Bocca di Brenta Pass and the parallel Bocca di Tuckett in the heart of the Brenta peaks and pinnacles, and for difficult climbs from them.   But even if you are a motorist who does not want to stray a yard from the road, there is a superb view of the whole group a couple of miles below the village of Madonna at the so-called Panorama Corner of the pass.   At this point, from a distance of only 4 miles, you look up across the gulf of a deep gorge carpeted and walled with the dark green of magnificent pine-forests into the amazing rock-world of the Brenta.   Beige and pink and blue, the huge wedges soar to the vertical Crozzon and the Cima Tosa (10,420 ft.), with its broad ice-cap, lifting to the right of the deep vertical V of the Bocca gap; and to its left the incredible towers and splinters of the Fulmini di Brenta curve forward again to join the bizarre masses of the Cima di Brenta cliffs.

Below Madonna, the Campiglio Pass road, on this side a beautifully surfaced bitumen road of modern construction, hairpin for 9 miles down the pretty Nambino valley to Pinzolo (2,525 ft.) and Tione (1,850 ft.), 10 miles farther on at its foot, a drop of about 3,000 ft.

Here the pass proper ends and the valley road runs southwards to the lowlands by way of the foothills to Brescia.   But if the motorist is following the route of linked passes I have suggested as a comprehensive Dolomite round he turns left at Tione and climbs again by a remarkable modern road, tunnelling and clinging through narrow and hilly impressive gorges between vertical walls of rock, past Stenico (2,190 ft.), to drop down again into the main Adige valley, striking the highway from the head of Lake Garda to Bolzano at Arco (300 ft.).

Here he turns northwards and follows the lovely Adige trough to Ora (Auer) (700 ft.), where the minor but attractive San Lugano Pass (3,610 ft.) strikes off to the right, eastwards into the Val Fiemme and by way of Cavalese to Predazzo, the joint springboard for San Martino over the Rolle Pass to the south-east and northwards for the great Dolomite road, by way of the Pordoi and Falzarego Passes to Cortina.

5. The Rolle Pass (6,463 ft.)

Entirely in Italy (Dolomites of Primiero).   Avisio Valley to Vale of Primiero.

From Predazzo (3,377 ft.) to Fiera di Primiero (2,350 ft.): 26 miles.

Detail.   Predazzo to Paneveggio (5,055 ft.): 8 miles, ascent 2,700 ft.
Paneveggio to Rolle Pass (6,463 ft.): 5 miles, ascent 1,400 ft.
Total ascent Predazzo to Rolle Pass: 13 miles, 3,100 ft.

Rolle Pass to San Martino (4,740 ft.): 4 miles, descent 1,800 ft.
San Martino to Primiero (2,350 ft.): 9 miles, descent 2,400 ft.
Total descent Rolle Pass to Primiero: 13 miles, 4,100 ft.

Usually open, chains sometimes necessary.   Maximum gradient: 1 in 14.

An excellent road from Predazzo to the pass (partly gravel), with well-graded hairpins of moderate width, followed by a somewhat narrow, winding section where great care is necessary. Then a magnificent modern section of broad, splendidly surfaced bitumen windings, almost to the pass.

The numerous hairpins on the southern side are sharp and moderate in width. The surface is gravel, and the upper corners were in poor condition in 1957: reconstruction will probably have remedied this defect.

Below San Martino the road winds gently down the valley, with only a few sharp corners, and is of reasonable breadth.

Traffic light to moderately heavy (sightseeing coaches in summer). An easy to moderate pass, with a few sectors requiring special care. Worth driving for its lovely scenery, especially the incomparable Dolomite views at the summit and on the San Martino side.

The Rolle Pass starts gently enough from Predazzo (3,337 ft.) in its green vale, but with no great peaks anywhere to be seen. For some miles the road heads up the quiet valley, passing a number of attractive villages as it goes, and rises steadily towards the projection of a long, pine-clothed spur, which seems to close its farther end. Above the spur, a remote, bizarre, saw-toothed outline appears in clear weather—the distant peaks of San Martino, 10 miles away.

Presently, finding there is no progress to be made at the level of the stream, the road swings diligently, by a series of fairly short hairpin bends, up the broad breast of the meadows which form the left-hand side of the valley till, after a climb of nearly 2,000 ft., it reaches the lower fringe of the pines and is faced with the passage of a narrow ravine ahead between their opposing banks.

Somewhere hereabouts, the jagged skyline, still some miles away, of the San Martino peaks suddenly heaves itself up above the dark rim of the pine-forests to unearthly heights. Towards evening, when the light has already left the long, flat-topped ridge of intervening pines and the valley below lies cool in a green shade, this can be one of the truly sensational mid-distance mountain views of the world. For then those four card-board-edged cut-outs of beige limestone, their sheer bases linked in a single shining wall, stand four-square to the western sun, aglow with an incandescent lave of living gold, high in the azure firmament above the twilit shadow world of trees and meadows and streams.

The road now winds delightfully on a high shelf along the left-hand face of the ravine, which for about a mile runs narrow and deep between the opposing pine-forests; and below the neat white guardian-stones at the outer rim of the carriage-way lies a little terrace of greensward in which at one point a dark lakelet sleeps unruffled. This is a narrow, twisting section of the road, requiring every care.

Once through the ravine, there is nothing left to do but to swing leisurely by great wide curves through the glorious forest till the top of the spur is surmounted. The road, now broad and modern, in contrast to its lower sectors, which have not changed a great deal in thirty years, here takes on a pleasant pinkish tone in nice contrast to the deep green of pines, a tribute to the local rock which has contributed to its splendid surface.

Then, beyond the topmost pines, the ribbon of the road curves up across the last slope to the bare, turfy saddle of the Rolle Pass and its fantastic background of the Cimone de la Pala—the 'Matterhorn of the Dolomites'. As you approach the tight cluster of buildings at the actual pass, the Vezzana and other adjoining cliffs lift above the grassy skyline; but at first the eye is entirely held by the sky-raking surge of the Cimone's narrow shaft, 4,000 ft. of slender uprightness and smooth, unbroken slabby verticality. I have often been told by friends that there is nothing beautiful about the Cimone; even that it looks like some supernatural factory chimney, fallen from top to bottom into ruin and decay, its per-pendiculars a little splayed out towards the wide base from which it soars. Very well, then; even if it were so, were I to come upon such a chimney, suddenly projecting above the intervening skyline 4,000 ft. into the sky, my heart would evidently miss a beat—especially if a great white sail of cloud 1,000 ft. high were leaning against its left-hand side, as so often and dramatically happens to the knife-edge of the Cimone. And, beauty is, after all, in the eye of the beholder.

By contrast, I see little or none in the knot of hotel and other tin-roofed buildings, with the road running level between them, at the sum-mit; but five minutes' stroll up the grassy knolls behind them on either hand will discover not only a charmingly situated chapel but also a variety of new views of the great wall ahead, including its extension to the startling crags and pinnacles of the Rosetta and the endless bastion of peaks beyond, overlooking San Martino and the long valley down to Primiero.

If there were nothing but the summit views to draw me to the Rolle Pass and its bare, humpy saddle, I should still turn east from Predazzo every time. Fortunately, it leads to more, and much more, though nothing quite so magnificent, beyond.

For a mile or so the road—gravel again and lately requiring renovation and repair on this side—skirts the base of the Cimone's broad eastern face through a narrow green funnel of turf slopes without losing much height. Then in a terraced series of spasmodic white hairpins it falls over the edge of a bluff, first to an alp and then to the wonderful mat of pine-forest sloping to the valley below.

Down and down it loops among gigantic firs, between whose upper tufts and branches vista after vista of beige and grey rock pinnacles flits by for 4 miles and 2,000 ft., till suddenly, at one of the innumerable hairpin bends, the topmost hotels of San Martino emerge from the woods.

San Martino (4,740 ft.) is a huddle of white-walled hotels, some vast, some small, occupying a meadow-slope below the pine-forests rising on three sides; to the south-east the open valley falls away gradually to the less-elevated peaks which close the vale of Primiero, 2,000 ft. and 10 miles lower down. Through its heart the Rolle road continues calmly in a bank of half a dozen hairpins; scattered about the terraces between them stand the shops, cafés, and hotels, interspersed with networks of little short-cut paths and steps. At the bottom of the loops is the ancient church tower and the bridge over the Cismone. Dominating the north-eastern side of the little clearing and bordering the length of the valley, rises the mighty precipitous wall of extraordinary towers, spires, crags, and pinnacles stretching for miles from the south-west face of the broad, castle-like Cimone, through the Rosetta, the Saas Maor, and the organ pipes of the Pala di San Martino and Cima di Ball summits.

This is a lovely spot for a short stay. The meadows among which it lies are a veritable sun-trap from early morning onwards; the pine-woods above them on every side, whose trees grow to exceptional heights, offer a cool shade and a glut of woodland strawberries at the side of their paths. There are strolls and short walks and long walks and, of course, mountaineering of all standards of severity.

Of the all-day expeditions which never stray from a path, undoubtedly the finest is that to the 9,000-ft. peak of the Rosetta—though by the time this assertion is in print it will probably be possible to cover all but the last easy 500 ft. by the cable ropeway already in construction; and for some years past it has been possible to dispose of the first 1,500 ft. by a chair-lift to above the tree level. This truly remarkable path is cut in the apparently vertical face of the mountains, skirting the base of the Cimone cliffs all the way to the broad and unsuspected plateau on which, between Cimone and Rosetta at 8,300 ft., stands the Rosetta Hut. A fairly steady head is an asset, though the few really exposed corners below the saddle are protected by railings or wire-ropes. From the hut an easy track leads up in half an hour through the almost snow-white, gently tilted slabs to the Rosetta's summit and the grand view from the rim of her 4,000-ft. frontal precipice.

For those who prefer a less vertical day with the blessing of woodland shade for much of the way, a broad and less steep path, and an entire absence of vertiginous places, there is the track to the very attractive Alp Tognola (6,510 ft.) on the gentler side of the valley, commanding wonderful views of the valley itself and the whole elongated chain of the San Martino peaks opposite.

Below San Martino, the Rolle road continues pleasantly down the long, straight valley for 9 miles, gradually leaving the wall of great jagged teeth behind till, at Fiera di Primiero, it reaches the floor of the wider Primiero valley, running at right-angles 1,500 ft. lower down.

From Primiero the long valley-roads lead southwards to Feltre, Treviso, and Venice; or eastwards to Belluno, skirting the southern fringes of the main Dolomite area and thence to Vittorio Veneto, Udine, and Trieste. But for me the southern end of the Rolle Pass is at San Martino; and when I have to leave that lovely spot it consoles me to have the steep, winding climb to the summit, close under the frowning crags of the Cimone's spire, and then the long drift down through the pines and meadows in the vale of Predazzo to look forward to.

APPENDIX I

GENERAL INFORMATION

No ATTEMPT has been made in this book to provide any detailed information about motoring on the Continent. The recognized motoring organizations (A.A. and R.A.C.) publish admirably produced foreign touring handbooks covering every aspect of the subject; they also offer full services of advice, the preparation of detailed routes, and, of course, undertake to arrange bookings on the various air- and sea-routes, as well as providing international carnets to cover the customs requirements of the countries involved.

Nor is there in this book any detailed reference to hotels, restaurants, art galleries, museums, or sightseeing generally. This information will be found in innumerable excellent guide-books available for different countries and regions, both in the general and the motoring field. The following is a brief selection of those found most useful by the author:

General

> *Baedeker's Guides* (all countries).
> *The Blue Guides* (*Guides Bleus*), English and French editions: Southern France, Northern Italy, Switzerland.
> *Muirhead's* Southern France (Benn).

Motoring

> *The Michelin Guides:* France, Belgium, and Luxembourg.
> *The Michelin Guides:* French Regional Guides (in French only).
> *Auberges de France* (Club des Sans Club): France.
> *Logis de France:* Annual Booklet.
> *Hallwag's C.H. Touring Guide:* Switzerland.
> *Grieben's Guide:* Austria.

There is also a very large choice of motoring maps, small and large scale, of which a few useful examples are listed below.

Europe

> *Hallwag's Europa Touring* (book). 37s. 6d.
> Bartholomew's Road Maps: *Western and Eastern Europe.* 48 miles to the inch. 7s. 6d.
> Kummerly and Frey: *Road Map of Alpine Countries.* 16 miles to the inch. 8s. 6d.
> Reise und Verkehrsverlag: *Road Map of Italy and the Alps.* 12½ miles to the inch. 8s. 6d.

Austria

> Austrian Touring Club: *Map.* 10 miles to the inch. 3s.
> Austrian Touring Club: *Section Road Maps.* 9 sheets. 3·15 miles to the inch. 4s. each.

Belgium and Luxembourg

    E. de Rouck.   *Road Map.*   5½ miles to the inch.   4s.
    Michelin Section Maps.   4 sheets.   3·15 miles to the inch.   2s. 6d. each.

France

    Michelin Map of Main Roads.   2 parts, North and South.   16 miles to the
        inch.   2s. 6d. each.
    Michelin Section Maps.   37 sheets.   3·15 miles to the inch.   2s. 6d. each.
    Freytag-Berndt.   The Riviera.   1 : 300,000.   7s.

Germany

    German Automobile Club.   *Road Map.*   16 miles to the inch.   2s. 6d.
    Michelin Section Maps of the Rhine Valley.   5 sheets.   3·15 miles to the
        inch.   2s. 6d. each.

Holland

    Dutch Touring Club.   *Sectional Road Map.*   3 sheets.   3·15 miles to the
        inch.   3s. 6d. each.
    Dutch Touring Club.   *Sectional Road Maps.*   3·15 miles to the inch.
        4s. 6d. each.
    Dutch Touring Club.   *A.I.T. North Italy.*   8 miles to the inch.   6s. 6d.

Switzerland

    Swiss Touring Club.   *Road Map.*   4·7 miles to the inch.   6s. 6d.
    Bartholomew.   *Contour Road Map.*   8 miles to the inch.   6s.
    Michelin Section Maps.   4 sheets.   3·15 miles to the inch.   2s. 6d. each.

A FEW USEFUL REMINDERS

Extra Clothing

It should always be remembered that, even in summer, the change of temperature between the valley-levels and that encountered at the top of a mountain pass
some thousands of feet higher up, especially if flanked by snow-fields and
glaciers, may be extreme.   It is therefore always wise to have spare warm
clothing, whether in the form of extra woollen pullovers or cardigans or of a
heavy top-coat, ready to hand, if chills are to be avoided during any sorties from
the car round and about the upper levels of a mountain road.

Rarefied Atmosphere

It is essential that all exercise, especially uphill walking, near the summit of
any pass higher than 6,000 ft. should be undertaken at a very gentle pace.   The
atmospheric difference between a sub-Alpine valley, left only an hour before,
and a mountain saddle at anything up to 9,000 ft. is very considerable, nor has
there been any opportunity for getting used to the much lower oxygen content
of the air while motoring up without the exertion of any physical effort on the
way.   Violent activity can in the circumstances produce unpleasant effects,
ranging merely from a slight diminution of enjoyment to actual 'mountain
sickness' at greater heights and if too much is attempted before adjustment has
been allowed to take place.

I once saw a party whose coach had broken down about 500 ft. below the
Col d'Iséran set off up the road towards the hospice full of enthusiasm, at the

normal gait of the plains and cities, laughing, shouting, and singing.   When we (also on foot) caught up with them again after about ½ mile they were all scattered disconsolately on rocks along the roadside, and when they eventually reached the hospice, some time after us, they did not appear to be enjoying themselves very much.

Single Meals and Wayside Catering

On the Continent as elsewhere, single meals are a relatively expensive item, as also are one-night stands along the road.   Even if you have no option but to stay at a different hotel every night, a considerable economy can be effected by carrying your own commissariat and so avoiding the disproportionate cost of restaurant lunches and other intermediate meals or snacks along the road. Quite apart from the financial angle, there are great advantages in the flexibility achieved by being able to stop anywhere you like along the road and picnic, choosing the exact points at which to break your day's run.   A medium-sized picnic basket or case, plenty of polythene bags, two or three Thermos flasks, and —if you are fussy about your tea—a couple of spoon-type infusers are sufficient equipment for a car-load of four.

When motoring across France as quickly as possible at the start of an Alpine holiday we usually start out with plenty of cold chicken, roasted the previous night, ham and tongue, salad and tomatoes, as well as fresh loaves and butter from home; in this way we are usually well into Switzerland before having to purchase a lunch or tea, or even separate items at a shop, except perhaps the luxury of *croissants* and a few *patisseries* at a *boulangerie* in some wayside town. Once the original supplies are exhausted it is relatively inexpensive to buy cut meats, sausages, bread, butter, and cakes sufficient for all the day's meals between a hotel breakfast and that night's hotel dinner before leaving the overnight stopping-place or at any convenient shopping-centre on the road.

Once in the mountains on *pension* or inclusive terms, the question no longer arises, as ample packed lunches will be provided to your exact directions, to cover every need of long days spent in motoring or other excursions.   And, after all, who would want to eat indoors if he can enjoy his meal under a blue sky, with a lake or mountain scene to encourage digestion?

Hotel Accommodation and Bookings

Up to about July 10th and after about August 20th it is normally possible to find accommodation in most towns and resorts in the mountain areas of Switzerland, France, Austria, and Italy without making reservations beforehand. Even then, telephoning in advance from a point on the day's run is a reasonable precaution when planning to visit any of the more popular tourist centres.

In the present era of ever-increasing holidays-with-pay and almost universal Continental travel, it is now essential for those who do not camp in or about their suitably adapted car, brake, or caravan to make certain of accommodation in advance, between the dates mentioned—especially in Switzerland, where the whole local watch-making industry closes down *en bloc* and falls upon all the more popular mountain resorts like a swarm of locusts.   Without this assurance, long and tedious searchings, frequently without ultimate success, are liable to cancel out all the enjoyment of the tired motorist at the end of a long and otherwise rewarding day.

It is a wise plan, too, to choose beforehand one's overnight stops on the main approach routes across France or Germany, as also on the return journey, and so make certain of a good night's rest on what will probably be the longest days of the tour by booking rooms well in advance. Late arrival, in the dark, at the height of the tourist season without having taken this simple precaution may lead to much anxiety, frustration, and discomfort.

Breakdowns and Repairs

Most British makers issue a list of agents and repair facilities on the Continent, while several make up a not unwieldy 'Continental Kit' package of the spares most likely to be required.

As the authorized repairers may be spaced out at wide distances, and local repairs to a 'foreign' car in out-of-the-way places can be difficult for want of the proper part or equipment, and are usually somewhat expensive, the provision of such a kit, or at least of adequate spares of minor items, such as lamp bulbs, fuses, and whatever the owner's experience leads him to think most likely to give trouble *en route*, is a wise insurance against frustration, expense, and delay.

Along the trunk roads there should be little difficulty about effecting running repairs at one of the many excellent garages placed at frequent distances along them; it is in the remote mountain areas that difficulties might be encountered.

Boiling on Passes

Even the best car will boil on the long ascent of a high mountain pass in mid-August under a broiling summer sun, heavily loaded, in rarefied air, if driven at high speed all the way up. Most modern cars will, however, keep surprisingly cool if the climb is taken at a reasonable speed and the gears are used intelligently.

If the car does boil there are nowadays ample watering facilities provided at frequent intervals along the major passes; elsewhere kindly nature will usually provide a convenient water-supply in the form of mountain stream or waterfalls.

Two things should always be remembered. It will do your car no good to pour ice-cold mountain or glacier water into it until it has stopped boiling and been given time to cool off a little. Secondly, it will do the driver no good—I have seen several burned and more than one nearly decapitated—to try to unscrew a red-hot radiator cap with ungloved hands and then to peer into the top of the boiling radiator with his face over the orifice. I have witnessed a cap blow fully 15 ft. into the air on such occasions; so go gently, protect your hands, and stand well away from the pressure and the jet of steam which may very probably emerge.

The Use of Brakes

If I had not seen two cars halted with heavily smoking brake-drums the last time I made the long descent of the north side of the Glockner road I should hardly dare to include this piece of advice under modern conditions of driving skill and knowledge.

Except as a control when changing down, use your brakes as sparingly as possible on the descents; your low gears are there to be used as braking-power just as much as for tractive power on the ascent. The continual use of the foot-brake is bound to lead to overheated drums, if not to eventual complete failure of the brakes just when it is most to be avoided.

In a recent descent of the Innsbruck side of the Brenner (an easy pass, it is true) I found it unnecessary to use the foot-brake for the first 15 miles; and, when at last compelled to use it at that point, it was entirely owing to a very bad piece of driving by a German just ahead of me.

Intelligent use of the gears is the secret of all mountain driving.

POSTAL MOTOR AND COACH SERVICES ON THE PASSES

POSTAL MOTOR and Coach Services operate over almost all the major passes of all the Alpine countries, thus enabling the non-motorist to enjoy these magnificent roads and their incomparable mountain scenery.

Switzerland

In Switzerland, where the roads are the responsibility of the Cantonal and municipal authorities tremendous pride is taken in the very highly organized network of Postal Motor Services, not only on the more famous passes, but also on innumerable subsidiary mountain routes. In the summer season whole fleets of the magnificent, modern Saurer-engined coaches operate daily over the entire mountain area, often, when the tourist traffic is at its height, in convoys, in order to accommodate every passenger who wishes to make the journey. Their presence on the road is advertised from afar by the sound of their distinctive three-note horn, which it is illegal for private cars to imitate, and which, like the bells on Bredon in summer-time, is a cheerful noise to hear.

These yellow-and-black Postal Motors have priority rights on the passes (which are marked accordingly, at the foot of the roads on which this priority operates, by a yellow-and-black sign depicting a postal horn), and motorists are bound in theory to obey any signals the drivers may give, including in certain cases instructions to take the precipice side of the road. In practice, the Postal drivers are extremely thoughtful for private road-users, and on the broader, major passes do not normally bother them at all; in fact, they are generally most courteous in signalling them to overtake when the road is clear enough to permit of passing. On some of the narrower mountain roads, however, even the smaller types of coaches, specially designed for their operation, are bound to occupy most of the roadway, and the private motorist should always be ready to give way to a Postal Motor coming in the opposite direction; where passing is impossible because of the narrowness of the road, the Postal driver has the absolute right to request him to manoeuvre or even to reverse for a considerable distance until it is possible for the Postal Motor to edge past.

Even greater care and attention than usual is therefore essential on the minor Postal Motor Routes, and it is a good tip to study the time-tables before starting on some of the really narrow roads, to be sure whether, and roughly where, a meeting is likely along the route. A few minutes' wait at a village may avoid one of these head-on clashes on a narrow section beyond, if intelligent planning and timing are employed. These extreme precautions are, however, quite unnecessary on the wide roadways of the major passes described in this book, where there is ample room for even the largest coaches to pass one another.

The men who drive these Postal Motors are hand-picked for the job, and in fact set a magnificent standard of driving on the mountain roads. They are highly trained experts, and subject to an extremely strict regime designed to maintain fitness and competence during the coaching season, under regulations which enforce a completely abstemious life.   As a result, the accident figures are, in spite of the difficulties of the roads and the great bulk and weight of the more modern vehicles, fantastically low.

Similar high standards are, indeed, in force in all the countries where coach services of various types operate daily in summer, in ever-increasing volume, over high and difficult mountain roads.   The accident record of the government and commercial services consequently compares very favourably with that among privately driven cars.

Besides the Postal Motors, innumerable private-enterprise coach services, local and international, ply regularly over the major passes of Switzerland and all the other Alpine countries.

Austria

Austria, like Switzerland, has its comprehensive network of Postal Motor Services, under the direct control of the Austrian Post Office Department. These cream-and-brown coaches cover all the major routes and operate far into the side valleys off the beaten track.

Besides the Postal Services there are numerous K.W.D. (Kraft Wagen Dienst) Services controlled and operated by the Austrian Railways, as well as a host of private-enterprise undertakings which run daily sightseeing tours to all the famous beauty-spots.

All alike are subject to the strictest safety regulations; the standard of driving is uniformly high and remarkably accident-free.

Italy

In Italy the operation of the coach services in the Alpine areas, as elsewhere all over the country, is left entirely in the hands of private enterprise, subject, of course, to strict supervision of drivers and vehicles alike under the regulations of the Italian Ministry of Transport.   Here again, the safety standard is high and the accident rate low.

Some of these services have a semi-official status, as, for instance, those of S.A.D. (Societa Automobilistica Dolomiti) based on Cortina, which operates on the main routes of the Dolomites and in the Ortler–Adige region.   Other important operators in the Dolomite area are Buzzatti of Agordo, who run services in the Belluno and Alleghe areas on the eastern side of the region.   All these services are, however, closely co-ordinated, and inter-connection is arranged to provide through-routes over long distances from one end of the area to the other.

In the area of the Stelvio, Aprica, and Tonale passes the main operator is Perego of Tirano in the Adda valley; while in the Aosta area the main services are provided by Tosco, operating over the Grand St. Bernard to Switzerland and the Little St. Bernard to France, to Courmayeur, and southwards up the valleys of the Graian Alps to Cogne and other well-known resorts.   Subsidiary independent services serve the valleys under the southern wall of the main Alpine chain, to Valtournanche, Breuil, and Gressoney.

France

In France, as in Italy, the coaching services are in the hands of private contractors.   The main routes are operated under concessions granted by the national railways (S.N.C.F.: Société Nationale des Chemins de Fer Français). Here again, exacting minimum standards and maximum safeguards are in force under a strict *cahier de charges*, and the accident statistics are as remarkably low as elsewhere.

Among the best-known operators in the Alpine areas are the Société Automobile des Grandes Alpes, which provides the main services over the passes of the Route des Alpes between Grenoble and Nice; another prominent operator in the Grenoble area is Traffort, along the less-exacting Route Napoléon and the Croix Haute routes to Nice, as well as locally over the Lautaret to Briançon.

In the Tarentaise area the Bernard services operate from Moutiers over the Little St. Bernard to Aosta in conjunction with Fosco (see above), and locally to Pralognan, Albertville, Chamonix, and elsewhere in the area, as do Martin et Boch.

The main operators in Savoy, based on Geneva and Chamonix, are S.A. Autos-Transports du Chablais et du Faucigny, Catella, and the Société Savoyarde d'Entreprises Automobiles.

Car Hire

In all the countries concerned car-hire arrangements can be made with a minimum of difficulty or formality by anyone who wishes to be driven or to drive himself (provided he has a valid car-driver's licence in his country of origin) over the roads described.

Conclusion

It will thus be seen that the great motor highways of the Alps can be equally enjoyed in safety and comfort by the non-motorist, who has no car of his own at his disposal, and the more fortunate owner-driver. The wonderful Alpine roads are there for the delectation of all who visit the mountains and wish to draw close to their ineffable heights.

THE MAIN ALPINE PASSES IN ORDER OF ALTITUDE

1. Iseran (France), 9,088 ft.
2. Stelvio (Italy), 9,042 ft.
3. Galibier (France), 8,399 ft.
4. {Grossglockner (Austria), 8,212 ft.
   {(Umbrail) (Switzerland), 8,212 ft.*
5. Grand St. Bernard (Switzerland–Italy), 8,110 ft.
6. Furka (Switzerland), 7,976 ft.
7. Flüela (Switzerland), 7,815 ft.
8. Izoard (France), 7,743 ft.
9. Bernina (Switzerland–Italy), 7,644 ft.
10. Cayolle (France), 7,630 ft.
11. Albula (Switzerland), 7,595 ft.
12. Julier (Switzerland), 7,493 ft.
13. Allos (France), 7,382 ft.
14. Pordoi (Italy), 7,346 ft.
15. Susten (Switzerland), 7,300 ft.
16. Sella (Italy), 7,264 ft.
17. Petit St. Bernard (France–Italy), 7,178 ft.
18. Grimsel (Switzerland), 7,100 ft.
19. Ofen (Switzerland), 7,070 ft.
20. Gardena (Italy), 6,959 ft.
21. Vars (France), 6,939 ft.
22. Splügen (Switzerland–Italy), 6,930 ft.
23. St. Gotthard (Switzerland), 6,926 ft.
24. Falzarego (Italy), 6,913 ft.
25. Mont Cenis (France–Italy), 6,834 ft.
26. San Bernardino (Switzerland), 6,768 ft.
27. Lautaret (France), 6,751 ft.
28. Oberalp (Switzerland), 6,720 ft.
29. Simplon (Switzerland–Italy), 6,594 ft.
30. Larche (France–Italy), 6,545 ft.
31. Rolle (Italy), 6,493 ft.
32. Klausen (Switzerland), 6,390 ft.
33. Lukmanier (Switzerland), 6,289 ft.
34. Mont Genèvre (France–Italy), 6,100 ft.
35. Maloja (Switzerland), 5,960 ft.
36. Tre Croci (Italy), 5,932 ft.
37. Arlberg (Austria), 5,912 ft.
38. Costalunga (Italy), 5,752 ft.
39. Tauern (Austria), 5,700 ft.
40. Campiglio (Italy), 5,580 ft.
41. Katschberg (Austria), 5,384 ft.

* Not a true pass.

42. Forclaz (Switzerland–France), 4,997 ft.
43. Resia (Austria–Italy), 4,947 ft.
44. Col des Montets (France), 4,793 ft.
45. Brenner (Austria–Italy), 4,495 ft.
46. Mendola (Italy), 4,475 ft.
47. Tenda (France–Italy), 4,331 ft.

SUMMARY

Over 9,000 ft. . . .	2
8,000–9,000 ft. . . .	3
7,000–8,000 ft. . . .	14
6,000–7,000 ft. . . .	15
5,000–6,000 ft. . . .	7
4,000–5,000 ft. . . .	6

Note. At 8,215 ft., the uncompleted Timmljoch (see App. IV) will become the fourth-highest of the Alpine Passes and will swell the total of those between 8 and 9,000 ft. to 4.

TUNNELS

There will, of course, be occasions when, owing to persistent bad weather in the mountains or the temporary blocking of the upper levels of the passes by snow, the motorist will be forced to use the railway tunnels.

The following car-conveyance services are available daily:—

SWITZERLAND–(ITALY)
Simplon. Brigue to Domodossola.
St. Gotthard. Erstfeld or Goeschenen to Airolo or Biasca.
Loetschberg. Kandersteg to Brigue.

FRANCE–ITALY
Mont Cernis. Modane to Bardonnechia.

AUSTRIA
Arlberg. Langen to St. Anton.
Tauern. Böckstein (Bad Gastein) to Mallnitz.

Full details can be found in the A.A. Foreign Touring Guide.

A NEW TRANS-ALPINE PASS—THE TIMMLJOCH (PASSO DEL ROMBO) (8,215 ft.)

A MAJOR ADDITION to the high passes across the Alpine Backbone should be open for traffic by 1959, bringing their number up to nineteen. This is the Timmljoch (Passo del Rombo), linking the western Austrian Tyrol with the Italian South Tyrol, and providing a direct route from Switzerland through Landeck at the eastern foot of the Arlberg (p. 184) to Merano, thus short-circuiting the present roundabout routes over the Reschen–Scheideck (Chapter XIX) to its west or by Innsbruck and the Brenner (Chapter IX) to its east, and considerably shortening the journey from Switzerland to Bolzano, the Dolomites, and Northern Italy beyond Lake Garda.

The new route will branch southwards from the main Landeck–Innsbruck highway along the Inn valley at the Oetztal turning (p. 184) and will follow the rebuilt and widened road up the lovely Oetztal through Sölden and Zwiesel-stein, ascending thence by its left-hand branch, the Gurgltal, as far as Unter Gurgl. From this point 8 finely engineered miles of completely new road have been thrust up the mountain-side to the east, to reach the 8,215-ft. Timml-joch, the mule-track over which has been used for centuries. An entirely new habitation, consisting of a cluster of hotel buildings, the last on the Austrian side, is being built at about 7,200 ft. and will probably be called Hochgurgl. The Austrian side of the pass should be opened in the summer of 1958.

The 10 miles of new road descending the huge Italian side from the saddle, through the villages of Corvara (4,500 ft.) and Moso (3,350 ft.) to S. Leon-ardo (2,250 ft.), the well-known resort in the Val Passeria, while less advanced, are scheduled for completion in 1959. From S. Leonardo to Merano is a distance of 12 miles along the good road which already exists down the valley; this sector will thus be shared with the San Giovo pass, which links S. Leonardo and (Vipiteno) Sterzing (p. 98).

This latest of the great roads will certainly be a most important and exciting addition to the trans-Alpine passes. Constructed to a minimum width of 20 ft., increasing to 30 ft. at the bends, with an average gradient of 8 per cent and a maximum of 11 per cent, the new pass crosses a saddle almost exactly the height of the true pass (Hochtor) on the Glockner road. Its approaches, as well as the 16 miles of the pass proper, traverse an area of glorious mountain scenery, penetrating the very heart of the snowy Oetztal Alps, which culminate in the lovely 12,300 ft. Wildspitze and Weisskugel, on the Austrian side; and on the Italian, skirting the southern wall of the slightly lower Stubai Group, whose highest peak is the 11,500-ft. Zuckerhütl.

Finally, owing to the protective character of the great Oetztal range to its west and peculiarly mild local weather conditions, the new pass should normally be free of snow, and therefore open to traffic, for two months longer in the year than the more-exposed Glockner road.

INDEX

R   257

'7